DYNAMICS OF
INTERCULTURAL
COMMUNICATION

SECOND EDITION

DYNAMICS OF
INTERCULTURAL
COMMUNICATION

CARLEY H. DODD
Abilene Christian University

wcb

Wm. C. Brown Publishers
Dubuque, Iowa

Copyright © 1982, 1987 by Wm. C. Brown
Publishers. All rights reserved

Library of Congress Catalog Card Number: 87–70027

ISBN 0-697-00800-2

Printed in the United States of America
10   9   8   7   6   5   4   3   2   1

Contents

Preface

Intercultural communication has become a truly exciting field of study. Experts in a number of fields are utilizing the insights and results from intercultural studies. This book is the second edition of the 1982 version and hopefully, here too, we have captured major findings in intercultural communication. In this edition there are new chapters on cognitive culture, intercultural communication effectiveness, and organizational culture. New introductory chapters open a discussion of the nature, scope, and importance of intercultural communication.

This book is an attempt to trace the imprint of culture in its effect on communication. As people from communication climates interact, the markings of cultural fragments and groupness have an impact on their interaction. In this work I look at how culture influences interaction patterns; an influence which ranges widely from information processing and cognitive culture to communication style. The book now more fully encompasses an understanding of cultural adaptation, interpersonal effectiveness, and communication relationships as they are wrapped in culture.

A number of people have been truly helpful in developing various aspects of the book. Cecile Garmon, Richard Paine, Peggy Kirby, Diane Schwalm, and Gary Hughes uncovered a great deal of primary research for me in the first edition for which I am truly grateful. Reviewers of the first edition of the book in 1982 who were most helpful include Bill Gudykunst, Young Kim, Nemi Jain, and Jess Yoder. Second edition manuscript reviews were provided by Mara Adelman, Don Boggs, Carolyn Wilkins Fountenberry, Wallace Schmidt, and Andrew Wolvin. Thank you for the very helpful insights you provided and the specific suggestions you offered.

The staff at Wm. C. Brown have been fantastic. I truly appreciate their many hours of work with special credit to Stan Stoga, Carla Aspelmeier, Mary Monner, and Judy Winter. I am sure there are others about whom I do not know whose tireless efforts contributed greatly. Also, I owe thanks to the staff and faculty in the Department of Communication at Abilene Christian University for their support and encouragement, especially to Anna Cloud and workers for their help in manuscript preparation. We gratefully acknowledge the ACU Department of Journalism and Mass Communication for various photographs.

I want to thank my parents, Carlysle and Leota Dodd, for the encouragement they have provided me all these years.

Most of all, I dedicate the book to my wife Ada, who is my best friend and counselor, and to our children Jeremy, Matthew, and Philip. They sacrificed for me to complete this project.

CHD

Introduction and Background to Intercultural Communication

Chapter 1

Introduction to Intercultural Communication

Objectives

After completing this chapter, you should be able to:

1. Define intercultural communication.

2. Describe crucial elements within the intercultural communication process.

3. Diagram and explain a model of intercultural communication.

4. Illustrate and explain the process involved as two persons from differing cultural backgrounds communicate.

5. Discuss levels of communication in differing subcultural settings, such as interethnic and interracial settings.

6. Define three possible intercultural communication outcomes.

This book is about a special kind of communication called intercultural communication. Since communication is a process, part of that process involves understanding the influence of culture upon such things as self-identity, values, patterns of speech, and nonverbal communication habits. If culture influences our communication, then obviously other people with whom we come in contact also have been influenced by their culture. Differences in those cultures underscore the reason why we study intercultural communication.

If someone is very similar to us, like a hometown friend or a family member, perhaps we understand one another fairly well. However, what about a person from another state? Another region of the country? Another nation? In such a circumstance, we may find that person thinking in a way different from our way, responding nonverbally in different ways, and holding values different from our values. Because of these differences, communication takes on a new dimension; now, we perhaps listen more perceptively than we listen to our close friends. When we talk with a close friend, we refer to common experiences, perhaps use jargon that we both understand, and talk freely because we know this person well. With a person from a different culture, however, we must listen and speak with a cultural consciousness. At first, we may feel somewhat awkward in conversing interculturally. Why? Because cultural differences can obscure our "certainty" and produce ambiguity with which we feel some psychological discomfort.

If we consider intercultural communication as a subset of general communication principles, we can reflect on the interpersonal nature of intercultural communication. That is, intercultural communication is actually interpersonal communication within a "special" context, namely a situation where we perceive cultural differences. Let us examine, for a moment, some cases that illustrate intercultural communication circumstances that are by their nature interpersonal and yet culturally conditioned.

A U.S. government official in a conversation with the Minister of Education from a Latin American country offers aid to assist what the former calls "backward" regions of the nation. The Latin American smiles wistfully and continues to talk in a friendly and positive manner. Upon returning to her office in Washington, D.C., the U.S. official finds a scathing letter from the Latin American condemning her for her paternalistic attitudes. How did communication fail?

The wife of a new foreign service officer in Sierra Leone is just learning to buy in the local marketplaces. She returns from an afternoon of shopping, her feelings hurt, because owners of market booths shouted at her during their bargaining transaction. She considers this behavior insulting. Was there misunderstanding?

An Iranian working in the United States wakes up ill. He sends his brother to work for him that day. The employer, shocked and angered, sends the brother home. What is the dynamic of this intercultural encounter?

Elite government officials from the ministry of agriculture in Bolivia spend days convincing farmers from the highlands of the Andes to add fertilizer to their potato crops to produce enough food for the village. The villagers respond that their ancestors would be disappointed should the villagers desecrate the earth with fertilizer. What would you recommend for future communication with the highlanders?

A black third-grade student lowers his head and casts his eyes downward when his teacher directly gazes at him. The teacher is insulted since the young boy "refuses" to look at the teacher. What nonverbal communication aspect has been overlooked?

An American businessman in Indonesia is constantly upset because the Indonesians arrive late for work and seem to work halfheartedly, enjoying joviality with each other on the job. The businessman finally tells the workers to "stop playing around and get down to work" or he will take drastic measures. A few workers quit, others deliberately work less efficiently. What type of communication is necessary to prevent this circumstance?

A Native American is interrogated by the police for allegedly stealing. The Anglo police officers are not certain the Indian is guilty, but the suspect refuses to say anything in his defense to the police or to a lawyer. Is there a cultural reason for this silence?

A Vietnam veteran seems withdrawn and distant to his family and old high school friends. They try to talk with him but consistently avoid the subject of the war. One by one, the veteran loses contact with these individuals. What dynamics are occurring?

Although these examples touch varied areas, such as international communication, development and social change, intercultural management, and interracial and interethnic communication, they highlight a single theme of intercultural communication. That theme, simply stated, is that culture and messages are inseparable. Intercultural communication does not consist merely of saying the right words in some language, be it English or Swahili. Rather, the study of intercultural communication springs from a recognition of how culture pervades so much of what we are, how we act, why we think as we do, and how we talk and listen.

The foreign service officer's wife has not yet learned that her host culture expects and enjoys intensive bargaining. There is no intent of animosity toward her; she does not yet understand interpersonal communication in that culture in that situation. The teacher apparently has not recognized cultural reasons for the student's lack of eye contact. The student has been taught that looking away is a sign of respect for authority, while the teacher's culture has emphasized respect by direct eye contact in interpersonal communication. The Vietnam veteran is facing a prolonged reverse cultural reentry adjustment problem. Unfortunately, his family and friends have no idea of what is happening to him, nor do they possess skills to deal with the situation. These examples suggest that intercultural communication deals not only with messages but with the cultural component within our communication relationships.

Let us explore some general concepts of communication that may consolidate your understanding of the nature of intercultural communication. An understanding of communication theory is important in understanding intercultural communication because intercultural communication is viewed here as a communication studies subset that deals with the imprint of social and cultural factors on any communication engagement between individuals, groups, and nations. Like any other area of communication, intercultural communication is concerned with the message, the channel or means of disclosing that message, the nature of the sender and the receiver of that message, the give-and-take process during communication that involves reciprocity and feedback, and the outcome after interaction between people. This process, easy as it sounds, is actually quite complex, for each element cited here can be expanded to include a plethora of detailed features. Many communication models, in fact, include numerous details outlining features of these basic components in communication, details available in textbooks especially designed to discuss communication theory.

Defining Intercultural Communication

In considering communication, however, there is an additional element that rather decisively influences the communication process. This element is culture with its many related aspects of societal life and social relationships. When culture significantly influences people in their communication, then the study of this process falls into the purview of intercultural communication. We are especially interested in cultural differences that intervene in that process.

Admittedly, when we try to capsulize communication into a few components linked by their relation to a message sent and received within some interface between people, we oversimplify the process. For example, intercultural communication is certainly two-way, since the sender becomes the receiver and the receiver becomes the sender in what is called a reciprocal process (figure 1.1). Thus, communicator roles of sender and receiver are fluid, switching, and operating simultaneously. So, communication is not just linear, or one-way. Also, communication, be it interpersonal, organizational, small-group, or intercultural communication, holds the potential for exposing deep-seated differences rather than narrowing gaps. Communication descriptions cannot portray hidden intentions or mask ulterior motives that may surface.

At the least, these warnings may underscore the understanding that describing communication is like taking a snapshot rather than shooting a moving

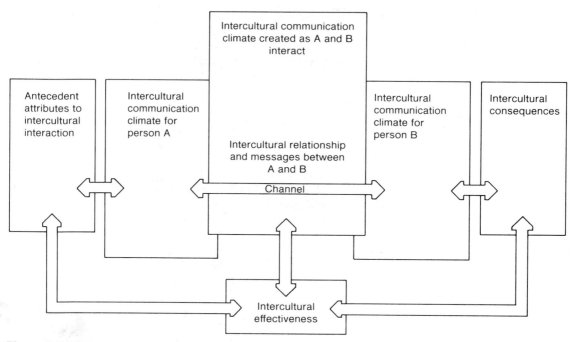

Figure 1.1
A model of intercultural communication.

film. The former merely freezes some view of reality and attempts to convey a minute portion of the total action. For good or ill, verbal descriptions or even illustrations fall into the snapshot syndrome. All definitions have potential limitations, but they do provide a general direction of inquiry. The following definition suggests conditions and variables that comprise intercultural communication:

> Intercultural communication is the process of message interaction between two or more people in which a communication climate characterized by cultural differences influences the outcome of the interaction.

Figure 1.1 illustrates a model of intercultural communication.

Intercultural Attributes to Initial Interaction

Intercultural communication, like other areas of communication, involves an interface between two or more communicating parties. Though one person must initiate communication, the persons involved simultaneously become senders and receivers, and a reciprocal process ensues. In addition to the encoding and decoding of messages, this process also involves characteristics each person perceives in the other and the kind of relationship the two people share, among other things. The perceived communication roles are initial antecedents influencing the interaction, as are the intention, personality, and receptivity of each person.

Communication roles are information role relationships that people in social settings tend to perceive in others. The evaluative tendencies, based on

Intercultural communication involves the interface of two or more people where culture becomes a dominant concern.

these communication roles, are enormous. Communication roles include communicator credibility, communicator similarity, communicator intentions, communicator personality, and communicator receptivity.

Communicator credibility. Research in communicator credibility reveals that the believability of another person depends upon a number of elements (see chapter 13). Among the factors people use to judge the worth of others are:

1. *Competence.* The degree of perceived task ability of another individual

2. *Character.* The perception of a communicator's morals, ethical values, and trustworthiness

3. *Co-orientation.* The degree of perceived similarity of goals and values

4. *Charisma.* The degree of belief in perceived special leadership qualities, particularly in crises or other exceptional circumstances

5. *Dynamism.* The degree of perceived enthusiasm and other nonverbal behavior

6. *Sociability.* The degree of perceived friendliness

The importance of these components depends on which factor a culture appreciates. For example, one culture may use competence as a measure of personal worth, while another may use friendliness. Or, in certain conditions, one factor simply may become dominant for awhile over other factors.

Credibility is not merely a matter of a listener perceiving the believability of a speaker; intercultural communication studies encompass the relational nature of credibility. That is, the credibility of each communicator, particularly on an interpersonal level, affects one's attitude toward another and thus permeates the conversation.

For example, President Carter's attribution of high credibility to Prime Minister Begin of Israel and his similar attitude toward President Sadat of Egypt seemed to set up a condition for effective intercultural communication during the negotiation of Egyptian-Israeli peace settlements during the Camp David talks in 1978. Perhaps because of mutual respect, there was a sense of high expectation and of great accomplishments. It is unlikely that many of the agreements that were reached would have developed had President Carter, for instance, held feelings of ethnocentrism, mistrust, or lack of respect for either of the other men. As it appeared, both verbally and nonverbally, mutual trust and other credibility factors played a major role in this historical event.

Communicator similarity. Homophily refers to areas of similarity between interacting individuals. Those similarities reflect commonality in such areas as attitudes and values, appearance, social standing, occupation, personality, and residence.

Heterophily refers to the degree of perceived dissimilarity between two individuals and is the opposite of homophily. When intercultural communication is marked by heterophily, the results are different than the results from communication between two people who share more similarity than difference. Think of your closest friend and your feelings toward this person. Try to think of some confidential information that you would feel comfortable telling this person. Now, take an inventory of your feelings toward an acquaintance, a person you really do not know very well. Are your feelings of closeness and willingness to confide in this person very strong? Probably not.

Two people from different cultures perceive in each other degrees of homophily and heterophily. Depending on the nature of the ensuing relationship following those perceptions, intercultural communication can take some interesting twists and turns. So again, this text stresses the importance of perceived relationships in intercultural communication.

Communicator intentions. Intercultural communication is influenced by perceived intentions. If a member of a host culture seems reluctant to listen to a person from another culture, perhaps the host simply perceives some kind of malevolent intentions; this perception may alter the intercultural communication outcomes. Peace Corps volunteers from the United States working in

Saudi Arabia inadvertently can stimulate suspicion solely because of their roles. Sometimes, the gap is so wide that a special trust and credibility must develop that involves empathy and leadership skills. In other cases, businesspeople from one culture living abroad may inadvertently arouse negative feelings on the part of the host culture because of a perception of the foreign businessperson's intentions. Sometimes, the gap is so wide that, again, a special trust and credibility must develop—usually through empathy—before effective intercultural communication can occur.

Intentionality counts interculturally. For instance, one ethnic group in the United States resisted the swine flu vaccination programs conducted nationally in 1976 because, according to informed sources, some group members believed the program to be a genocidal plot against this group. Thus, we can see that a relationship influenced by credibility, homophily, and intentionality forms a framework by which intercultural participants view each other as they communicate.

Communicator personality. An individual's personality, highly influenced by that person's culture, is still another factor in intercultural communication. Consider, for instance, the "quiet" nonverbal behavior exhibited by a Japanese man who prefers to go unnoticed in a crowd. Contrast this with a North American who values assertiveness and who believes that self-created recognition may to some extent relate to success. Acceptable personality behaviors in one culture may be offensive in another culture. Cultural types and cultural heroes, including folk heroes, provide a rich reservoir for learning the ideal types for a given culture, for so often, the ideal stands as a model for individual personality development in a given culture. The American who insists on handshaking and backslapping within a nontouching culture, such as Laotian culture, may find that his personality type is repugnant to Laotians. So, it behooves each student of intercultural communication to learn as much as possible about ideal role and cultural behavior.

Communicator receptivity. Research studies in intercultural communication identify individuals and groups that manifest openness or resistance toward new ideas. In fact, many practitioners have advanced the notion that cultural receptivity may be the single most important element in social change (Tippett 1975).

Not only is receptivity important on a systems level, but on an interpersonal-intercultural level as well. Because of social, economic, political, or religious differences, intercultural encounters may at first be stiff, unnatural, or in other ways strained. Developing intercultural communication relationships despite the initial resistance sometimes caused by these differences is one of the challenges of intercultural relationships discussed later in this text.

Obviously, the message—whether verbal, nonverbal, or paralinguistic—remains a central feature of the interchange between people of contrasting cultures. But in what ways can we conceive of messages? Although later chapters in this text deal extensively with these concepts, we briefly discuss types of symbolic stimuli or messages here.

Intercultural Messages and Interaction

Cultural differences allow us to learn from each other and to interpersonally interact in a creative manner.

Verbal stimuli. When speaking and listening or writing and reading, we have a pool of vocabulary and a set of grammatical tools for transmitting our thoughts. Simply speaking or writing the appropriate words in proper sequence, however, does not signal the intended meanings unless two people share a common code. For example, were a NASA worker to tell an Australian aborigine about a space shuttle, we might expect less than ideal communication unless both engaged in extended elaboration. Yet, two NASA workers would probably have little difficulty discussing space vehicles since that domain of technology and code for talking about them is common to both.

Nonverbal stimuli. Just as verbal stimuli act symbolically to elicit meaning, another set of stimuli operates in communication—nonverbal stimuli. Nonverbal behaviors refer to our use of body, time, and space. Like the verbal code, some nonverbal behaviors elicit meaning and thus become a kind of code system. The point is illustrated by deaf persons who communicate by a highly formalized, totally nonverbal system. To a lesser extent, each culture develops a highly stylized set of informal behaviors that elicit meaning, although the user often produces these behaviors unconsciously.

In addition, people use nonverbal behaviors in coordination with their total communication behavior. Some of these nonverbal behaviors elicit meanings implicit in the behavior, such as a beckoning gesture; others emerge in coordination with verbal communication as auxiliary messages, such as a frown accompanying words of disappointment. Above all, nonverbal communication is highly culture-specific—different cultures have different meanings for the same nonverbal behaviors. For that reason, this text introduces some basic concepts in nonverbal communication. Some of the major categories in the study of nonverbal communication include:

Kinesics. Kinesics is the study of body language, consisting of body position, body orientation, facial expressions, gestures, and the like. Although we usually infer meanings from a unit of body movement, such as a complete gesture, technically, each body movement has dozens of slight variations that the trained eye, with the use of a slow-motion camera, can detect and analyze (Mehrabian 1981). Most kinesic behaviors occur in concert with the total context of our speech at any one moment of utterance (Birdwhistell 1966).

Oculesics. Oculesics research concerns the study of eye movement and position. Amazingly, there are up to twenty-three distinct eyebrow movements with unique meanings. It is probably more obvious to most of us that eye movements indicate a variety of messages, such as disgust, surprise, boredom, and so forth. One example of intercultural differences in oculesic behaviors is the subtle belief among North Americans not to trust anyone who does not "look them in the eye." By contrast, many Cambodians believe that meeting the gaze of another is insulting—something akin to invading one's privacy—so that unobtrusiveness with the eyes is considered polite.

Haptics. Touch, or the study of haptics, provides a rich area of intercultural communication insight. Many North Americans feel uncomfortable when a person from a culture whose members touch a lot greets the North American by touching the shoulders, arms, and sometimes the waist for what seems like a long time. A North American who lived in Botswana once expressed his discomfort when he said, "As I shake hands with Botswanian villagers, I have to remind myself, 'this is not America,' when they hold my hand for several minutes after an initial handshake." Conversely, many members of a "haptically active" host culture feel equally uncomfortable when the visitor maintains a lack of touch and distance, since this behavior is perceived as unfriendly and cold!

Proxemics. The study of proxemics, or spatial relationships between people, is another significant nonverbal communication category (Hall 1973). The human tendency to establish a zone of geographical area that one sometimes renders "my own" is called territoriality. This trait has also been observed in a number of other species. More recently, the private self has been applied to territoriality in research concerning personal space. The resulting structure is something like a "body bubble" that can be invaded or withstood. For example, the normal North American conversational zone is about three feet. To converse at a lesser distance may invade another's privacy and be annoying, although to stand at too great a distance is to appear unfriendly.

Chronemics. The study of time or temporality is called chronemics. Like the other nonverbal communication behaviors, chronemics is highly culture bound—which probably explains the countless intercultural misunderstandings. Often, stereotypes stem from insensitivity to the milieu of contrasting cultural clocks, resulting in such words and phrases as "irresponsibility," "laziness," "never on time," and "how do these people operate?" being applied to cultural groups whose orientation toward time differs from some North Americans' view of time. As one Latin American stated it, "People in my country believe people are more important than time, schedules, and events." Like other nonverbal communication phenomena, chronemics also touches the innermost fiber of culture and is discussed more thoroughly in a subsequent chapter.

Paralinguistic stimuli. In addition to verbal and nonverbal stimuli, a third type of stimulus also becomes a message to evoke meanings in intercultural communication. Paralanguage is the set of vocal, nonvocabulary utterances that carry meaning. Such utterances include inflections, rate, pitch, volume, grunts, and other vocalized utterances. Were it not for paralinguistic stimuli, such as the need for a vocal pitch rise at the end of a sentence to connote a question in English, many messages would be imprecise, if not totally incomprehensible. Paralanguage can convey such emotions as sarcasm, disgust, and humor, to name a few.

Intercultural Communication Climate Characterized by Cultural Differences

As we will see in a later chapter, culture is a set of customs, behaviors, beliefs, patterns, and codes or language that socially define a group of individuals. Communication patterns are inherent in a culture as well. Thus, we can describe culture as a kind of climate with communication tendencies or, simply, an intercultural communication climate.

We study intercultural communication to recognize cultural differences that have to be dealt with before effective intercultural communication can occur. Culture is like a kaleidoscope with similar shapes but different colors, or at other times, with different shapes and similar colors. The point of studying culture is to be able to recognize the communication climates that have an impact on intercultural relations.

Macrocultural Systems

Obviously, there are large regions that are structurally and organically bound together into a social system where people have developed a cultural network. Examples include what might be globally described as North American culture, Latin American culture, African culture, Middle Eastern culture, European culture, Asian culture, and so on. These global differences, marked by geopolitical factors, fit into the study of international communication.

Quite naturally, lumping people together obscures the numerous subcultural differences. However, throughout points of historic commonality, there are webs of similarity in certain cultural patterns that generate enough bonding to be considered a common culture. We can talk about "modality" of cultures—the most frequently occurring pattern of behavior or personality—that allows some accurate predictability of cultures. Yet, great care must be exercised to avoid incorrect stereotyping. Individuals should not be hastily judged.

Microcultures simultaneously operating within a macroculture are sometimes referred to as subcultures. As used throughout this text, the term *subculture* does not in any way connote "less than" or "below." It means a culture within a culture. For instance, within the American culture, we might identify an elderly subculture, a cowboy subculture, an Appalachian subculture, and so on. Each subculture contains some similarities to the large parent culture but also has some differences. In this sense, specific groups, occupations or professions, ages, and social classes can be described as subcultures. For example, within the Ibo tribal culture of Nigeria, there are subcultures marked by social class, education, traditionalism, and so on.

One element constituting a subculture is the members' mutual self-perception. Other characteristics used to define subcultures include race, religion, geography, economy, linguistics, national origin, and age differences. Ethnic and racial classifications have also been identified as subcultural communication (Brooks and Emmert 1976). The paragraphs that follow discuss subcultural communication conditions.

Interethnic communication. Ethnic groups are identifiable bodies of people uniquely noted for their common heritage and cultural tradition, which are often national in origin. Interethnic communication is communication between two or more persons from different ethnic backgrounds. Although any listing of ethnic heritage is certain to omit some significant group, the following exemplify ethnic groups in the United States: American Indian, Polish American, Italian American, Irish American, Asian American, Mexican American, and Puerto Rican American.

Interracial communication. Race is genetically transmitted and inherited traits of physical appearance. Therefore, interracial communication is communication between two or more persons of differing racial backgrounds. The important concern here is that racial differences trigger perceptual differences that cut off potential communication before communication attempts have been made. At one university, an administrator in the office of student affairs argued in a meeting with a black fraternity leader. Only after a cooling-down period did both men realize and freely admit that their racial differences had produced an immediate and mutually negative response in each, even before either had spoken a word. The conceptual baggage we often carry with us, such as stereotypes toward other racial groups, can easily act as a filter that blinds us to the fact that, in many instances, few cultural differences exist between two people. Real cultural differences do not always exist beyond ethnicity and race—we simply magnify the immediate out of proportion through the looking glass of stereotypes.

Countercultural communication. Countercultural communication involves persons from a parent culture communicating with persons from a subculture within the parent culture. Prosser (1978) defines it as

> that interaction between members of a subcultural or cultural group whose members largely are alienated from the dominant culture. Members of the group not only reject the values of the dominant culture or society, but may actively work against these values. Conflict is often the result. (p. 69)

Prosser cites the example of the Amish, a countercultural group whose members have reacted passively, withdrawing from the dominant culture. Or consider Polish laborers who, without historical precedent and at risk of life from the Soviet Union's antistrike policies, went on a well-publicized strike to seek to free labor unions from government control. Many of the communication encounters that followed could be considered countercultural types of intercultural communication, at least in terms of rejecting establishment values existing up to that time.

Social class communication. Some of the differences between people are based on status inferred from income, occupation, and education. Communication between these classes is appropriately labeled social class communication. The gap between the elite and the masses as well as between the rich and the poor is large in many parts of the world. Often accompanying this gap are significant differences in outlook, customs, and other features. Although these social classes share some aspects of a common culture, their differences become a type of subcultural concern.

Group membership communication. In many instances, social participation and group membership are significant subcultural units marked by their homogeneity on ideological characteristics. Many intergroup differences, fueled by group loyalties, explode into serious concerns for subcultural communication. The fighting between Protestants and Catholics in Northern Ireland and between Moslems and Christians in Lebanon are examples of the importance of group membership as a subcultural system within the larger culture. Sex, residence (such as urban and rural), and age (such as senior citizens) are also receiving increasing attention and exemplify circumstances where group differences prevail.

Rural-urban communication. Rural and urban life-styles are noted for differences in pace of life, fatalistic tendencies, philosophy, interpersonal relationship formation, and other qualities. Exploration of the communication styles distinguishing these groups and of their cognitive category differences is highly functional in working with some of the communication problems that can develop when rural and urban individuals interact.

Regional communication. Often, people from one region of the United States have serious communication problems with people from another region. A reserved New Englander is sometimes put off by a syrupy-sweet southern style of communication because he takes it to be a sign of insincerity. On the other hand, a Southerner may interpret the reserved style of her northern friend as a sign of rudeness. In other words, regional cultural styles differ.

Male-female communication. Mounting evidence confirms how communication patterns markedly differ between men and women. From examples in management to cases in the family, data remind us that there are male and female subcultures. The different communication styles of males and females can be a source of enormous interpersonal misunderstanding. An understanding of the cultural differences involved can improve intercultural skills.

Organizational cultural communication. Another kind of cultural communication climate in which most of us interact is organizational culture—

Trends in international terrorism add a challenging dimension to the importance of international as well as intercultural communication.

that is, the culture of an organization which includes its accompanying norms, procedures, and communication patterns. Every organization has an accumulation of its own customs and rules, which along with the mind-set of corporate members, profoundly influences the way organizational members operate among themselves and how they interact with people from other organizational cultures.

The study of corporate culture has illuminated the need for looking at corporations in terms of how they can better improve their public image and their business in the international market. For example, an organization that emphasizes task and performance orientation above other factors will likely experience some frustration in communication with or in doing business with an organization that has a more laid-back approach that emphasizes personal relationships, even at the expense of time and productivity. Of course, it is not really the organizations that communicate—it is the people who represent those organizations. And one of the discoveries in the field of intercultural relations is that corporate organizational norms vastly influence how organizational members talk to other people, how they feel about themselves, and how successful they are when dealing with someone from a different cultural orientation.

Intercultural communication has immediate and long-range effects. Sometimes, those effects occur only as limited feedback, but at other times the effects are more obvious.

There are three intercultural communication outcomes about which we are concerned: task, relationship, and personal adjustment. Task outcome is the result of intercultural communication on performance. *Task* means accomplishing a work-related purpose, and clearly a lot of intercultural communication involves people working together.

Intercultural Communication Outcomes

Another outcome is relationship outcome, which is to say that we are concerned about what others think of us. Do they like us? Dislike us? Can we continue to work together? Understanding and friendship are two important subsets of relationship. Increased understanding makes mutual influence and accurate understanding possible (Ruhly 1976). One of the goals, in fact, of studying intercultural communication is to increase understanding and to decrease tensions.

Friendship is also a relationship outcome of intercultural communication. An effective application of intercultural principles noted throughout this text hopefully will inspire interpersonal attraction and friendship. Effective intercultural communication occurs when self-disclosure, trust, and liking result because each of us has tried a little harder to let cultural differences provide an opportunity for developing friendship.

A third possible outcome of intercultural communication is personal adjustment. We have learned a great deal in the last few years about the process of going through transitions and overcoming the cultural stresses that accompany communication in a culture different than our own. Learning to cope—and in the case of long-term permanent moves, learning to acculturate into the new culture—is a major outcome.

Task, relationship, and personal adjustment outcomes are certainly effects of intercultural communication. However, the nature of the perceived relationships in a communication climate and the degree of cultural adjustment we experience influence the entire intercultural process. In other words, the kind of relationship we have with the person with whom we are communicating touches the communication experience either positively or negatively. Similarly, a person who is adjusting well to culture shock is usually a more effective intercultural communicator and relationship builder.

As we will discuss later in this book, intercultural effectiveness is the goal of intercultural communication. The research on effectiveness highlights the variables that can make us more successful in our interactions. In the long run, success at task, relationship building, and personal adjustment is a matter of outweighing negative attributes with positive intercultural processes.

This text takes a "culture general" rather than a "culture specific" approach and contains numerous examples and illustrations from a significant number of cultures. Throughout the book, however, the theme of principles is salient. Hopefully, the positive outcome principle will be helpful.

Developing Intercultural Skills in Initiating Intercultural Communication

The principles and concepts introduced in this chapter lead to the following practical skills. By enhancing skill levels, we hope to improve our intercultural relationships.

1. *Assume the burden of communication to be yours.* Many people simply avoid the sometimes difficult task of communicating with someone from a culture different than their own. Assuming the burden for making the attempt is an important first step in improving intercultural communication skills. When intercultural "breakdowns" occur, try to take responsibility for finding creative ways of solving the problem.

2. *Try to look beyond surface conditions, such as dress, custom, and environmental conditions (too cold, too hot, too humid, too dry, etc.)* Most of us tend to see and process new places on a tourist level.

3. *Develop a curiosity about the internals of culture, such as cultural structure, cultural thought patterns and logic, and cultural relationships.* A sense of internal culture can heighten intercultural experiences and foster better relationships.

4. *Look for ways in which various communication sources mold perceptions of groups.* Family, friends, media, and educational sources all leave us with information about cultural groups. Question your communication sources to develop a sharp focus on the accuracy of their stereotypes. A jaundiced view of all of our communication sources would likely be dysfunctional, but allowing ourselves a healthy critique of the perceptions handed to us invites growth.

5. *Discover ways that relationships affect content and content affects relationships.* Obviously, how we feel about someone colors the message, and conversely, messages can heighten or flatten how we feel about a person. Unfortunately, not everyone means what he or she says, so working through the person versus the message issue can be an important aspect of communicating.

6. *Broaden your views of culture from something "foreign" to the notion of collectives.* Where people relate and have tasks, communication bonds emerge. And with these bonds develop a set of norms, structure, thought, procedure of relationship, and communication style. One measure of a person's intercultural growth is his or her ability to visualize those kinds of factors in a number of groups and to look for the ways in which a culture exists for that group.

7. *Where a set of negative attributes exists for you toward a group or a person within a certain group, work on balancing the negative attributes with positive attributes.* Unfortunately, many people selectively perceive negative features about others, or better put, what they define as negative features. The idea here is to develop the discipline to select and search out positive attributes to weigh alongside the negative.

This Chapter in Perspective

Intercultural communication involves person A interfacing with person B in a reciprocal process of sending and receiving messages in a context of cultural differences with various potential effects. The term *intercultural communication* is somewhat inclusive, and purposefully so. It is important to discover the imprint of culture on communication. That tracing of culture's "footprints" in the sands of each human's experience is partly this book's theme. What we say and do has a cultural concomitant, and as you read each chapter, hopefully, you will discover the important roles of cultural and social influences on communication.

You may not live in Pongo Pongo, but you may live in Chicago, or in a rural area of the United States, or in a region of the United States culturally different from the place where you grew up. So, intercultural communication should encompass a number of dimensions where culture and communication come together. This text takes you through the dimensions that should assist you in sorting out how talking and listening are affected by culture and other social variables. The text begins by introducing you to the dynamics and nature of culture. It then goes on to explain how our interpersonal relationships with others in the context of culture affect our communication, a central concern in the material presented.

Exercises

1. Conduct a newspaper scan for bias toward groups. How can you spot these reflections? How can you define them? What words or symbols would you use to alter perceptions of these groups if you were writing the newspaper story?

2. In a small group, list as many subcultures as you can within the United States. Pick two or three of these cultures and identify the form, structure, and symbols of these groups. How do their forms and symbols foster or inhibit communication with other cultural groups?

3. Rent a video movie of *The Witness* (about the Amish culture). After viewing the movie, discuss the perceptual limitations people have of the Amish subculture. What perceptual limitations do the Amish have of the larger macroculture? If you were in a position to resolve problem areas in intercultural communication between the Amish and others, what would you do?

4. Write at least ten headlines from a newspaper that indicate culture or groupness. How do they define culture?

Resources

Berlo, David K. *The Process of Communication: An Introduction to Theory and Practice.* New York: Holt, Rinehart and Winston, 1960.

Bernard, H. Russel, and Pertti Pelto. *Technology and Social Change.* New York: Macmillan, 1972.

Birdwhistell, Ray L. "Some Relations between American Kinesics and Spoken American English." In *Communication and Culture,* edited by Alfred G. Smith. New York: Holt, Rinehart and Winston, 1966.

Brooks, William D., and Philip Emmert. *Interpersonal Communication.* Dubuque, Iowa: Wm. C. Brown Company Publishers, 1976.

Gudykunst, William B., and Young Yun Kim. *Communicating with Strangers.* New York: Random House, 1984.

Hall, Edward T. *The Silent Language.* New York: Anchor, 1973.

Mehrabian, Albert. *Silent Messages.* 2d ed. Belmont, Calif.: Wadsworth, 1981.

Prosser, Michael. *The Cultural Dialogue.* Boston: Houghton Mifflin, 1978.

Rogers, Everett M., and F. Floyd Shoemaker. *Communication of Innovations: A Cross-Cultural Approach.* New York: Free Press, 1971.

Rogers, Everett M., with Lynn Svenning. *Modernization among Peasants: The Impact of Communication.* New York: Holt, Rinehart and Winston, 1969.

Ruhly, Sharon. *Orientations to Intercultural Communication.* Chicago: SRA, 1976.

Samovar, Larry A., and Richard E. Porter. *Intercultural Communication: A Reader.* 4th ed. Belmont, Calif.: Wadsworth, 1985.

Sharp, Lauriston. "Steel Axes for Stone Age Australians." In *Human Problems in Technological Change,* edited by Edward H. Spicer. New York: Russell Sage Foundation, 1952.

Smith, Alfred G. (ed). *Communication and Culture.* New York: Holt, Rinehart and Winston, 1966.

Tippett, Alan. "A Mexican Flashback." *Missiology* 3(1975):259–64.

Chapter 2

Presuppositions to Intercultural Communication

Objectives

After completing this chapter, you should be able to:

1. Discuss some general historical trends leading to interest in intercultural communication.

2. Generalize about some of the situations in which intercultural communication is important.

3. List eight axioms about the intercultural communication process.

This chapter opens with an examination of a few historical trends that influenced the development of the study of intercultural communication. From there, the chapter discusses some of the situations in which intercultural communication is important. Throughout the years of intercultural communication research, trends have indicated some major threads underlying the intercultural communication process. These basic assumptions, axioms, or presuppositions are fundamental principles of intercultural relationships and interactions and are discussed in detail in the final section of this chapter.

While you may have some concrete ideas about speech and communication theory, you may never have had any exposure to intercultural communication, which is a relatively new area of communication studies. So, let us explore this portion of the speech and communication disciplines by first discussing what conditions led to the serious investigation of intercultural communication.

The Origins of Intercultural Communication

Some observers claim that, prior to World War II, many people in the United States seemed to lack a kind of world perspective. It is true that we had the Monroe Doctrine, embracing people in the world because it was our "manifest destiny" to extend the doctrines of "democracy." We also learned from the experiences of travelers, missionaries, and the like. However, the Second World War seemed to jolt us, even more than the First World War, into a national consciousness that there really was another world out there. This nation's isolationist views continued to evolve toward a path of global awareness. For instance, foreign language classes following World War II took on new enthusiasm, partly perhaps because language had become more "functional."

As our national attitudes toward the world began to change toward a more global view, our understanding about culture also began a gradual change that was long overdue. In 1909, for instance, the Bureau of Indian Affairs, working with other persons, had arranged "The Last Great Indian Council," a meeting that was supposed to be a type of farewell to the "vanishing race" of Indians, despite the fact that Indians had been increasing in numbers, not decreasing (Faherty 1976). This lack of cultural awareness was augmented by various national programs intended to assimilate the Indians into white society. Often, the handling of educational, welfare, and medical programs on Indian reservations, for instance, revealed little awareness of certain Indian cultures. Such examples typified the way in which a number of programs for minorities in the United States and foreign programs for citizens in Third World nations had been handled in the past. The formal study of culture up until the Second World War focused to a large extent upon political-geographical aspects of culture, not upon cultural anthropology. Although there were some notable exceptions among British and European social anthropologists, such as Malinowsky and others, and among American cultural anthropologists, such as Sapir, Margaret Mead, and Ruth Benedict, by and large, cultural anthropology lacked a general citizenry acceptance until World War II.

Not only did the war cause our soldiers to return home with stories of Pongo Pongo, Bali, and Algiers and with a broader view of the world, but, during the war, American leaders were faced with a practical strategic problem. How could the United States secure the cooperation of some island residents, for instance, when the U.S. leaders knew practically nothing about the language or the culture? At that point, anthropologists were invited to study and discover the culture of many of these new places. Through these investigations, the focus of cultural anthropology for the populace in the United States took on new meaning. Thus, the study of culture became somewhat more generally accepted, and many people in a number of government agencies, academic disciplines, and the like began discussing the importance of culture.

After the Second World War, a number of programs focusing on world situations and U.S. policy abroad influenced the development of intercultural communication studies. Of course, the establishment of the United Nations became a significant concern of U.S. foreign policy. With the United Nations occupying a prominent role in world events, the U.S. government felt obliged to initiate new programs in interacting with leaders from nations throughout the world. This situation created a need to learn about the political, social, economic, and cultural life surrounding the representatives of these many nations. With the advent of the World Health Organization, the United Nations' assistance programs, the World Bank, and other agencies, the need to understand the culture of many developing nations and to interact meaningfully with citizens from these nations became one goal of some government agencies. Unfortunately, many of their attempts at communication across these cultural boundaries were superficial and sometimes dominated by economic theories of development that cast some dispersion upon cross-cultural theories of social change. Often, some of the sincere attempts of United Nations' agencies and other organizations were overshadowed by the lack of cultural understanding of the peoples they were trying to serve.

Because the activity of the United Nations and other organizations inadvertently created a need to understand the interface of culture and communication, Congress passed an act in 1953 that instituted the United States Information Agency (USIA). The name was changed in 1977 to the International Communication Agency. This agency was charged with providing information about the United States through various communication media to nations of the world. One familiar medium is the "Voice of America," but there are magazines and other materials as well.

Early pioneers in this effort during the 1950s, such as Edward T. Hall, found that the USIA sometimes lacked cultural information. The image of the ugly American seemed linked to poorly trained foreign service officers and travelers who lacked awareness of other cultures and insight into issues that could be dealt with by some knowledge of intercultural communication. During this decade, Edward T. Hall drew upon his vast experience with the Hopi and Navaho Indians during the 1930s and 1940s and with foreign service officers in his capacity with the USIA and wrote the classic *Silent Language,* originally published in 1959. In some ways, this publication marked the birth of intercultural communication since it synthesized some crucial and fundamental issues in understanding culture and communication, cultural perceptions of interpersonal distance and of time, and their relationships to numerous intercultural misunderstandings.

The 1960s in the United States also marked a kind of cultural awakening. With the passage of the Civil Rights Act in 1964, the nation more seriously than ever before discovered its pockets of minorities. The same decade gave birth to many human rights issues and to the emergence of many countercultures in the United States. The questions, and sometimes the fights, made us painfully aware that communication between groups and cultures was no longer a matter of international expediency, but a problem of domestic urgency. And it appears that events in the 1990s will cause us to determine our future in part by our abilities to understand and to interact interculturally.

Perhaps the most recent event with the severest repercussions for intercultural communication was the Vietnam War. The interactions with Southeast Asians under the conditions imposed by the war overwhelmingly influenced the participants. Then, the consequent overflow of refugees thrust a new generation of Americans into cultural contact never before known to them, for suddenly, elementary, high school, and college students were now in classrooms with counterparts from Cambodia, Laos, and Vietnam. Educators faced a challenge with a cultural group with whom experience was lacking, and communication challenges loomed at an all-time high following these postwar adjustments.

Of historical importance, too, is the continuing influx of political and economic refugees from the Caribbean, Central America, and Mexico. The intercultural demands have opened additional opportunities and problems in rural and urban areas throughout the United States.

From these historical points, investigations began to accrue, along with compilations of essays revolving around intercultural communication. For instance, in 1966, anthropologist Alfred Smith edited *Communication and Culture,* a resource that brought together essays from a number of fields, including communication theory, mathematics, social psychology, psychiatry, linguistics, anthropology, and sociology. Later, many volumes appeared, each exploring dimensions of the quickly emerging field of intercultural communication.

Meanwhile, the field of speech was rapidly changing, sometimes being newly named communication and speech communication. The directions in many speech departments, starting with name changes in the early 1960s, added to rhetorical theories and public address concerns of speech and communication in its many contexts—such as interpersonal communication, small group communication, and organizational communication. Then, in the later 1960s and early 1970s, a number of U.S. colleges and universities added coursework in intercultural communication, as well as in social communication, because of the large number of sociologically oriented communication studies from the 1940s to the present.

Thus, from the work of anthropologists, linguists, psychologists, sociologists, and communication specialists, there has arisen an ever-growing body of literature on the interface of people talking with people, within and between cultural frameworks. Now, intercultural communication research does not focus exclusively on issues from any one discipline but combines insights and theory concerning the message and its impact wherever people are communicating across cultural distinctions.

When Intercultural Communication Is Important

One ultimate goal of understanding intercultural communication dynamics is to recognize circumstances when intercultural needs dominate. Perhaps you have already begun to picture numerous occasions in which intercultural communication is needed, and perhaps the situations that follow will encourage even further thinking about concrete ways in which this text can be helpful. Keep in mind that culture predominates many situations. Therefore, principles of intercultural communication may apply broadly, as some of the following points concerning intercultural communication saliency demonstrate.

Interacting within Subcultures

Many of us live in culturally diverse cities, regions, and schools. Too often, many people treat those conditions with mild tolerance and with little awareness of how to communicate with individuals from a contrasting subculture. For example, a member of an Appalachian subculture may feel uncomfortable talking with a visitor from Maine. Both people can experience positive communication, but initial impressions and stereotyping must be overcome. Negative categorizations of "Yankee" and "hillbilly" must give way to positive motivations to speak, listen, and understand before effective communication occurs.

Interacting within a Host Culture

Whenever we travel in another country, we have two ways of handling our visit. One way is to stay with friends or family and never venture forth into the culture. Or we can experience the new culture, utilizing the things we have learned from this text and through experience. One naval officer, for example, found that applying several insights from his study of intercultural communication enabled him to interact quickly and competently during his stay in Italy.

Intercultural communication involves skills that facilitate relationships, break down barriers, and create foundations for new visions.

A major challenge of intercultural communication involves reformulating our preconceived impressions of "foreign" students and their impressions of North Americans. Overcoming stereotypes, understanding culture, and empathizing with the international student are but a few ways we can make friends and enrich our own experiences interculturally and educationally.

Interacting with International Students

Interacting within Organizations	Hundreds of U.S. organizations are multinational corporations employing many workers from the United States to travel and work in a host country. You may discover new careers and exciting opportunities in business, education, or governmental organizations in different cultures. An understanding of intercultural communication can address many of the challenges you may face if you work overseas.
Interacting Internationally	If you choose to work in international agencies or in broadcasting, for instance, the principles of culture and intercultural communication will again be useful. Understanding the variables and the theories noted in this text will provide insight for your analysis of a culture and should assist you at those times you must rhetorically shape messages to achieve effectiveness.
Interacting within One's Own Culture	An understanding of intercultural communication can help us to understand others and ourselves in our own culture. These principles of communication should prove useful for self-awareness.
Interacting within the Classroom	The pluralism of cultures within a culture clearly carries into classroom communication. The social roles, competition, cliques, and stereotyping can give rise to negative, dysfunctional classroom communication. On the other hand, experiencing cultural differences in a classroom can become an enormous resource for personal, social, and intellectual growth. The classroom, in fact, may be our most immediate environment for exploring intercultural communication.
Axioms about the Intercultural Communication Process	Research in intercultural communication has revealed eight axioms, or basic assumptions, about intercultural relationships and interactions. The paragraphs that follow review each of these axioms in detail.
Intercultural Communication Assumes the Principle of Difference	That communication exists in a climate of cultural differences is a presupposition for the entire range of intercultural principles. The whole process begins with the perception that differences exist. Consequently, we focus on the message linkage between individuals or groups from two different cultural situations. Naturally, there are a number of antecedents and consequences to that interaction, but it is the bridging of the intercultural gap that gives intercultural communication its fullest meaning.

The principle of difference implies that people often do not immediately share norms, thought patterns, structures, and systems. However, dealing with cultural differences alone and studying cross-cultural comparisons, while valuable, do not get to the point of contact and communication (Kim 1984).

Rather, it is precisely the principle of difference that explains communication tendencies. We may be motivated to avoid intercultural interactions because being confronted with difference may be uncomfortable for us. On the other hand, an effective intercultural manager recognizes difference as a positive motivational approach to create skills to work through and overcome misunderstanding and poor communication. So the difference, once recognized, can have positive or negative motivational qualities. To be successful in intercultural relationships, we must recognize differences as resources. An exact copy of ourselves can prove only to multiply our own flaws—the differences of others can provide a renewed resource of insight.

By the nature of the process, intercultural communication is rooted in the social relationships that accompany our interactions. That is, communication has content and relationship. Watzlawick, Beavin, and Jackson (1967) emphasize that communication does not exist in content isolation. Communication, and ultimately meaning, is cemented with the two essential notions of content and relationship. In other words, our relationship with the person with whom we are communicating affects how the message is interpreted. For example, if our best friend said, "Could we get started on this project?" we would probably interpret the statement as a simple request for starting or perhaps completing a task. However, if our boss said, "Could we get started?" the meaning would likely be different. From the boss, the statement sounds more demanding and is much more likely to be treated with greater deference than our close friend's request.

Messages also alter relationships. For example, we probably would feel friendlier toward a co-worker who compliments us than someone who constantly criticizes.

Another perceived relationship occurs when we evaluate others in terms of their credibility and their similarity to us. These evaluative tendencies are especially important in communication because they lead to informal information relationships in which we receive, give, evaluate, and act upon information. The qualities we perceive in others are unique social relationships in cultures and subtly wield enormous communication influence. For instance, an international student from Thailand recently expressed her negative evaluation of a certain American young man. However, once she reevaluated her attribution of various qualities about him, she perceived him as much more believable in ways that were credible for her home culture. Once that credibility was established, she began to view this same young man's messages as "very important." In the process, her alteration of the credibility relationship subsequently influenced the messages between the two.

Intercultural Communication Has Content and Interpersonal Relationship

Intercultural communication can be described in terms of the cognitive, social, and communication styles that people use. Some people have a dominant communicator style; others have a submissive style. Some are warm and caring; others are cold and unfeeling. Some are authoritarianlike; others are open-minded. Some communicators are preoccupied; others are attentive. People view themselves in various psychological communication roles, and this perception leads to some dramatic relationship styles in social communication. A few other communication styles include being extremely friendly, being a mediator between people, being a counselor, being a critic, being a question-asker,

Communicator Style Affects Intercultural Communication

being an informed opinion-giver, being a victim, and so on. Each of these psychological roles also creates a stylized social relationship role. Furthermore, very few of us remain unaffected by the positions others put us in during their communication attempts from these role positions.

The point is that the intercultural communicator functions through the psychological and social roles that people play. And some of these relationships serve information roles—either by providing information, by sharing and/or evaluating information, or by the very style of communication used in the interpersonal communication and in the development of the relationship.

Intercultural Communication Involves Reducing Uncertainty

From one perspective, intercultural communication depends upon reducing uncertainty levels about other people. In our interpersonal encounters, there is always some ambiguity about the relationship: "How does he feel about me?" "What are her attitudes?" "What can I expect to happen next in this relationship?" As human beings, we experience discomfort with questions about relationships, and so to reduce our discomfort, we engage in behaviors that enhance our chances of maximum understanding with the fewest possible questions.

In the field of communication, information theory leads us to conclude that predictability is an important aspect of relationships. We seem to need a certain amount of redundancy to lessen the entropy in communication. Consequently, predictability, redundancy, and low entropy leave us in a more comfortable psychological state. In other words, the less guesswork about a relationship, usually the better we feel about the situation.

All communication relationships, however, have some ambiguities. Within our own cultures, the ambiguity is lessened by some standard areas of predictability. When we greet someone, for instance, there is a range of acceptable cultural greetings that we expect and understand. Other cultural rules guide the conversation, even to the style of saying good-bye. If we share the same culture, the communication rules are implicitly understood and the job of deciphering and interpreting the other person is significantly easier.

Interaction with someone from another culture, however, means that we do not necessarily share the same communication rules—and the ambiguity increases dramatically. There are significantly more possible behaviors during intercultural communication than during intracultural communication.

Gudykunst and Kim (1984) point out that with strangers we work significantly harder to reduce ambiguities than with familiar people. The process of uncertainty reduction involves three interaction phases: precontact, initial contact and impression, and closure.

Precontact. The first phase of reducing uncertainty involves precontact impression formation. In coming in contact with another person, we proceed from an unfocused scanning of the environment to a focused scanning (Barnlund 1968). That is, we become aware that another person is suddenly a part of our immediate communication climate. At that point, we gain interpretation information from the appearance and mannerisms of the other person,

Interaction between people from different cultural backgrounds creates a system between them that demands an understanding of each participant's need to reduce uncertainty.

while the other person does the same with us. This is called reciprocal scanning. A number of active and passive strategies can reduce uncertainty, mostly by gathering information through indirect channels (Berger, Gardner, Parks, Shulman, and Miller 1976). The point is that a precontact stage of interpretation begins immediately and thus enables us to initiate the process of uncertainty reduction.

Initial contact and impression. The second phase of the uncertainty reduction process in intercultural communication involves the initial impression that occurs within the first few minutes of the verbal communication. Brooks and Emmert (1976) suggest that, during the first four minutes, a decision is made to continue or discontinue the relationship. Even within the first two minutes, we form some rather important judgments: "Do I like him?" "Is she understanding me?" "Am I wasting my time?" "He sure doesn't look like much." This impression procedure may not take exactly four minutes, but it does not take long to form long-lasting attitudes.

Closure. The third phase of uncertainty reduction involves our need for closure, or completion, in our interpersonal relationships. We exhibit a rather intriguing behavior of trying to categorize others into some pattern meaningful for our personal understanding. Some people feel cognitively uncomfortable until they have developed a summary of the person with whom they are communicating—at least a kind of mental pigeonhole that helps to evaluate the other person. Closure involves two interaction principles: attribution and implicit personality development.

Attribution theory suggests that we attempt to understand the behaviors of others, and in the process, make inferences about their motivations (DeVito 1986). If someone does something we like, we attribute a positive motivation to that person because, after all, they practiced what we valued. Negative actions, however, cause us to infer a negative motivation—"He doesn't like me," "She's out to get me," "He's manipulative," "She really is working for a different position in the company."

Related to attribution processes is implicit personality theory. This theory implies that we seek closure in a way consistent with our first personality assessment of another individual. If our first impressions of another person are positive, then we tend to continue to ascribe positive qualities to that person. For instance, if Jim is energetic and assertive, then he will also be _____.
What word did you think about inserting? Courageous? Intelligent? The theory predicts that some positive word will follow. In the same way, if the first-known qualities are negative, then a tendency exists to close the assessment with more negative features. If Jim is dumb and clumsy, what other personality-oriented adjectives might be included? In other words, there is a positive or negative halo surrounding our first information about someone. This extended halo effect leaves us with comfortable closure and consistency.

The closure principle is so salient that we even draw upon impersonal (often in-group) information available to us to make a judgment. Without firsthand knowledge, we sometimes find our culture's interpretation valuable for reducing uncertainty. Unfortunately, capsules of information passed on through our culture about other groups can be erroneous stereotypes. A stereotype can be positive ("Asians are polite and hardworking") or negative ("Multinational corporations are nefarious").

Communication Is
Central to Culture

Cultures inherently contain communication systems. Many years ago, Smith (1966) observed that "communication and culture are inseparable." The first implication of this insight is that culture itself contains systems and dynamics pertaining to the sharing of symbols. For instance, cultures have procedures for achievement and attainment within the culture. In American culture, the symbols of these "rites of passage" include degrees, promotions, and the like. In the culture that typifies much of the Western world, material objects, technology, and symbols of material wealth signal our attainments. A plaque of recognition, a certificate of merit, and a gold watch at retirement all represent examples of how we use symbols as a part of our culture's communication system. Natives of Botswana use physical symbols also, but the symbols represent recognition in tribal terms and are symbolic of pride in the primary

Communication is central to any culture. Intercultural communication involves relationship development that is sufficient to bridge intercultural gaps.

group and not just individual attainment. So, communication systems have something to do with the symbols we use in a culture.

Each culture also has communication styles appropriate for that culture. For instance, in Saudia Arabia, interpersonal communication style is marked by flowery language, numerous compliments, and profuse thanks. Rarely does one publicly criticize fellow workers in that culture because that would smack of disloyalty and disrespect (Harris and Moran 1979). Africans tend to exhibit an extremely friendly and warm interpersonal communication style. Asians appear rule oriented and reserved because of procedural and cultural displays of respect and honor. Americans are informal, somewhat uninhibited, and get down to the main point fairly quickly in a kind of linear, evidential manner. Britons seem to have a reserved subtlety, preferring understatement and control in interpersonal interaction. These examples remind us that it is crucial to understand the intercultural style of the people with whom we communicate.

Another axiom of intercultural communication involves communication effectiveness. This concept underscores intercultural success as a goal. That success can take many forms: improved relationships, effective management, friendship, training, technology dissemination, conflict reduction, and the like.

Communication behavior links with a set of outcomes that can be reasonably successful with the right awareness and skills. Intercultural communication involves bridging cultural differences, and the essential notion of intercultural performance is to realize our best in these communication situations.

Intercultural Effectiveness Involves Intercultural Communication Success

The skills necessary for intercultural effectiveness and the variables that influence effectiveness are examined in a later chapter. In the long run, performance is based on a cultural awareness model that task needs and people needs work in concert.

Intercultural Communication Relates to Cultural Adjustment and Stress Management

Research in the area of culture shock, cultural transition, and cultural stress management has mushroomed in recent years. This rather exciting body of literature indicates that intercultural communication is successful proportionate to our ability to adjust to transitional experiences and new cultural environments. In fact, there are some rather predictable patterns in the adjustment process. Without some prior awareness, the cultural stresses can be overwhelming, dramatically altering our intercultural behaviors and experiences. Fortunately, researchers have analyzed a number of methods of modifying culture shock and adjustment phenomena. The correlation between intercultural adjustment and intercultural effectiveness is fundamental to the study of cultural differences and the underlying interactional communication climate and also to an examination of the adaptation process itself.

Intercultural Communication Is Not Always Completely Successful

Those who study communication theory and principles would like to believe that understanding of these concepts will always result in successful intercultural communication. Quite naturally, however, this is not always possible. Simply put, if we approach clarity, we really have done our best. If we reduce relationship ambiguities, then we have facilitated communication. If we foster cultural acceptance, then we have approached a critical pathway in a world of converging values. Success may come to those who *attempt* to interculturally communicate; it will *not* come to those who never even try to bridge intercultural gaps.

Developing Skills in Processing Intercultural Assumptions

The following suggestions may prove helpful in improving your skills in processing intercultural assumptions:

1. *Work on developing a theory-oriented mind-set.* This book emphasizes doing and practicing, not just knowing principles of intercultural communication. However, this chapter is a good place for examining assumptions behind an idea. Looking for single and multiple causes and effects, ascertaining social and historical forces behind the origination of a new concept, and creating new concepts are part of a theory-oriented mind-set. Reasoning, looking for facts, analyzing facts, synthesizing, and offering critiques are also important skills for the intercultural communication process.

2. *Develop fluency in thought.* Surprisingly, many people find that their communication skills are not weak in what they think but in articulating their thoughts ("I know what I think—I just can't say it"). The ability to develop a communication richness of concept and to express that diversity is important. Especially during intercultural communication, we

must explain our meanings in more than one way. Forcing ourselves into multiple ways of describing our feelings, thoughts, and behaviors is a step in initiating improved intercultural communication skills.

3. *See success in people as success with task.* In other words, effective intercultural communication begins with a recognition that a focus on task alone is insufficient. The communication relationships must be planted, watered, and cultivated along with our task orientation for successful intercultural communication experiences. Intercultural relationship success is an important ingredient for task success.

4. *Try to be a facilitator with people.* Another skill that can be helpful in intercultural relations is the ability to link persons who have not yet met. By simple introductions, by emphasis on their commonalities, and by staying with people long enough, we can serve an important liaison role. Sometimes, just knowing the right questions to ask can spotlight others in a positive way. We do not have to be glib or effervescent, just sincere and willing to invest time and energy in others. Then, by sharing our positive insights during an informal introduction to another person, we can build relationships between others that can be exciting for us and more helpful to them.

This Chapter in Perspective

This chapter develops a historical trend analysis explaining the importance of intercultural communication. Intercultural communication is especially important when interacting within subcultures, within host cultures, with international students, within organizations, with international development, with people from our own culture, and with individuals in classrooms.

The following eight axioms concerning intercultural communication are introduced in this chapter:

1. The principle of difference is fundamental to understanding the need for intercultural communication.

2. Intercultural communication has both content and relationship.

3. Personal cognitive communication style affects the intercultural communication process.

4. Intercultural communication is a process partly of reducing uncertainty about relationships and messages.

5. Communication is assumed to be central to culture.

6. Intercultural effectiveness, or performing at our best and with the best tools available, is an important part of intercultural communication.

7. Intercultural adjustment is assumed to be a part of the intercultural process.

8. Intercultural communication does not always lead to clarity but to misunderstanding.

Exercises

1. How have recent trends in terrorism affected foreign travel? Perceptions toward other nations? People who are from different countries?

2. Interview an international student on changing patterns of communication style within his or her country. What are the differences in communication style between that person's home culture and the current culture in which he or she lives?

3. Your instructor will assign an intercultural communication book to each student. Scan and list all of the assumptions about communication that you can find in the book. Compare your list with the lists of other students and compile a master list of assumptions. Evaluate the items on the master list and then redraft a final list of the communication assumptions that you think really say it best.

Resources

Barnlund, Dean C., ed. *Interpersonal Communication: Surveys and Studies.* Boston: Houghton Mifflin, 1968.

Berger, Charles R., R. R. Gardner, Malcolm R. Parks, L. Shulman, and Gerald R. Miller. "Interpersonal Epistemology and Interpersonal Communication." In *Explorations in Interpersonal Communication,* edited by Gerald R. Miller. Beverly Hills, Calif.: Sage, 1976.

Brooks, William D., and Philip Emmert. *Interpersonal Communication.* Dubuque, Iowa: Wm. C. Brown Company Publishers, 1976.

DeVito, Joseph A. *The Interpersonal Communication Book.* 4th ed. New York: Harper and Row, 1986.

Faherty, Robert. "The American Indian: An Overview." In *Intercultural Communication: A Reader,* 2d ed., edited by Larry Samovar and Richard Porter. Belmont, Calif.: Wadsworth, 1976.

Gudykunst, William B., and Young Yun Kim. *Communicating with Strangers.* New York: Random House, 1984.

Hall, Edward T. *Beyond Culture.* New York: Anchor, 1977.

Harris, Philip R., and Robert T. Moran. *Managing Cultural Differences.* Houston: Gulf, 1979.

Kim, Young Yun. "Searching for Creative Integration." In *Methods for Intercultural Communication Research,* edited by William B. Gudykunst and Young Yun Kim. Beverly Hills, Calif.: Sage, 1984. (This is the Intercultural and International Communication Annual, volume 8.)

Smith, Alfred G., ed. *Communication and Culture.* New York: Holt, Rinehart and Winston, 1966.

Watzlawick, Paul, Janet H. Beavin, and Don D. Jackson. *Pragmatics of Human Communication.* New York: Norton, 1967.

Cultural Systems Impacting on Intercultural Communication

Chapter 3

Intercultural Communication and the Organizing Facets of Culture

Objectives

After completing this chapter, you should be able to:

1. Define culture.

2. Identify and utilize elements of culture.

3. Describe various systems of culture.

4. Describe the means by which culture is transmitted.

Perhaps the idea of cultural differences strikes some readers strangely, since, after all, we live in a world of mass media, where we can watch the evening news on television and see for ourselves the modernization among nations and peoples. But the mesmerizing blue light of television may have dulled our sensibilities into thinking there are no differences across cultures. Cold realities continually remind us of groups of people, nations, continents, and a world divided not merely by political boundaries but by cultural barriers.

For example, during a nationwide news interview in 1978, Barbara Walters interviewed the Prime Minister of India, who explained a cultural practice of imbibing one's liquid waste. He described its salutary effects, its ceremonial significance, and its widespread practice. In 1979 and the early 1980s, dissenters to the resurgence of a Moslem nation, during the turmoil of Iran's political life, left a trail of executions; like thieves, their hands were chopped off as a means of social control. Perhaps such a practice of law should be no more shocking than practices in portions of the United States, not so many years ago, where men were hung for stealing a horse, but released or mildly punished for taking a life. The mass suicide of over nine hundred persons in a religious cult in Jonestown, Guyana, also reminds us that we live in a world of different cultures.

A recognition of cultural differences can create in us a desire to understand those differences and to communicate effectively when we contact members from contrasting cultures. This chapter describes the basic foundations of cultures around the world and the organizing principles around which cultures are built. These basics should enable us to more fully realize the dynamics of culture—which in turn should direct our efforts at intercultural communication.

Culture is to the cultural anthropologist what attitudes are to the social psychologist. To the intercultural communicator, an understanding of another culture is necessary to ensure message flow, understanding, and satisfying results from our communication efforts. Just as scholars refine theories of communication to describe the communication flow between doctor and patient, the intercultural practitioner needs a systematic way of understanding messages between individuals of differing cultures. An understanding of culture, then, unlocks a key to more effective intercultural communication.

In this chapter, we first define culture and then identify elements common to all cultures. Various systems of culture are then examined, along with a number of theories about how culture develops.

What Is Culture?

To some people, "culture" refers to some obscure group of people in a distant land; to others, "culture" simply means economic or class differences in their own community. The term includes these things but applies more broadly. Culture has been variously defined by theorists in so many fields of inquiry that over 150 definitions of culture exist. Obviously, a complete compilation of these numerous definitions exceeds the scope of this text. For our purposes, however, culture is defined as follows:

Culture is the total accumulation of many beliefs, customs, activities, institutions and communication patterns of an identifiable group of people.

This definition moves through a continuum from cognitions and beliefs about others and self, including values, to patterns of behavior. Customs and activities are part of a culture's norms, that is, accepted and prescribed models of behavior. The systematization of these norms and beliefs is evident in a culture's institutions. The most frequent pattern of behavior is linguistic, wherein the use of verbal and nonverbal messages represents a feature of daily life. Culture is also reflected in thought, speech, and action. Furthermore, cultural members are identifiable; they can also define themselves perceptually as members of the group, which can be described as a culture.

Culture is generally accepted to be learned rather than inherited. Our immediate context, education, language, and interactions from childhood onward influence us. Much of the behavior of lower animals is instinctive, but human behavior is primarily learned. We learn in a social context, not in isolation. Certainly, culture is group-oriented—a social phenomenon with learning occurring through role models, usually teaching by example.

Cultures also reinforce basic values of good and evil, custom, and ritual. The understanding of personal relations and responsibility to family members is learned; often, this learning occurs in the family, where children imitate family members' beliefs, customs, and behaviors. Thus, a child grows up understanding the world and his or her life through the eyes of the family, which in turn reflects the cultural system. Among the Kissi tribe of Kenya, for example, the grandmother assumes special responsibility for telling her grandchildren stories about the importance of family honesty, loyalty, and the nature of good and evil.

Alfred Smith (1966) emphasized the relationship between communication and culture when he wrote:

Our perception is behavior that is learned and shared, and it is mediated by symbols. Culture is a code we learn and share, and learning and sharing require communication. And communication requires coding and symbols, which must be learned and shared. Communication and culture are inseparable. (p. 7)

Culture is more than a place or an institution, for culture encompasses the life patterns, customs, and beliefs of an identifiable group of people.

Culture is more than a mosaic of customs, for culture teaches behavior:

> Attitudes toward time, property, dress, food, and even the proper distance between people talking to each other all have been determined by culture. Your culture tells you what is beautiful, ugly, sexy, or exciting. Your culture teaches you the value of hard work, thrift, privacy, competition, frankness, and fair play. (*Overseas Diplomacy,* 28)

And just as naturally as these things, our culture also teaches us how to communicate—the code to use and the mode to facilitate that code.

Overall, an important axiom about culture is its inherent communication climate—cognitions, patterns, styles, and behaviors of communication are all linked with culture. That is why we speak of an intercultural communication climate, where cultural interactions involve communication tendencies, conditioned by unique cultures.

A large part of our experience in our own culture involves learning the rules about proper behavior. Our mothers may have warned us "not to point at people" and reinforced their point if we pointed anyway. With thousands of cultural rules—many of which we are not consciously aware—we may have spent much of our life learning to function with these rules and maybe even refining them. Since we invest so much time in culture, it is no wonder we use our culture as a yardstick to judge others.

Culture is something like a glue that bonds people together. A person who refers to a Mexican-American culture probably is thinking of a large population with some commonalities of world view, attitudes, concept of self, and language, who live in the United States as a minority. Obviously, one problem in identifying culture is overgeneralization, since numerous differences among individuals exist in any one culture. But, to avoid this problem of stereotyping, we cannot then swing to an opposite extreme and argue for no commonalities. On the contrary, there is a middle ground where we can respectably speak of central tendencies among groups of people, a modality tendency. The precise boundary where one culture ends and another culture begins is obscure. Nevertheless, we can approach the concept of culture perhaps as we approach the notion of groupness in small group communication, where we recognize its prevalence and then mark its feature.

Now, we will study the elements of culture. By understanding the features that constitute a culture, we can excel in communicating with a member of that culture. Discussing every culture would be impossible in this text. However, in this chapter, we examine ways by which each culture develops customs "natural" to that culture in meeting its needs. We probably cannot learn and remember the do's and don'ts of every culture, but we can sensitize ourselves to the common substance of virtually every culture.

Elements of Culture

Over the years, experts have identified the elements common to all cultures. These elements are very general, but familiarity with these elements across cultures can help us to understand why cultures differ, since cultures may differ widely on their specific characteristics within any one item. And recognizing these differences is a beginning point for intercultural communication.*

The elements of culture that we review here include: cultural history, cultural personality, material culture, role relationships, art, language, cultural stability, cultural beliefs, ethnocentrism, nonverbal behavior, spatial relations, time, recognition and reward, and thought patterns.

Cultural History

Historical development and tradition for a people are foundation stones for analysis—basic cues to understanding a culture. In the United States, for example, a family tree and family lineage afford identity and purpose, perhaps more in some regions than in others. Cultural history generates insight into norms of group and individual behavior and explains many attitudes that seem to be shared by cultural members.

For example, African tribes, such as the Ga and Ewe tribes of Ghana, highly respect the neighboring Ashanti because, as one non-Ashanti indicated, "The Ashanti are strong." Their respect has historical origins. In the slave-trading days, the Ashanti outnumbered and conquered neighboring tribes and

*Ethnographical research can be found in the Human Relations Area File, which is carried by many libraries and offers numerous opportunities for in-depth research of specific cultures.

sold them on the coast as slaves to European and American dealers. Apparently, a historical origin permeates contemporary relationships of the Ashanti and their tribal neighbors. As another example, communication with various tribal Indians from Central and South America would be incomplete without a knowledge of their ancestral heritage, which includes being conquered by Spaniards and a 450-year history of submissiveness to social and economic domination.

Cultures have various ways of expressing their history, heritage, and traditions. Among some African cultures, a totem—often portrayed with elaborate artistry—is used to graphically display tribal history. The totem's importance lies in its symbol as a record of the past, a reminder that for some cultures is a pervasive part of the present. The roots of history for almost every culture are so long that, from the past, come norms and taboos for the present. A group's history provides a social continuity, an identity, as if to say, "This is who I am."

In some cultures, the past is recorded in books—or in some cases by local historians who specialize in memorization of a culture's history. For example, American Alex Haley's quest for his black heritage led to interviews with West African tribal members who specialize in memorizing generations of orally recorded history. In other cultures, temples, mosques, cathedrals, and other historic sites may symbolize significant cultural features.

No matter how a culture records its history, the point for the intercultural communicator is to appreciate a culture's past. For example, many European visitors to the United States wonder at the North American's fascination for the new and innovative. Our enthusiasm for more efficient buildings—to replace old structures that could be remodeled—along with our quest for the latest gadgetry or technology contrast with cultures that believe in preservation and sufficiency of existing material objects. In fact, in many cultures, tradition is so important that anything new is viewed suspiciously. The effective intercultural communicator appreciates these emphases and sources of cultural pride and seeks to learn the history and geography of another person in order to know that person's possible attitudes and values—essential elements in intercultural communication.

Closely linked with history is the culture's general character, its sense of group personality. In other words, cultures can be described as having a certain social characteristic likened to a personal behavior, only expanded to an entire group. The idea is akin to Cattell's (1951) syntality theory, in which he explained that groups are like individuals, since both have generalized orientations to behavioral tendencies, likes and dislikes, myths and ideals. Raymond Rodgers (1978) explained that, through its folklore, a culture or subculture identifies itself with archetypal figures, such as heroes, and that these ideals become a yardstick by which we measure personal and group prowess.

The cultural personality affects interpersonal relationships and expected models of individual personality behavior. For example, in some cultures, decisions are collective rather than individual—even to the point of giving up

Cultural Personality

Traditions and historical roots are a part of culture that contribute to the current life of a group of people, illustrated by these Mayan ruins in Guatemala.

individual rights in favor of decisions made by the leaders in that culture. To speak up against a village chieftain's decision, for instance, would be inappropriate and inconsistent with African villagers' conceptions of behavior. Among the Ashanti tribe, individual decisions are made with the approval of the maternal uncle, maternal grandfather, and one's father.

As a result, interpersonal communication style is highly fashioned after the appropriateness of cultural personality. For example, loudness, pitch, rate, certain stances, gestures, and the like characterize communication behaviors. The specific way a cultural communicator utilizes these may depend on that person's conception of the ideal cultural personality. The North American who speaks in what he considers a normal voice contrasts with a Thai national who is accustomed to lower volume and who considers the former to be talking angrily. In this case, the ideal cultural personality types are in conflict, reflected in their intercultural communication.

Material Culture

Probably the most salient features of most tourist trips abroad are the differences in material culture—food, clothing, and methods of travel, as well as differences in machine technology. Unfortunately, some travelers offend host cultures by making light of their cultural methods of working out basic universal needs. For example, since technology is usually a matter of cultural invention and of intercultural contact with other technologies, it might be argued that no opportunities have arisen for acculturation of a technology, or perhaps the culture has rejected the technology.

Too often, we prematurely judge a culture by its material features. A person who values technological features may overlook a rich cultural heritage in such areas as art, language, interpersonal relationships, and so on. Unfortunately, such myopia can damage intercultural communication.

Material culture is a significant part of culture. However, material culture alone does not provide an adequate yardstick by which to measure culture and to reflect upon the aspects of a culture that lie deep below the surface.

One question in analyzing a culture's technology (such as tools, machines, and so on) concerns the social function of traditional methods for conducting cultural tasks. For instance, one observer described how women in one East African country walked over half a mile to a river that supplied their families with water—two buckets at a time. One of this nation's governmental agencies decided that a water pump and a central water supply system would enormously benefit the villagers. However, the water-gathering routine was a means of social interaction and a very important method of making new relationships, enjoying friendship, and keeping up with village news. The government field staff also did not recognize the fact that routine excretory functions were performed off the beaten paths to and from the river. When the new water system failed—since no one used it—the government was shocked to learn the reasons. The water system was abandoned, and life continued as before. This illustrates that some methods and procedures are not always amenable to change without entire cultural imbalance and repercussions.

Material culture does not exist merely as a feature with functional value. *Overt* material culture may reflect a more subtle, *covert* peculiarity (much like the tip of an iceberg revealing only a small part of the total iceberg). For example, the Yir Yoront tribe of Australia had a central tool—the stone axe— for securing food, shelter, and warmth. Beyond its function of value as a material object, however, the stone axe symbolized masculinity and respect for elders. In short, the stone axe represented authority, which was a controlling feature for these people, bonding together elements of their culture. Although the men owned the stone axes, women and children borrowed and used the tool according to customary rules of social relationships, and, in the process, reinforced the cultural glue of respect and authority. In fact, this artifact of material culture had such symbolic value that the subsequent introduction of the steel axe totally disrupted the social and economic bases of the culture (Sharp 1952). The culture literally disintegrated as thievery, drunkenness, and men selling their wives and daughters as prostitutes became commonplace once social order was removed.

This discussion is not meant to merely warn against judgmental attitudes but to suggest that customs surrounding material culture are complex and their reasons are intricate. Effective intercultural communication begins by looking, first, at what customs exist and, second, at how to avoid reacting negatively when confronting these situations. Material cultural patterns vary dramatically among cultures—the early dinner in some Northern European cultures strikingly contrasts with the late evening meals in Spain, for instance. Simple observation and adaptation are keys to interacting in any host culture.

Role Relationships

Cultures maintain certain attitudes toward categories of persons and their behaviors, which often are expected to conform to predetermined patterns. The prescribed or, at least, expected behaviors toward various cultural members are called roles, and role relationships are another element of culture.

One obvious example of how culture determines role relationships centers on views toward the aged. Japanese students show respect for their elderly in various ways, including the use of various language greeting terms that show respect. The Ashanti of Ghana have a form of greeting any elderly man that is roughly translated "my grandfather." The numerous examples demonstrating respect for the elderly and ancestral generations are well documented. By contrast, many people in our culture lack respect for the elderly; they sometimes view a person past sixty-five as nonproductive, an intruder in the lives of a busy, younger generation. This attitude seems to be changing, but these feelings can cause an elderly person to act upon these societal conceptions. In a type of self-fulfilling prophecy, some elderly people actually perform less efficiently, develop more health problems, and feel alienated because of societal expectations.

Occupational and social role behaviors are also culturally defined. A person in a certain occupation ought to perform in a role-prescribed manner, so the expectation goes. Police officers, lawyers, doctors, and salespersons, to name a few, play a certain role congruent with social expectations. For instance, a police officer usually does not crack jokes while handing out a citation, not because he or she lacks a sense of humor, but because of social roles expected at that moment. Incidentally, personal stress is generally reduced once we narrow the gap among the multiple roles in which many of us perform.

Even our relationships with friends, professors, family, and strangers are mediated by societal expectations. And we usually communicate in full accordance with those unspoken but expected cultural rules for each role. For instance, bowing in Asian cultures correlates with the perceived social relationship: The higher the status of the person, the lower one should bow.

Role differences also involve the differing expectations of males and females. Not only are sex roles organizing factors for a culture, but sex roles are widely variant and culturally dependent. Almost every culture, for example, has a division of labor decisively determined by the individual's sex. Among the Boran herdsmen of Kenya, women are expected to complete all household duties, gardening, and milking while the men tend to the herds. In another example, Vietnamese women are expected to eat smaller quantities of food than men at each meal, no matter how hungry they are (Hong 1976). One performs in such a culture according to appropriate role expectations for one's own sex within the family.

Decision making and authority fall on the shoulders of male societal members in what anthropologists call *patriarchal* societies. Societies where women are in authority, called *matriarchal* societies, do not formally exist. British anthropologist Robin Fox (1971) summarized this position:

> Early writers called any system that looked to them as though "kinship was through females only" either matriarchal or a system of mother-right (to contrast with the patrilineal, patriarchal, or father-right). This implied that power and authority were in the hands of women in such a system. This is, of course, just not true. . . . Such a sinister practice exists only in the imagination, although most people have at some time or another accused their neighbors of it, or at least of being in some way "matriarchal." Thus, Athens accused Sparta, France accused England, and now we are accusing the Americans. It probably arises from a deep-rooted fear on the part of men that they will lose their position, and the fear is projected onto disliked nations. Be this as it may, the true Amazonian solution is unknown. (p. 113)

The decision-making and authority positions of women are obviously changing in a number of cultures. Power, of course, comes in variant forms. Consider, for example, Boran women of Kenya who decide who in the family gets the greatest allotment of milk. Or consider women who are world leaders. In either case, the importance and power-status relationship of women in a culture vary with the norms of the culture.

Art

Another universal element for cultural analysis is the relevant artistic expressions of a particular culture. When we consider music, sculpture, painting, weaving, and so on as reflections of underlying themes of a culture at a given time in its history, this element assumes deeper significance. The myriad of aesthetic differences and explanations of why one culture's view of "beautiful" is another culture's view of "ugly" go far beyond the mere scope of the artistic object or its manifestations. Serious probing usually leads to the discovery of an underlying meaning of various aspects of art. Artistic expression can reflect current, relevant themes of a culture, by which the investigator gathers more and better insight. Or an investigator may discover a bit of artistic work to hold only vestigial significance, in that a particular design of cloth, for instance, at one time had special religious significance but perhaps currently only holds tourist-attraction significance.

A culture's artistic expressions become one keyhole through which to view and understand a culture.

Play and recreation as art forms usually develop in two ways. Indigenous games develop from within the culture. Other games and forms of play are borrowed from contact with other cultures.

Language

Language is another element of culture. The descriptive linguist strives to discover and report the basic sound system (*phonology*), meaningful sound combinations (*morphology*), and grammar (*syntax*) of a language. The anthropologically trained linguist usually also investigates the relations between the language and the culture.

The relation between language and culture is important, inasmuch as language and its categories filter our reality, shaping ideas and organizing reality by the lines and boundaries that linguistic systems draw. Every culture has a language, although of the more than three thousand language communities on earth, over one-fourth have yet to be written.

Cultural Stability

Just as we can characterize cultures according to various structural and attitudinal categories, we can go a step further and discuss briefly norms of cultural stability and change. It is not immediately obvious why this is true, but another element of culture is that cultures can be characterized as innovative or resistant. For apparent historical and traditional reasons, some cultures have propensity for change; others do not. For example, Japan has demonstrated extraordinary adaptation into the world economy since World War II. Apparently, Japanese values stress flexibility, perhaps a cultural feature from warlord days. The precise boundaries of highly adaptive cultures is not well known. Current research efforts will probably reveal methods of delineating cultural stability and change.

Communication depends extensively on perception. Our perceptual *frame of reference* is like a screen through which information passes. Since the frame of reference filters our encoding and decoding, we can account for different interpretations of reality by considering perceptual "windows" through which we view our world and the universe and by which specific beliefs about that view develop. Values and cultural themes also constitute the belief system, which is another unique element of each culture.

Cultural Beliefs

While specific perceptual frames of reference, or ways of seeing things, depend on our total life experience, it is possible to pinpoint a foundation for our frame of reference. The core of our frame of reference is *world view,* a term referring to accepted beliefs about the nature of the universe. More than just an "outlook" or "philosophy of life," world view appears to be a function of several interwoven factors.

Ethnocentrism, another element of culture, refers to a group or individual attitude of superiority over other groups or individuals. In almost every culture, tendencies exist to judge others. The "us" versus "them" attitude is especially prevalent among subcultures. In many nations, urbans look down upon rurals, elites scorn peasants, and white-collar employees negatively evaluate blue-collar employees. National cultures also practice ethnocentrism. For instance, Iranis feel superior to Iraqis, Indians ethnocentrically look down on Pakistanis, Thai devaluate Malaysians, and so on. On thousands of occasions throughout history, ethnocentrism has led to wars, takeovers, and a host of negative behaviors. This tendency to judge appears universal and is part of the attitude system sometimes lurking in intercultural communication climates. High ethnocentrism leads to negative stereotypes. What better way to prove one's superiority than to rely on negative caricatures to confirm the negative attributes of another, but disliked group.

Ethnocentrism

Every culture has some system of nonverbal behaviors—gesture, touch, facial expression, eye movement, and so on. The collective pattern of such behaviors, while usually in concert with spoken communication, is itself a symbol system. Nonverbal behavior, in this sense, becomes nonverbal communication. Many researchers agree that a culture's nonverbal communication system is the most powerful communication system available, although not without its liabilities. The differences in nonverbal behavior among cultures can cause breakdowns in intercultural communication.

Nonverbal Behavior

Another element of culture involves our use of space. Use of space is considered a part of the nonverbal communication system within cultures since we infer information and meaning from an individual's structuring and use of space. Spatial relationships refer to the interpersonal uses of space between communicators. In fact, a great deal of communication research highlights relationship dimensions of space: perception of roles, perception of feelings

Spatial Relations

and moods, inferences about intentions, and generalizations about personality. Like nonverbal behaviors, inferences about spatial usage leave wide ambiguities even within our own culture. This important variable also accounts for a significant amount of cultural variance, as reflected in a number of our intercultural communication failures.

Time

Time is also considered an element of culture and is a category of the nonverbal communication system within cultures. Time's implications for cultural communication, however, are more cognitive with tendencies toward consequent behavior. In other words, our view of time is culturally rooted—and our use of time is wedded to our culture's cognitive perceptions surrounding time. For instance, some cultures view time with great precision, and members of that culture often react interpersonally with behaviors congruent with the culture's cognitive view of time. Americans, Britons, Canadians, and Germans, to name a few, expect punctuality. A large share of these peoples' relationships are governed by the clock—and with some rigor: "Sorry I arrived a few minutes late," "Wow, look at the time! I've got to go." Furthermore, impression management in a time-oriented culture is based on one's ability to adhere to cultural rules about the time system.

By contrast, some cultures, such as Africans, Latin Americans, and Malaysians, are less time oriented. In these cultures, time obviously exists, and, of course, in various situations, punctuality is the rule. But norms in the less time-oriented cultures seem to address the issue of people first, schedules second. Cultural rules in these cases are centered around internal relationships rather than external schedules.

Intercultural communication problems between time-oriented cultures and less time-oriented cultures involve task-oriented people, externally shaping their relationships with time and schedules, and interpersonal-relationship-oriented people, motivated by saving face and social lubrication. The task-oriented individual communicating with the people-oriented individual may experience unexplainable rebuffs—such cool relationships are expected when our cultural time rules do not match those of the cultural system in which we are communicating.

Recognition and Reward

Every culture has norms for understanding success and failure. Within the boundaries of cultural social systems, relationships exist that express recognition and reward. Initiation rites, when successfully completed, represent a cultural method for advancement in tribes and clans. Proper behavior is usually rewarded in some way. Of course, what constitutes "proper" behavior is culturally variable. What constitutes "rewarding" is also culturally dependent. An American manager working in a Japanese cultural climate who insists on individually recognizing an outstanding employee may inadvertently create embarrassment. Japanese norms emphasize the individual in relation to his or her group, not usually individuals singled in isolation.

The kind of reward or recognition that is appropriate is a significant cultural difference. Money is appropriate in some cultures. Gifts, personal praise, written statements, future contracts, new titles, promotions in rank, acceptance into a group, initiation completion, and equality are but a few additional ways of showing recognition.

The most usual problem in intercultural communication concerning reward is that an intercultural participant simply does not know the cultural method for honor or praise. Consequently, a manager representing a multinational corporation, for instance, hires, makes assignments, and offers promotions according to his or her corporate culture's methods: management by objectives, participatory decision making, and the like. However, the methods by which such techniques are administered, or even the techniques themselves, often fail because they simply lack cultural fit. The same goals can be achieved with culturally acceptable adjustments.

A final cultural element is a culture's pattern of thought, which refers to the way a cultural group views such things as decision making, the kind of logical system practiced, the nature of truth, and cognitive pathways of thought. For instance, many people in the Western hemisphere accept cause-effect reasoning—that is, for every effect there must be a cause. Solutions to problems are simply a matter, they reason, of altering or controlling the causes to alter or control the desired effects. In contrast, a differing culture may reason that no one can know the causes of life events and that the events are part of a natural plan that humans should not try to understand completely but accept. Thus, the intercultural difference in this example is the divergent approach the interactants have toward the use of evidence, the way the universe operates, and consequently, the most useful communication styles for discussing solutions to problems.

Thought Patterns

Furthermore, members of some cultures think in terms of linear sequential, time-ordered patterns (1, 2, 3, or *A, B, C*). In contrast, members of configurational cultures think in terms of pictures or configurations. The individual with a configurational pattern of thought follows a different order of attention to stimulus items than the linear thinker. Here, the stimulus items may follow an attention pattern unique to that culture; for example, 1, 16, 37, 2, or *A, M, Z, B*. The issue involves how a person collects and processes information and is being addressed by Bandler (1985) in the psychiatric literature. The method of information processing appears to be culturally dependent as well as individually derived, and thus a significant part of understanding cultural differences involves examining methods of thought.

Cultures have various systems, including economic systems, kinship systems, political systems, systems of social control, health management systems, educational systems, and religious systems. Clearly, cultural variations in just how these systems are organized affect intercultural communication situations. Keep in mind that, since culture refers to macroculture, organizations,

Systems of Culture

subsystems, families, regions, and so on, these systems of culture provide useful categories for a number of groups. We now discuss each of the systems of culture in detail.

Economic Systems

A practice among farmers in certain parts of the United States is to "swap out" work, whereby one farmer helps another harvest crops and the second reciprocates. Money is seldom exchanged in this process, although a system of informal, mental record keeping develops so that both parties are fully aware of who owes whom. While monetary economic systems play a dominant role in most cultures today, this example reminds us that other methods of exchange exist according to unique cultural situations. For instance, the highlanders of Papua New Guinea traditionally use the sweet potato as one unit of exchange. A missionary once described the mild surprise of foreign visitors to a church meeting where the indigenous church members contributed their sweet potatoes in a large pile within their circle of meeting.

Hallmarks of economic systems consist not only of divergent methods of economic exchange but also of concepts of property ownership and utilization. It is not uncommon for tribal groups to jointly work their land and share communally in the profits. Various communal living arrangements in the United States during the 1960s portrayed joint property themes, particularly among some countercultures. For example, an unusual subculture called the Children of God, a radical religious communal movement, required new converts to give up all possessions (including cars and bank accounts) and live on the commune's property. Secular jobs and earning money were considered inherently evil—only communally located jobs were approved. Although they held no secular outside jobs, the total group was divided into "tribes" corresponding to Israel's heritage. Each tribe had specific duties, such as the five tribes of girls (Ephraim, Manasseh, Naphtali, Asher, and Benjamin) who worked at laundry, sewing, table serving, and child tending. Among the men, tribal functions included farming (Zebulun), mechanics (Issachar), maintenance (Dan), kitchen (Simeon), all-around work (Reuben), printing and photo (Gad), food procurement (Joseph), carpentry (Joseph), and administration (Levi) (Dodd 1975).

Kinship Systems

Like many cultural elements, concepts of "family" frequently are compared only with our own cultural experience. Our culture becomes a measuring rod with which to compare and contrast cultural views of social organization and marriage. The family is more important to many cultures around the world than to many North Americans. Successful intercultural communication involves, again, an understanding of the other person's total set of experiences. For a number of cultures, kinship is a highly integrated part of that set of experiences.

The forms and institutions surrounding the existence of the family differ from culture to culture, but the existence of the family is certain and universal. The historical evidence for the exact formation of many cultural groups is

Systems of culture generate individual and group interdependence, leading to achievement as defined in each culture's system.

scanty, lost in the annals of time, obscured by few records of changing models of family organization. However, theorists believe that the family serves functionally to meet the demands of a particular cultural group. Anthropologist Robin Fox (1971) summarized this position:

> I have tried to show how kinship systems are responses to various recognizable pressures within a framework of biological, psychological, ecological, and social limitations. Many anthropologists write as though kinship systems have dropped from the sky onto societies—they're there because they're there because. . . . In truth, they are there because they answer certain needs—do certain jobs. When these change, the systems change—but only within certain limits. (p. 25)

Clearly, then, societies organize the family as they would any other aspect of social organization to meet many needs in a practical way.

Because they face common problems and needs, family units sometimes evolve to meet those needs. For example, if a cultural need exists for farm labor, a person from that cultural situation might deduce that having many children could supply that need. To foster that goal, the marriage practice of *polygeny* (one man with many wives) may result as that culture's way of meeting its needs. Superstitions, magic, and various religious beliefs supporting such a marital norm may ultimately develop, thus making it, in a sense, an "institution." Other basic modes of marital units, such as *polyandry* (one woman with more than one husband), *monogamy* (one husband and one wife), and *serial monogamy* (a series of monogamous marriages with different partners), develop in a similar way.

Researchers describe family units under two major classes. The first unit is the *nuclear family,* a unit referring to father, mother, and siblings. The second unit is the *extended family,* which includes the nuclear family and extends to incorporate the grandparents, uncles, aunts, cousins, and so on. Beyond these two classes, the trained cultural observer is concerned with the actual lineage, wherein group membership can be actually demonstrated from some common ancestor. *Descent groups* refer to groups where a common ancestor is assumed and where group members have ritual, property, or activity in common. A collection of lineages where common descent is assumed but not necessarily demonstrated is a *clan* (Fox 1971, 47–50). Collections of clans may become a *tribe*.

The fundamental family unit of course, accrues only after *marriage procurement,* a process that also varies culturally. For example, some clans adhere to strict prohibitions, allowing marriage only within the clan (or even some other significant unit), a practice called *endogamy*. One reason for endogamy is the containment of property or perhaps sacred qualities connected with a lineage. For instance, the ideal marriage of a Yoruk of Turkey is between first cousins (Bates 1974). Another variation of marriage availability is the procurement of marriage partners from outside the clan (or other significant unit), a practice called *exogamy*. Sometimes, exogamy occurs to strengthen ties with other clans or to ensure the exchange of economic resources through marriage. Unlike the Yoruk, the Tzetal tribe of Mexico opposes intrafamily marriages, including marriage to even very distant kin (Stross 1974).

Kinship systems also involve the role of authority. Male-oriented authority patterns in the family are called *patriarchy,* while female-oriented authority patterns are called *matriarchy*. Qualities of inheritance and/or naming that come through the mother's side are found in *matrilineal* systems. *Patrilineal* systems foster inheritance and/or naming emphasizing the father's side.

Political Systems

Universally, societies have some form of governing organization functioning on a formal level and an informal level. On the formal level, such governing organizations originate because of self-appointment, inherited rights, vote, consensus, or political takeover. A less obvious method of accruing perceived power, status, and leadership also exists. In various cultural groups, for example, some leaders are assumed to have a certain degree of supernatural power. Many years ago, a group of South Sea islanders considered the power of *mana* to dwell in certain individuals. This impersonal power was believed to cause its recipients to possess the equivalent of what we might term "power," since persons who were perceived to have high degrees of mana usually had greater financial prowess, inherent status, and attributed power. Individuals believed this power also resided because of some special charm or incantation formula. The term for this perceived power stuck—today the word still can refer to a special leadership.

Aside from the concept of impersonal supernatural power residing in or near a person, traditional leadership in political organizations among traditional cultures seems closely linked with age and economic qualities. In Ghana, for example, village chieftainship and eldership appear to be related closely to father's role (inheritance factor), age, and economic ability. Reyburn's (1953) ethnographic report among the Sierra Quechua of Ecuador indicates that village leadership is a function of economic ability, marital status (only married men are considered for the post of *prioste,* responsible for fiestas), and priestly appointment.

Another form of leadership exerted in political organizations is informal "opinion leadership." Every cultural group has people to whom others go for information and advice. These opinion leaders are not necessarily the formal leaders of a group. For instance, the mayor and councilpeople are not necessarily the ones who influence the masses in their town on political issues. In fact, the formal leaders may be influenced by the informal opinion leaders.

Systems of Social Control

All cultures have methods of dealing with violations of norms (accepted modes of behavior) and laws. Societal punishment appears universal in scope, although consequences vary from fines to banishment or death. For example, two visitors to an African country unknowingly walked through sacred African *ju-ju* ground, a religiously special place, and were fined the native equivalent of one month's wages. Dismemberment and capital punishment also exemplify differing cultural solutions to the universal need for order.

Like every other element of culture, social control develops from specific cultural contexts. Thus, difficulty arises when we compare social control in one culture with its counterpart in another culture. Many international persons, for example, believe that the United States is far too lenient in its punishment for certain crimes; conversely, many U.S. citizens believe that some countries have enacted overly strict laws. Evaluation of cultural methods of social control depends on examining each culture from its own perspective.

Health Management Systems

How a culture addresses the health of cultural members also poses a significant cultural system. As Harris and Moran (1979) observed, the very concept of meaningful health can differ among cultures. The methodologies by which people are medically treated can range from chemical medication by highly educated medical specialists to herbal application by witch doctors.

Hospitals and medical clinics are relatively new innovations in some cultures, and sometimes an interesting mixture of the traditional medicines with the modern arise in hospital rooms. In Papua New Guinea, family medical tradition has sometimes combined with modern hospitalization as family members take turns in groups staying with a patient, cooking food and practically camping out for days at a time in the patient's room. Health information is a topic currently significant for those working in developing countries. Not only is it important to understand the health system of a culture, in order to manage it effectively from within, but it is equally important to be able to disseminate health information.

Educational Systems

Cultural educational systems differ widely. In the British educational system, for instance, students are either university bound or vocational bound, determined by testing in about the sixth or eighth grades. Also, some European education is conducted bilingually. Many foreign universities are structured differently from those in the United States. At some universities, subjects are studied a year at a time, not by semester or quarter unit credits. We cannot examine every system of education here, but it is important to understand that they are usually not the same as our own cultural educational system.

Religious Systems

Religious systems involve holidays, ceremonies, places of worship, norms of respect, and linguistic concepts that can cause great embarrassment if one does not understand the system. Many visitors to mosques and temples, for instance, neglect basic etiquette by failing to remove their shoes or observe other norms of respect. Recognizing the external elements of religiosity in a particular culture not only prevents cultural mistakes but also can affect insights into macrocultural patterns, cultural beliefs, and cultural values. For example, during a certain holy month, Moslems must fast from dawn to dusk. Their fasting includes no hint of imbibing their own saliva, so the Islamic followers are constantly spitting on the floor during that time. Thai executives who supervise Moslem workers describe this situation with great horror and concern, while the Moslems proclaim the righteousness of this procedure. Consequently, the organizational cultural climate during the holy month is filled with strained tensions between the Buddhists and the Moslems, a tension that easily flavors communication patterns, work productivity, and morale.

Theories of Culture

We have identified some elements and systems around which cultures are organized. Now we discuss the theories that explain cultural patterns.

Cultural Borrowing

External contact of one culture meeting another can produce change in one or the other or both. When the Pilgrims ventured to the United States, some of their habits changed; partially because of culture contact, they borrowed some survival skills from the American Indians, such as planting and eating corn and other foods. Sometimes, cultural borrowing occurs deliberately, sometimes incidentally. In the case of the Australian stone axe culture, mentioned earlier in this chapter, acceptance of a culturally foreign object proved disastrous.

Many years ago, blackbirds were brought into the United States from England to control insects. However, today in a number of midsouthern states, these birds are creating an enormous health problem and millions of dollars of grain loss each year. Another example also illustrates this point. A hearty ground cover useful in Japan was imported to the United States for planting along roadsides. For some reason, the plant life grew so well that it became uncontrollable, covering fence lines, large trees, and waterways.

Similarly, cultural borrowing can significantly alter culture. Acceptance of imported calculators is a contemporary example of the powerful cultural borrowing and acculturation to create cultural change and development.

Sometimes, cultural changes are the result of uncontrollable forces, such as floods, hurricanes, volcanic eruptions, and other spontaneous events that cause physical relocation or psychological alteration. Just as disasters create a need for cultural realignment, these cataclysmic changes in the life and history of a group of people can also forge a new culture from the old. For example, the severe Guatemalan earthquakes of 1977, which toppled entire barrios down hillsides and engulfed mountain villages, caused relocation. The settled villagers of the mountains became the new settlers in plains regions. And this shift has caused alteration of endogamy, authority structure, and even language.

Cultural Cataclysm

Contrived, manmade forces can be just as cataclysmic and at least as forceful as natural disasters in shaping cultural destinies. Wars, political coups, and even installation of high dams along rivers seriously alter culture. For example, war-torn Vietnam, among other things, left a trail of refugees, many of whom settled in the United States. In some cases, highly skilled physicians, lawyers, or engineers worked at menial jobs as a result of their immigration. Family structures also were altered. For example, many of the younger Vietnamese showed greater acculturation capabilities than their elders. Despite family pressure to let the elders make decisions, pressure from the new culture sometimes pushed the younger generation toward individualism.

In another example, as World War II encroached upon the South Pacific, New Guinea islanders were confronted dramatically with strange new ways. The war brought guns, machines of sorts, vehicles, and hundreds of other things needed for life support and battle. The alien aircraft dropping their packaged cargoes from the sky surprised the islanders and yet enticed them toward these "miracles." When the hardware was removed at the war's end, an unusual cult developed. This new culture was termed the "cargo cult," and one of its tenets rested on the expectation of a return of the cargo. To this day, this quasi-religious subculture still anticipates the return of the cargo.

Similarly, waterways have altered cultures. Many U.S. citizens are familiar with the effects of new lakes and canals in this country. Not only do these innovations bring economic change, but they induce social change. In another instance, the Aswān High Dam on the Nile River has seriously affected Egypt. Some observers believe that the many economic benefits of the dam may be balanced partially by its social effects. Many villagers have shifted occupations and live in newly formed towns, a move which has eroded traditional lines of authority. The farmer who is now the factory worker at a fertilizer plant sometimes loses his personal pride as his superiors devaluate his former life. Once prosperous river villages now lie under water, swept by the currents of a lake newly formed for a developing nation.

The intercultural communicator must realize that these forces shape not only the culture but also the cultural perceptions of a potential communication partner. That is why understanding culture is so important for communication.

Cultural Ecological Theory

While cultural cataclysms have an immediate crisis-centered impact on a culture's development, cultural experts recognize that a culture's ecology also has a long-term, gradual impact. Certain environmental features may influence a culture's diet, dress, religion, and marriage partnerships.

Ecological environment is important to culture for at least two reasons. One is that, as population increases, available land decreases. This population pressure pushes natural boundaries to their limit. Consequently, new frontiers are colonized. As a result of the new frontier environment, changes in agricultural practices, dress, diet, word usages, and so on emerge. Also, hierarchical societies sometimes send lower-status members to colonize. As a result, new ranks emerge in the newly changing culture.

A second reason why environment influences culture involves the distribution of products, services, and materials of neighboring cultures. For example, if the environment of culture C contains necessary items for cultures B and A, a symbiotic relationship develops. *Symbiosis* refers to fulfilling mutual needs between two or more cultures. Suppose that clans A, B, and C contain environmental productions of timber (A), construction stones (B), and fish (C) (figure 3.1). Inasmuch as all three of these subcultures desire these things, economic exchanges develop and symbiotic relationships crystallize.

As economic interplay heightens, significant cultural features may be borrowed or adapted, leading to divergence from tradition in cultural development. For example, members of a submissive culture may now become fierce bargainers. Or symbiosis may escalate, whereby exogamous clans (clans marrying outside their own clan) exchange those available for marriage.

Both symbiotic relationships and territorial pioneering produce adapted cultures. The important key for cultural ecological theorists is that environmental-ecological pressures cause gradual but steady changes.

Cognitive Anthropology

The cognitive anthropology approach to culture tries to get inside the mind of the culture (Harris 1968). Traditional ethnography proposes cultural analysis by examining material manifestations, such as economic systems, kinship

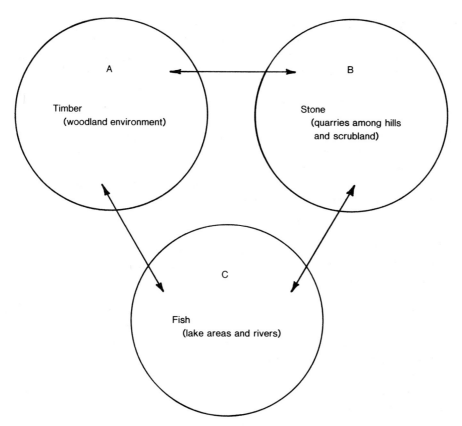

Figure 3.1
Economic symbiosis
based on
environmental
production.

relations, and so on. One criticism of such an approach is that *a priori* categorizations are culturally conditioned and thereby biased. Also, an ethnog-
rapher may fail to see systems from a national point of view. Hence, the analysis
is attached to ethnocentrism. The cognitive anthropology approach, in contrast, attempts to get "inside the human skin" to fully understand culture.

Tyler (1969) highlighted a significant cognitive anthropology perspective
compared with traditional ethnography. Ethnography underscores structure,
form, norms, and patterns. By contrast, the cognitive anthropology position
focuses on and discovers how people organize and use their cultures. The assumption is that cultures have unique systems for perceiving and then organizing events, behaviors, and emotions (Frake 1969).

Another theory for explaining culture examines major themes of culture. According to Benedict (1934), a dominant idea of a culture can reveal cultural
members' fundamental attitudes. Furthermore, these fundamental themes are
more important than the functional relationship of cultural items to each other.

Among the Zuni Indians, for instance, two cultural themes stand out. According to Zuni tradition, men submerge their activities into those of the entire group and claim no personal authority. A second theme is nonviolence.

**Dominant Theme
Analysis**

Even under attacks of insult and abuse, accepted behavioral systems provide nonviolent outlets. For example, if a man is unfaithful to his wife in Zuni culture, the wife may simply not wash his clothes, thus indicating to her husband and to the community that she knows of the affair. In one case, this nonviolent, even nondirect, method caused the husband to relinquish his extramarital affair.

Functionalism

Another theory of culture is called functionalism, developed by Bronislaw Malinowski (1944). From his work with the Trobriand islanders, he reasoned that cultural systems are an outgrowth of three underlying human needs: basic, derived, and integrative. Basic needs refer to survival needs, such as food, water, and shelter. Derived needs refer to "social coordination," as Nanda (1980) went on to describe, including division of labor, distribution of food, and social control. The third need is integrative, or as Nanda continued, the need for security and social harmony met by magic, knowledge, myth, and art, for instance. Malinowski's fundamental notion was that every aspect of culture can be summarized by one of these three needs and that cultures develop to satisfy these needs in ways functional for their situation and with their particular resources. In other words, cultural features and social institutions arise out of individual needs. There are other kinds of functionalism, but the point is that this theory proposes to explain norms, rules, and social interaction (Harris 1983).

Developing Intercultural Skills in Understanding Culture

You may find some of the following suggestions helpful. They are suggested with imperative verb forms for ease of suggestion. If one is not useful, pass for one that fits your situation.

1. *Respect the dignity and personhood of others.* Even if you find yourself disagreeing with some values or other aspect of a culture, you may wish to avoid arguing. Respect the rights of others in their cultural situation and seek to understand the culture rather than to criticize it. Try to enjoy people, looking at their personhood rather than their cultural background.

2. *Do not let others' criticism get you down.* In your attempts to learn a new culture, you will always find people who criticize your attempts to adapt and practice skills in intercultural communication. Be a bit thick-skinned. Do not let even your friends criticize your attempts if they are unwilling to try to understand a new culture themselves. Of course, if they are trying to tell you that you are reacting unduly, then be aware of their honest feedback. Keep in mind that you may be experiencing some forms of culture shock, and friends can help you with that experience.

3. *Do not feel as if you have to be liked everywhere by everyone.* The outgoing American may feel alienated in some cultures where members do not act as gregarious as the visitor may prefer. Everyone cannot be liked everywhere. Even if you feel that people do not like you, keep on trying to communicate.

4. *Be careful in discussing monetary matters.* If you are visiting in another culture, you will soon discover that a number of other cultures believe that you are rich. Some southern Europeans perceive Americans to be loud, boastful, and ignorant of local customs. So, do your best not to support that stereotype. Avoid talk of money and financial matters, except in clearly appropriate circumstances.

5. *Work on adaptability.* Studies show that being able to adapt quickly to new and different situations is essential to becoming a good intercultural communicator. In many circumstances, you may prefer to suspend judgment and listen to other people—and avoid merely reacting. Emotions blind us quickly, especially when frustration and emotional tensions are high anyway because of our arrival in a new culture.

6. *Work on initiative.* Be willing to take social risks. Try to open yourself to new cultural experiences. Undoubtedly, you realize that the principles in this chapter, including this suggestion, do not apply only to cultures outside the United States. Showing initiative and creativity can help you in everyday interpersonal communication and relationships. The words of Shakespeare seem particularly important as you ingratiate yourself with others: "Our doubts are traitors and cause us to lose the good we oft might win by fearing to attempt."

7. *Be observant.* Obviously, part of becoming proficient in intercultural communication involves watching and listening. You may find it helpful each day to write in a diary or notebook the things you observed that day. Write down things people say, stories you hear, or anything you think is important. Then, every couple of days, look over your diary or notes and reflect. You will be amazed at what you learn.

8. *Be ready for lack of privacy.* One of the things you probably value, sometimes without realizing, is your personal privacy. In another culture, privacy as you may conceive of it may be less than you prefer. Be ready for anything, and let things happen as they will without spending too much time preoccupying yourself with your "rights." Your personal privacy simply may not be a factor in another culture's way of thinking.

9. *Do not superimpose your political values.* All too often a person in an intercultural contact converses about political systems to the exclusion of other topics of conversation. In fact, some people get into violent arguments about politics and misjudge a culture because of its political norms. Remember, a culture can be appreciated for topics and areas other than politics.

10. *Recognize perceived roles of women.* A number of cultures hold attitudes toward the role of women that are variant from our attitudes. Though you may disagree with these attitudes, try to demonstrate respect for cultural traditions, whether you think they are right or wrong. Many intercultural

relationships are lost trying to win ideological battles. You may win the battle but lose the war of building relationships.

11. *Respect tradition.* Most of us who grew up in the United States have not learned the same respect for tradition that many members from other cultures hold. Many cultural members believe that traditional ways are "tried and proven" and that to disregard these matters is highly disrespectful.

12. *Get used to long lines.* Many cultures do not have systems that handle things as efficiently as you think they should be handled. Sometimes, if you travel very much, for example, you will find yourself waiting in long lines. Thus, be prepared and keep your frustration level down if you are impatient.

13. *Learn to give of yourself and to receive.* One reaction to facing differences in intercultural contact is to become reticent. This pattern of withdrawal, however, prevents interaction needed to learn a new culture.

This Chapter in Perspective

The chapter discusses a number of divergent cultural practices and has treated cultural elements in a way that hopefully answers puzzling questions about some of these cultural practices. Beyond an appreciation for cultural elements, the goal has been to introduce the meaning of a culture's history, personality, material features, role relationships, economic methods, kinship and other social and political organizational patterns, social control, artistic expression, language, changeability and stability, belief system, and a number of cultural attitudes. The chapter also examines the numerous theories on how culture develops.

Obviously, we do not become experts in intercultural communication because we know some categories of culture. But this discussion may help set the stage for understanding. Sensitization to another person's culture is a prerequisite to effective intercultural communication.

Exercises

1. Secure from some resource person a simulation or game that emphasizes cultural differences, such as BA FA BA FA, and Heelots and Hokias. After playing the game or simulation, try to spend some time debriefing. What made the exercise meaningful or not meaningful as far as learning about culture? What cultural variables came to light during the simulation?

2. Interview an international student on your campus. Then explain a cultural element, a cultural theory, or a system of culture from the international student's home culture to your class or a small group.

3. In almost every issue of *National Geographic* are articles on other cultures. Pick an article that describes a culture of some interest to you and give a brief synopsis. What theoretical point of view did the author of the article take concerning his or her description of the culture? Can you identify the major cultural variables uncovered in the article?

Resources

Arensberg, Conrad M., and Arthur H. Niehoff. *Introducing Social Change.* Chicago: Aldine, 1964.

Ayres, Barbara. "Bride Theft and Raiding for Wives in Cross-Cultural Perspective." *Anthropological Quarterly* 47 (1974): 238–51.

Bandler, Richard. *Using Your Brain for a Change: Neurolinguistic Programming.* Moab, Utah: Real People Press, 1985.

Bates, Daniel G. "Normative and Alternative Systems of Marriage among the Yoruk of Southeastern Turkey." *Anthropological Quarterly* 47 (1974): 270–87.

Benedict, Ruth. *Patterns of Culture.* Boston: Houghton Mifflin, 1934.

Burke, Jerry. "An Explanation and Evaluation of Cognitive Anthropology." *International and Intercultural Communication Annual* 1 (1974): 24–38.

Cattell, R. "New Concepts for Measuring Leadership, in Terms of Group Syntality." *Human Relations* 2 (1951): 161–84.

Dodd, Carley H. "Social Structure and Communication Behavior among the Children of God." A paper presented to the International Communication Association Convention, Chicago, April 16, 1975.

Dodd, Carley H., and Kay E. Payne. "The Effects of Culture and Sex on Time Concepts between Black and White Children." A paper presented to the Southern Speech Communication Association Convention, San Antonio, April 9, 1976.

Firth, Raymond. *Human Types.* New York: Mentor, 1958.

Fox, Robin. *Kinship and Marriage.* Baltimore, Md.: Penguin, 1971.

Frake, C. "The Ethnographic Study of Cognitive Studies." In *Cognitive Anthropology,* edited by Steven Tyler. New York: Holt, Rinehart and Winston, 1969.

Goodenough, Ward. "Componential Analysis and the Study of Meaning." *Language* 35 (1956): 195–216.

Harris, Marvin. *The Rise of Anthropological Theory.* New York: Thomas Crowell, 1968.

Harris, Marvin. *Cultural Anthropology.* New York: Harper and Row, 1983.

Harris, Philip R., and Robert T. Moran. *Managing Cultural Differences.* Houston: Gulf, 1979.

Hong, Nguyen Kim. "Vietnamese Themes." A paper presented to the Regional Indochinese Task Force Workshop for the New York City Board of Education, New York, January 19–21, 1976.

Katz, Elihu. "The Two-Step Flow of Communication: An Up-To-Date Report on Hypothesis." *Public Opinion Quarterly* 21 (1957): 61–78.

Malinowski, Bronislaw. *A Scientific Theory of Culture and Other Essays.* Chapel Hill, N.C.: University of North Carolina Press, 1944.

Nanda, Serena. *Cultural Anthropology.* New York: Van Nostrand, 1980.

Overseas Diplomacy. Bureau of Naval Personnel, 1973.

Reyburn, Marie F. "Applied Anthropology among the Sierra Quechua of Ecuador." *Practical Anthropology* 1 (1953): 15–22.

Rodgers, Raymond. "Folklore Analysis and Subcultural Communication Research: Another View of World View." Paper presented to Society for Intercultural Education, Training, and Research, Phoenix, February 25, 1978.

Sharp, Lauriston. "Steel Axes for Stone Age Australians." In *Human Problems in Technological Change,* edited by Edward H. Spicer. New York: Russell Sage Foundation, 1952.

Smith, Alfred G. *Communication and Culture.* New York: Holt, Rinehart and Winston, 1966.

Stross, Brian. "Tzetal Marriage by Capture." *Anthropological Quarterly* 47 (1974): 328–46.

Tyler, Stephen, ed. *Cognitive Anthropology.* New York: Holt, Rinehart and Winston, 1969.

Chapter 4

Intercultural Communication and Subcultures

After completing this chapter, you should be able to:

1. Define subculture and understand its various components.

2. Identify key features of reference group membership and its effect on individual behaviors, including communication.

3. Understand the effects of residence (regional, rural, urban) and socioeconomic class on communication behavior.

4. Identify the causes of barriers in interracial and interethnic communication.

5. Identify the basic steps necessary to improve interracial and interethnic communication.

6. Identify the dynamic elements of a counterculture and apply those elements to specific groups.

7. Identify attitudes of poverty-level and traditional subcultures around the world.

A fundamental principle of social communication is that we do not live in isolation but, inevitably, must coordinate our behaviors with other societal members. Social support for attitudes and behaviors stems from significant others and from salient reference groups, including subcultural groups. Even in the most individualistic cultures, subcultural groups act as reference points for individual thought and action. For example, a person deciding how to vote in a major election in the United States is often heavily influenced by family, peers, unions, and recreational associates.

Even though we properly speak of similarities of customs and the like that constitute a culture, a web of subcultures within a culture mediate cultural influence. For example, North America contains numerous subcultural groups that act as reference groups, mediating thought and behavior. A Mexican American in South Texas may reject culturally expected participation in a fiesta because of his loyalty to an educational group, a religious sect, or upper-middle-class ideals—all of which represent subcultures.

This chapter focuses on reference group influence and some individual characteristics of various subcultures. Since many intercultural communication problems stem from intergroup or subcultural communication situations, to understand reference group influence is to more fully appreciate microcosms that make up the whole of a culture.

What Is a Subculture?

As chapter 1 indicated, the term *subculture* does not connote any notion of less than or below but is a term used throughout this text to mean a smaller cultural unit within a larger culture. The definition connotes groupness and includes a host of units, such as occupation, ethnicity, age, and the like. Rodgers (1978) advanced an eclectic definition of subculture, suggesting that:

> A subculture is any collectivity of persons who possess conscious membership in identifiable units of an encompassing cultural unit as well as the larger cultural unit itself. (pp. 4–5)

Since they are consciously aware of their membership in a behaviorally defined subunit of a definite larger unit, American coal miners were described by Rodgers as a clear example of a subculture. Rodgers also referred to Boulding's work, who discussed a key ingredient in defining subcultures—shared self-image:

> Within any complex societies, there are groups more or less isolated from the rest of the community which develop public images which they share within the group, but do not share with outsiders. From the street corner to the executive suite, our own society is honeycombed with these subcultures. The image around which they are organized is not so much a spatial, temporal, or relational image; these images they tend to share with the world around them. It is rather a value image. (Boulding 1972, 143–44)

Boulding also argued that communication serves to reinforce these images, making them self-supporting and self-propagating.

Subcultures exist in a larger culture and yet maintain unique purpose and self-image.

The criteria that follow take the previous definitions of subculture a step further. (Keep in mind that we must allow for some flexibility where exact parameters cannot be established.)

1. *Members may be self-identifiable.* That is, they may perceive themselves to at least intellectually, if not behaviorally, have membership in the subculture. If we identify ourselves as a member of a "poor" class, then our self-perception is as one index of membership in the subculture of the poor.

2. *Members are often behaviorally identifiable.* Some characteristic must exist that can be behaviorally perceived by others. For example, a person who is part Sioux Indian may document her heritage but lack behavioral involvement as a member in that subculture. For all practical purposes, therefore, that person is not really a member of that subculture since she chooses not to personally identify.

3. *Members are often contemporaneously identifiable.* While not the only criterion, this point suggests that, to the extent that contemporary society has developed its own coinage for the subculture, there is corroboration in defining the group as a subculture. For example, the news media coined the label "Children of God" for a right-wing religious communal movement, and the label was adopted by the members of the group to identify themselves (Dodd 1975).

Reference Group Communication

Reference groups are highly important to us and influence many of our decisions. These groups act as mediating influences upon a given communication. In essence, they serve as a focal point for interpreting messages and affect perceptions of issues and events.

Defining Reference Groups

In this text, the term *reference group* refers to the group anchor point. Individual behavior is not fully understood without a knowledge of the influence exerted by a person's group. This influence is so strong that it not only touches our opinions but results in the group itself becoming a reference point by whose norms we judge ourselves. The group may become a symbol of personal self-worth and identification. We do not necessarily come in physical contact with a group, for we may simply think of ourselves as a member of the "intellectual class" or the "average middle class" and act accordingly.

Most reference groups center around family, play or peer groups, co-workers, and co-members in voluntary organizations (Smith, Bruner, and White 1956; Sherif and Sherif 1967). Berelson and Steiner (1964) identified the following reference groups:

1. The autonomous group, such as a circle of close friends, built on free choice and voluntary association

2. The institutionalized small group, such as family

3. The small group within a large organization, often called a mediating group because of its linking position between the individual and the organization, such as a work group in a factory or office, or a group of soldiers (buddies) in the army

4. The problem-solving group, illustrated by a committee with a task to perform

These groups are highly significant in passing information. As we will see next, they are also influential. For that reason, we often call them primary groups.

Role and Function of the Reference Group

Most of us belong to many groups that support numerous and sometimes divergent norms and policies. In fact, as we have already stated, one of the major functions of the reference group is to set and enforce norms or other standards of behavior. Norms vary from culture to culture and from group to group, but they determine behavior by becoming a reference point for the individual. Furthermore, all of our group memberships simultaneously add to our perceptions and sometimes press us into conformity. By conforming to group norms, we receive two rewards: (1) acceptance by the group and (2) title to group beliefs, to which we can cling as a way of interpreting life's events (Abelson 1959, 25–26).

But just what effect does the group have upon communication? As a reference point, the group basically performs the task of mediating communication, usually in the direction of messages that reinforce group opinion. In other words, the group acts as a source, reinforcement, and support, bolstering old attitudes and providing a context for future conversion to new positions (Sherif, Sherif, and Nebergall 1965). This social communication provides a frame of reference, but this "web of influence" is most meaningful when we consider the following important group variables that influence communication, change, and control:

Group size. The smaller the reference group, the greater the pressure to conform. The larger the reference group, the more formal its proceedings and the greater the probability that a formal leader will emerge. The larger the group, the greater the possibility of splinter groups or cliques; these are prevented in a smaller group because of social pressures. If there is persuasive communication occurring in the group, the mode of presentation changes as the group gets larger. Within a large group, for example, less interpersonal interaction occurs, and thus the group looks to a central leader to structure the communication (Bettinghaus 1980). The size of the group influences the amount and type of participation potentially available to members. Thus, small-group members are more easily involved in discussion, but large-group members are limited in their participation.

Frequency of contact. Another group characteristic is the relationship between attitudes and frequency of contact. Researchers have observed that the more interaction within a group, the more likely that members have positive feelings toward other group members. Also, when some group members share opinions, they often predispose other group members toward acceptance of these opinions (Berelson and Steiner 1964). Furthermore, increased contact strengthens friendships and produces opportunity for similar attitudes and behaviors to develop.

Studies of subcultural or intergroup contact generally support the idea that positive attitudes follow intergroup contact. For example, one generally accepted approach to easing tense race relations has been to induce interracial contact, during which erroneous preconceptions about members of the other group diminish. Once group members actually communicate face-to-face, they realize that the negative stereotypes are inaccurate and therefore seek to correct the prejudice. As Gudykunst (1977) pointed out, however, subcultural contact may produce positive attitudes only under certain favorable conditions—the intensity of the effect depends upon several factors, some of which follow:

1. When the status of persons of both groups is similar, positive attitudes result.

2. When someone in charge promotes intergroup contact, positive attitudes result.

3. When the intergroup contact is personal, rather than casual or impersonal, positive attitudes result.

4. When the intergroup contact seems rewarding and pleasant, positive attitudes result.

5. When the individuals within each group differ markedly from commonly held negative stereotypes, positive attitudes result.

Intercultural contact is one important way of reducing stereotypic impressions and establishing positive attitudes toward members from other cultures or subcultures.

Furthermore, Gudykunst (1977) showed that intercultural contact, such as international visits, foreign travel in a host culture, and talking with international students, also induces positive attitudes. Of course, the exact nature of these positive attitudes depends upon the amount of contact, the setting, the quality of contact, and the reason for the contact.*

Cohesiveness. Another factor in group influence is cohesiveness, which most frequently is defined as the degree of group attraction for group members. Cohesion implies a unity of group-centeredness and loyalty. In Back's (1958) classic study of cohesive and noncohesive groups, (1) cohesive members showed efforts toward uniformity and agreement, (2) fewer individual differences emerged in the highly cohesive groups, and (3) discussion was more effective, producing more influence and change than in noncohesive groups. By contrast, members of low-cohesive groups appeared to act independently, disregarding the needs and desires of other group members.

Group cohesiveness extends to several general principles that can be summarized as follows (Bettinghaus 1980):

1. Highly cohesive groups have fewer deviants in their decisions.

*The effect of intergroup or intercultural contact on attitude or behavioral change is termed the "contact hypothesis." Early studies noted contact effects on attitudes toward ethnic groups (Amir 1969), different races, and countercultures. Work by Kim (1977) outlined a number of variables that influence acculturation, including intercultural contact.

2. Cohesive groups are more likely to be influenced by persuasive communication.

3. Members of a highly cohesive group communicate frequently, and the communication is distributed more evenly among group members.

4. Members of a highly cohesive group offer mutual support and tend to reject threatening messages.

5. The higher the cohesiveness of the group, the stronger the pressure to conform.

Group salience. Salience refers to the importance of a group and, therefore, the value the individual places upon the group. In another sense, salience specifies personal awareness of the group and perceptions of its importance. Researchers tell us that resistance to change of group norms and attitudes is in direct proportion to the group's degree of salience. For example, Middle East terrorist groups would be expected to resist outside communication because of the salience the groups hold for their members.

In addition, research has demonstrated that the more interested the individual is in becoming a member of a group and the more salient the group, the more he or she tends to conform to its norms of behavior. An example of this principle is the Jonestown, Guyana, religious community, where group salience may have been a factor leading to an ultimate cohesive behavior—mass suicide of nine hundred victims.

Clarity of group norms. Studies concerning group norms have shown that, in general, the more ambiguous the group norms and standards of conduct, the less control the group has over its members. However, if the standards are clear and unambiguous, the pressure to conform is greater. Also, when ambiguity is prevalent within a group, interaction among group members increases to reduce the ambiguity (Berelson and Steiner 1964). For example, in college life, if the rules for fraternity membership are unclear, then it is unlikely that the fraternity will influence its members.

Homogeneity. While homophily refers to degree of similarity on various characteristics between two people, homogeneity refers to similarity among many group members. We know that small groups tend toward uniformity in actions and attitudes as homogeneity increases. Group homogeneity also contributes toward cohesiveness. Also, when homogeneous attitudes prevail, an individual tends to hold personal attitudes more tenaciously. Homogeneity of opinion is most directly observable in reference groups, such as family, friends, and co-workers (Katz 1963).

Issues. The issues that confront the reference group influence group members. As the importance of a particular issue increases, we tend to conform in attitudes, behaviors, and values. On the other hand, when an issue is ambiguous, or even overly complex, we find consolation in conforming to views consistent with the majority, especially when we lack experience in dealing with that particular issue.

Affiliative needs of group members. Reference group influence extends only as far as the boundaries of the human personality allow. Personality affects individual response in concert with group influences. For example, whenever group members depend strongly upon the group for satisfying various needs, they conform to group expectations, if they understand the norms. And this conformity may result from a need to resemble highly esteemed persons, to sustain social approval, or to avoid unpleasant circumstances, such as loss of membership (Hovland, Janis, and Kelley 1953). In such situations, communication may become overly self-serving, since dependent members may offer frequent "positive strokes" to win the favor of high-status members and receive positive strokes themselves.

Affiliative personalities experience a high need for acceptance. The more strongly we are motivated to stay in a group, for example, the more susceptible we are to persuasion from the group. Also, individuals who are strongly attached to the group are least influenced by later communication that attacks their group norms. A high need for acceptance and fear of rejection may explain why some people are compulsive "joiners"—they seek acceptance through group affiliation.

Individuals' reasons for joining group. As we have already stated, although groups influence individuals, some people join groups for the primary purpose of reinforcing their existing beliefs. For example, a person who already holds a position consistent with the goals of the organization may join a civic club. Membership may deepen this person's beliefs and strengthen commitment, but a favorable predisposition existed before joining.

A secondary individual purpose for joining groups concerns the person's using the group for personal goals. The person who joins the civic club may indeed associate with the group because the group shares similar viewpoints, but the same person may identify with the group because of less idealistic motives. For example, a salesperson may wish to make contacts, useful later for sales appointments. In this sense, reference groups serve instrumentally, mostly as a stepping-stone for individual purposes.

Regional Cultures and Communication

People filter messages through what DeFleur and Ball-Rokeach (1976) called the "social categories" of communication. The inherent idea of this approach is that certain groupings of people are sufficiently similar to think alike and to respond uniformly to messages. This assumption appears correct in spite of the heterogeneity of modern society. In large measure, some subcultures can be considered social categories. Or, we may wish to think of these categories, as some researchers do, as demographic groupings, which are another dimension describing subcultures and communication.

Regional differences, therefore, can represent differences in outlook. The intercultural communicator must understand regional cultural differences and be able to suspend any negative stereotypes. Even speech patterns and dialectical differences can produce feelings of disrespect toward others. Because negative perceptual filters mislead a person, each intercultural communication event should be viewed in light of the uniqueness of each separate interaction.

Evidence indicates that regional cultures (for example, West Coast versus East Coast) apply different approaches to information management and particularly to intercultural relationship style here in the United States. Some of the dimensions that mark the differences in communicator style are:

1. Perceived abruptness

2. Speed of speech communication delivery

3. Amount of verbal buffering or preparation with introductory phrases in a sentence

4. Amount of interpersonal buffering where informal rapport is built to various extents

5. Amount of eye contact, touch, space, and verbal pausing

6. Amount of verbal and nonverbal behavior surrounding phrases and messages before leaving a conversation

7. Amount of warmth and openness

8. Amount of animation

9. Amount of dominance

10. Amount of contentiousness (see Norton 1978)

While these categories do not represent all possible regional differences, they highlight some of the most common areas of communication difference, besides accent. Regional differences can silently keep people apart. Some of the most sophisticated people seemingly let the nonobvious prejudices of regional differences affect their attitudes, relationships, and communication style. This unfortunate waste of human resources is preventable.

Rural Cultures and Communication

In addition to regional differences, it is possible to identify characteristic norms of rurality. Norms of rural cultures include an emphasis on personal know-how, practicality, and simplicity over complexity in approaching decisions. Skills at "doing" rather than "being" or "knowing" are often valued. Of course, cultural norms in some rural cultures may favor innovation and change, while others resist change and embrace traditionalism. Even in those cases, though, an emphasis on skills and action is still evident.

A strong norm toward interpersonal relationships also exists within rural cultures. Indications are that bonds of friendship last longer. Friendship is rooted deeper. And not surprisingly, norms of rurality extend into traditional American values and themes.

Of further research interest is the recent notion that rurality is a mindset. For example, there are pockets of rural Southerners in the greater Detroit area. In many cases, their cognitive, behavioral, and linguistic subculture is as it was fifty years ago when migration from South to North was high.

A study by Tichenor (1981) showed a higher degree of communication apprehension among rural cultural people. She also found higher cognitive complexity for rural individuals, which indicates a higher ability to form accurate interpersonal impressions. This also means that rural individuals possess a more diverse set of categories by which to finely judge interpersonal relations. In fact, as Perrin (1980) writes in his book *Second Person Rural,* rural people can judge rather quickly according to the interpersonal rules.

Communication style differences of rural individuals involve cultural norms blended with regional practices. For instance, a GM plant relocated into a traditional Southern rural area from an urban, midwestern region. Most of the management team was oriented toward urban culture, while most of the machinists and other members of the work force were native to that rural area. The problems that were most evident were the communication style differences. Beyond accent and dialectical differences, there were some diverse approaches to managerial style of communication.

Overall, characteristics of rural communication style, based on personal observations and on the work by Perrin (1980), include:

1. Requests and other forms of communication are not made in a demanding style.

2. Messages tend to be phrased in personal terms, rather than objective terms.

3. Respect is shown for the free will of the other person.

4. Story, image, and describing background scenarios play an important role in the communication style. Communication is filled with anecdotes and stories, often about family or friends, though in a number of cases about "out-groups."

5. Messages are usually related to a unified whole. There is a kind of implicit theory about how this person or that event fits into the whole picture from a cultural point of view. For instance, "He acted kinda crazy, most likely because he's been working long hours."

6. History behind events, people, and conditions serve an organizing role for messages, as, for instance, "He perty near fell off the hay wagon, but that's no wonder, 'cause his grandpa did the same thing twice when he was a boy."

Urban Cultures and Communication

Metropolitan communities seem characterized as composed of members needing identification. For example, from a census of Catholic mass attenders in Montreal, Serge Carlos (1970) discovered that the frequency of church attendance increased as people moved from the central areas of the city to the periphery. Although a certain amount of quality in religious practices diminished, Carlos explained higher church attendance as a need for community integration when people moved from the urban core to the suburbs.

Certain forms of neighborhood identification, such as when neighbors stand together on an issue, lead to cohesive neighborhoods. Also, when people have high identification needs, they tend to be joiners, which leads to more neighborhood cohesiveness. Strong upward mobility and an emphasis on success symbols are also associated with urban cultures (McDonald 1985).

Inner-city communities, however, may be characterized as composed of isolated members with little group cohesion. Few social participation outlets are available, and isolation seems to remain entrenched unless other group memberships override the isolation. Housing problems and high crime rates affect social participation in urban areas and foster less dependence on interpersonal communication networks.

Anomia, a generalized isolation and loneliness, may result partly from crowded physical surroundings. Such conditions can easily lead to urban fears and suspicions predicated upon an urban dweller's experience with such things as increased crime and decreased personal territoriality.

Socioeconomic Cultures and Communication

Social systems often become stratified as a result of socioeconomic variables, such as occupation, income, and education. That is, members of a society rank people into higher or lower social positions, producing a rank order of respect and prestige. Respect is conferred to individuals according to their conformity to a society's ideals. *Class* is a role-related position determined by the prestige, esteem, and value that other members of the social system place on the individual's position and, therefore, on the individual. Some intercultural communication problems result from misunderstandings among socioeconomic subcultures.

Overall, classes are inclined to depreciate the social differences between themselves and higher classes and to magnify differences with lower classes. Sometimes, this perceptual set is heightened so that a certain unity of outlook exists by allusions to "people like us" and to persons "not our kind." A feeling of "we-ness" especially occurs when expressing dissatisfaction with the upward mobility of the lower classes or resentment toward the higher classes. Unity is further intensified through common beliefs and patterns of overt behavior. The Indian caste system is an example of a highly ordered and rigidly determined class ranking, which in turn predicts attitudes and communication between different castes within the larger context of India's culture. Labor and management differences also reflect the attitudes that some classes hold toward other classes and of the importance of communication in resolving those differences.

Research reveals unique tendencies concerning where socioeconomic differences emerge. First, compared with stationary members, those members climbing upward in the class system are not as likely to maintain close personal friendships. This phenomenon can partly be traced to their more frequent geographical movement, as Alvin Toffler's *Future Shock* reminds us. Second, prestige and achievement become more valuable to middle-class members than to lower-class members and, especially, to middle-class persons

Subcultures, such as those marked by generation, status, sex, and racial differences, are easily susceptible to misperceptions about other subcultures.

who are moving upward. Third, lower classes seem to be more distrustful of authority utilized by more powerful classes. Accordingly, they are also more resigned to suffering, both physically and psychologically, than are higher classes (Berelson and Steiner 1964).

Interracial and Interethnic Communication

As you may remember from chapter 1, interracial and interethnic communication are also types of subcultural communication, since racial and ethnic groups typically are smaller, distinctive units within the larger culture. As you may also remember from chapter 1, *race* is a genetically transmitted and inherited trait of physical appearance. *Ethnicity* refers to a people's common heritage and cultural tradition, usually stemming from some national and/or religious origin.

Three characteristics appear common to both interracial communication and interethnic communication. While far more information exists about these specialized forms of communication,* the following three areas touch a chord of commonality and serve to draw together significant aspects about interracial and interethnic communication:

Suspicion

Interracial and interethnic situations are frequently marked by mutual suspicions of group *A* toward group *B*. The era of the 1960s serves to illustrate the intense feelings of a number of racial and ethnic groups toward contrasting groups. The level of suspicion aroused is clearly irrational in most cases and is fueled by specific features, such as the "we-they" syndrome and mistrust.

We-They dichotomy. An accompanying characteristic of suspicion in the interracial and interethnic context is the distinction between "we" and "they."

*Works by Smith (1973), Rich (1974), and Blubaugh and Pennington (1976), for instance, describe in detail the process of interracial communication.

Such a distinction clearly heightens a sense of loyalty and group identity, both of which are necessary for social change. The words of Malcom X illustrate this principle:

> No, I'm not an American. I'm one of the 22 million black people who are victims of Americanism. One of the 22 million black people who are victims of democracy. . . . (Minnick 1979, 143)

Mistrust. Suspicion is also aroused by attitudes of mistrust. Unfortunately, since contacts are often limited, people selectively perceive racial and ethnic groups that contrast with their own in such a way to create mutual mistrust. The mistrust, however, is often predicated upon not only selective perception but also upon negative, erroneous stereotypes.

Stereotypes develop as a way of organizing our world. Categorizing is a necessary part of daily functioning. However, stereotyping categories of people is often misleading, since all people within a category are not alike and since we may not always fully understand what we perceive.

Stereotypes

Experimental studies confirm anecdotal notions of stereotypes and specify the ways in which those stereotypes operate. For example, in his study of stereotypic attitudes toward Mexican Americans, England (1977) used two groups of matched respondents. Both groups were shown a series of eight slides. The central figure in the slides shown to group 1 was a Mexican American male in various scenes—in a yard behind a frame house, carrying trash cans, raking leaves around a tree, and putting the leaves into a wagon. He was dressed in a work shirt, work pants, and an outdoor work hat. Group 2 was shown exactly the same scenes, except that the man in the slides was an Anglo male dressed exactly as the Mexican American stimulus figure. Subjects were told they would be shown some slides and were then asked to evaluate what they saw. The slides were shown twice in succession with no narration.

On a series of questions, several significant test results revealed perceived differences toward the Mexican American and the Anglo. As figure 4.1 portrays, the subjects perceived the Mexican American as having a larger family and less education than the Anglo. They further perceived the Mexican American as being engaged in the process of working for someone else in that person's backyard. These data clearly revealed that the perception of ethnic background alone precipitates significant differences in assessing a person's characteristics, a finding that has been documented numerous times.

The solution to the problem of negative stereotypes, in terms of communication, is complex, as evidenced by the volumes written on the subject. However, the following simple but direct observations are helpful in indicating where to begin:

1. *Seek a common code.* Frequently, linquistic variations and dialectical differences cause people to close the door to further understanding and communication attempts. By seeking a common code, we can maximize our

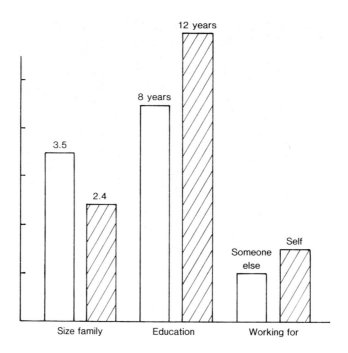

Figure 4.1
Perceived
differences toward
Mexican-American
and Anglo.
(Adapted from
England 1977.)

☐ Mexican-American

▨ Anglo

All categories compared are significantly different at P < .05.

chances for a heightened overlap of experiences. Communication in establishing a common code should become two-way; asking questions and seeking to clarify are excellent ways to begin the process.

2. *Seek to build trust.* Trust comes from showing trust. An accompanying sense of empathy toward others can turn hostility into a meaningful relationship.

3. *Suspend judgments.* If interaction with a person from a different racial or ethnic background raises negative attitudes toward that group, then make a conscious effort to suspend those attitudes. Consider the uniqueness of each individual by carefully listening, expressing your view honestly, and then continuing to listen.

Solidarity

A third characteristic of interracial and interethnic communication is the group's solidarity, often corresponding to a group's self-identity, as noted earlier in this chapter. This solidarity was well illustrated in the words of Martin Luther King when he declared:

Interracial and interethnic communication are too easily marked by suspicions, stereotypes, and a wall of solidarity that blocks out healthy intercultural communication.

But one hundred years later, the Negro still is not free. One hundred years later, the life of the Negro is still sadly crippled by the manacles of segregation and the chains of discrimination.

One hundred years later, the Negro lives on a lonely island of poverty in the midst of a vast ocean of material prosperity. One hundred years later, the Negro is still languished in the corners of American society and finds himself an exile in his own land. So we have come here today to dramatize a shameful condition.

In a sense, we have come to our nation's capital to cash a check. When the architects of our republic wrote the magnificent words of the Constitution and the Declaration of Independence, they were signing a promissory note to which every American was to fall heir. (Minnick 1979, 140–41)

The point of commonality, so eloquently stressed in this excerpt, was the mutual suffering and the future promise of mutual reward to a group showing solidarity (emphasized by the "we").

Countercultural Communication

A counterculture is a unit that stands in opposition to the larger culture, though it may be somewhat similar to the larger culture. Various communal subcultures represent clear examples of countercultural groups. The exploration of countercultural communication is largely a matter of understanding the counterculture itself. To best understand a counterculture, let us discuss some features that serve to bind its members: common code, common enemy, and common symbols.

Common Code

Counterculture group members gravitate toward a common set of linguistic usages, such as jargon, slang, and so on, that are meaningfully interpreted

Subcultures often create norms, codes, symbols, and styles to reflect and even preserve their uniqueness.

usually only in light of the group members' assigned meanings to the code system. Street language, while constantly changing, is an example of specialized code usage in antisocial groups such as gangs.

Common Enemy

In a number of countercultures, there is a perceived common enemy, such as the dominant culture, big business, the world and its "rat race," and so on. When attention is focused on the common enemy, who incidently is allegedly responsible for some ill affecting the countercultural group, the group then has a rallying point. In this way, group members are reinforced for their beliefs, and the reinforcement tends to bond the group into an even more cohesive unit. The "M-19" terrorist group in Bogotá, Colombia, who captured some forty diplomats on February 27, 1980 and held them hostage, clearly expressed images of a common enemy.

Common Symbols

Many countercultural members use symbolic objects, such as flags, graphic art, highly prized objects, drugs, and so forth, to emphasize commonality. The symbols become another rallying point—and thus provide not only a sense of unification but a tangible reflection of personal and group identity.

Another subculture is the poverty culture, which is marked by lack of financial and material resources. The economic condition of the poverty culture, however, correlates with several value and attitudinal beliefs. Rogers (1969) described several factors that indicate a profile of attitudes among the poor. In some ways, these factors can be attributed to all of the subcultures described thus far in this chapter. They are included at this point in the chapter to provide a thought-provoking conclusion to understanding subcultures, at least those defined as traditional subcultures and poverty-level subcultures.

Poverty Cultures and Communication

Members of many traditional subcultures believe the world's goods to be something like a pie with a limited number of slices. Consequently, if someone prospers, that prosperity is perceived to occur only at others' expense, since it is assumed that prosperity means one has taken an inordinate amount of the pie. It follows that neighbors may become suspicious of a community member who financially succeeds and thus violates the unspoken norms of this subculture.

Perceived Limited Good

Members of many traditional subcultures subordinate personal goals to the wishes and perceived good of the family. These people typically do not think of themselves apart from the family, and this heavy emphasis upon the family is called familism.

Familism

Fatalism is the degree to which we cannot control our future. In many traditional subcultures, the future is often viewed as humanly unknown and certainly uncontrollable.

Fatalism

Members of traditional subcultures typically react negatively, rather than positively, to innovations. In the case of technological innovations, the resistance may be purely economic, although a strong element of traditionalism also dictates that, despite the cost, most things need to be done according to the past ways, which have been tried and proven by predecessors.

Lack of Innovativeness

Members of many subcultures in the poverty cycle have a low motivation for achievement. They simply do not think of raising themselves in this world in an economic or status sense. That a poverty-level person does not actively seek a job should not be surprising in light of the lowered goals accompanying the debilitating effects of poverty.

Limited Aspirations

Apparently, members of poverty subcultures and traditional societies find it difficult to think about deferring gratifying experiences until the future. The concept of saving money for a later time has few takers in this subcultural

Lack of Deferred Gratification

Table 4.1 Perceptions of the Poverty Culture in the United States

Concept	Poverty Culture's View
Success	Generally unattainable, limited only to people with a lot of luck
Failure	Inevitable, no hope to overcome inherent failure
Emotions	Emotions are made to be expressed, publicly or privately
Future	Difficult to envision, so live for now
Money	To be used before it gets away, not saved for the future
Police	Unfriendly, out to get us, and should be avoided
Education	Useful for poor people with upward aspirations, an obstacle for individuals with low aspirations
Fate	Dominates some people since various seen and unseen forces control our destiny

pattern. Perhaps the immediacy of personal subsistence leads to a "here-and-now" syndrome of reward, rather than postponement of immediate satisfaction to await future rewards. Also, some traditional cultures may not have linguistic notions of future time.

Low Empathy

Members of poverty subcultures seem unable to project themselves into any situation or role other than their present one. This lack of projection may be why traditional subcultures around the world resist attempts at modernization.

Table 4.1 shows how various concepts are viewed by the poverty culture in the United States.

Developing Intercultural Communication Skills with Subcultures

We invite you to consider some suggestions for intercultural skills. We hope this list will stimulate your own response to your endeavors.

1. *Test your stereotypes.* As this chapter indicates, we may have negative impressions of others that are based on incorrect information. Ask yourself why you feel as you do, and try to correct false impressions.

2. *Treat cultural differences as a resource.* All too often, we treat cultural differences as something highly negative and thus approach intercultural communication with something of a "jaundiced eye." We should look upon differences as an opportunity, a resource from which to learn exciting things about a new culture, a new person, and ourselves.

3. *Develop ways of handling uncertainty.* Intercultural communication by its nature poses various degrees of uncertainty—uncertainty about ourselves, about what to say, and what to do. Thus, each of us needs to develop an ability to handle contradictions and uncertainty with grace and ease.

4. *Develop self-respect.* One of the best things that can help us in developing intercultural contacts is to take an extra dose of self-confidence. Be positive about others, and that will help you become positive about yourself. Criticism and resentment only serve to hurt you, the intercultural communicator.

5. *Do not rely on past experiences to deal with every new situation.* The past comes from your own cultural background. But the new culture represents a situation where your familiar cues are not present, and thus, to respond to features in the new culture as if you were in the old culture would be misleading.

6. *Outgoingness may not work.* If you handle new situations in your own culture with outgoingness, you may be surprised to find that being extra friendly does not necessarily work in the subculture where you are currently interacting.

7. *Competition may not work.* If you like competitiveness, do not be surprised if cultural differences preclude this value from being mutually appreciated.

8. *Progressivism may not work.* You may also hold strong attitudes toward goal orientation and "progressivism." That is, you may expect a subculture to be moving in a linear manner straight toward some goals that you have predetermined are good. Do not be surprised should such a direction not work for you.

9. *Stress areas of positive relations.* As we have already indicated throughout this chapter, look for ways to build bridges of understanding.

10. *Do not assume your needs are like everyone else's needs.* Because you feel a certain way, do not assume that your feelings reflect anyone else's opinion. By listening and asking questions, you can quickly discover how your personal frame of reference does not match another person's viewpoint. And that discovery is the beginning of effective intercultural communication within subcultures.

11. *Learn the rules of the subculture.* You may think that subcultures do not have a systematized way of behaving, but a subculture, like a culture, has rules. Effective intercultural communication requires an understanding of the system.

This chapter highlights awareness of group membership and identification as essential microcomponents of a larger culture. To understand group differences is to increase our insight into cross-cultural communication. Many intercultural communication problems emerge from reference group barriers.

This Chapter in Perspective

Understanding the dynamics of reference groups is partially a matter of realizing their importance. Under a number of conditions, reference groups have an enormous influence on individuals. Also, individuals can affect reference groups.

This chapter also described regional, rural, urban, and socioeconomic subcultures and their relation to communication. Members of various geographic locations, social classes, and age groupings can perceive messages in somewhat similar ways. The barriers in interracial and interethnic communication include the effects of suspicion, stereotypes, and solidarity. The common elements among countercultural groups, another type of subculture, are common codes, perceived common enemy, and perceived common symbols. Finally, the following attitudes found in cultures around the world among rural, traditional villages may also apply to any subculture of the poor: perceived limited good, familism, fatalism, lack of innovativeness, limited aspirations, lack of deferred gratification, and low empathy. Observations of North American poverty groups show significant attitudinal differences between middle- and low-class poverty-level persons.

Exercises

1. Look at a cross-sample of television programs, especially reruns of older programs. Are there some stereotypic profiles that come across in these programs? For instance, how are elderly people portrayed? Blacks? Mexican Americans? Do these stereotypes still exist on television today?

2. In a public place, like your campus student center, observe people interacting with various subcultural members. What patterns of behavior and interaction do you observe?

3. Interview someone from an ethnic minority. Ask that person questions about his or her minority. What misconceptions do people have about the group? What misconceptions does the minority member have concerning members of other ethnic groups or of the dominant culture?

Resources

Abelson, Herbert I. *Persuasion.* New York: Springer, 1959.

Amir, Y. "Contact Hypothesis in Ethnic Relations." *Psychological Bulletin* 71 (1969): 319–41.

Arensberg, Conrad M., and Arthur H. Niehoff. *Introducing Social Change.* Chicago: Aldine, 1964.

Asch, Solomon E. "Effects of Group Pressures upon the Modification and Distortion of Judgments." In *Readings in Social Psychology,* edited by Eleanor E. Maccoby, Theordore M. Newcomb, and Eugene L. Hartley. New York: Henry Holt, 1958.

Back, Kurt. "Influence through Social Communication." In *Readings in Social Psychology,* edited by Eleanor E. Maccoby, Theodore M. Newcomb, and Eugene L. Hartley. New York: Henry Holt, 1958.

Berelson, Bernard R., Paul F. Lazarsfeld, and William N. McPhee. *Voting.* Chicago: University of Chicago, 1954.

Berelson, Bernard, and Gary A. Steiner. *Human Behavior: An Inventory of Scientific Findings.* New York: Harcourt, Brace & World, 1964.

Bettinghaus, Erwin P. *Persuasive Communication.* 3d ed. New York: Holt, Rinehart and Winston, 1980.

Blubaugh, Jon, and Dorothy Pennington. *Crossing Difference: Interracial Communication.* Columbus: Charles Merrill, 1976.

Boulding, Kenneth. *The Image.* Ann Arbor, Mich.: University of Michigan Press, 1972.

Carlos, Serge. "Religious Participation and the Urban-Suburban Continuum." *American Journal of Sociology* 75 (1970): 742.

Cohen, Arthur R. *Attitude Change and Social Influence.* New York: Basic Books, 1964.

Daniel, Jack. "The Poor: Aliens in an Affluent Society." In *Intercultural Communication: A Reader,* 2d ed., edited by Larry Samovar and Richard Porter. Belmont, Calif.: Wadsworth, 1976.

Davis, Allison, Burleigh B. Garner, and Mary R. Gardner. "The Class System of the White Caste." In *Readings in Social Psychology,* edited by Eleanor E. Maccoby, Theodore M. Newcomb, and Eugene L. Hartley. New York: Henry Holt, 1958.

DeFleur, Melvin L., and Sandra Ball-Rokeach. *Theories of Mass Communication.* 3d ed. New York: David McKay, 1976.

Dodd, Carley H. "Social Structure and Communication Behavior among the Children of God." A paper presented to the International Communication Association Convention, Chicago, April 16, 1975.

England, William. "The Stereotype of a Mexican American: Analysis by Semantic Differential Technique." Unpublished paper, Department of Anthropology, University of Texas, 1977.

Erbe, William. "Gregariousness, Group Membership, and the Flow of Information." *American Journal of Sociology* 67 (1962): 502–16.

Festinger, Leon. *A Theory of Cognitive Dissonance.* Stanford, Calif.: Stanford University Press, 1957.

Freedman, Ronald, et al. *Principles of Sociology.* New York: Henry Holt, 1952.

Goldstein, Sidney. "Socioeconomic Differentials among Religious Groups in the United States." *American Journal of Sociology* 74 (1969): 612–31.

Goode, Erich. "Social Class and Church Participation." *American Journal of Sociology* 72 (1966): 102–11.

Gudykunst, William B. "Intercultural Contact and Attitude Change: A Review of Literature and Suggestions for Future Research." *International and Intercultural Communication Annual* 4 (1977): 1–16.

Homans, George C. *Social Behavior: Its Elementary Forms.* New York: Harcourt, Brace & World, 1961.

Hovland, Carl I., Irving L. Janis, and Harold H. Kelley. *Communication and Persuasion.* New Haven: Yale University Press, 1953.

Katz, Elihu. "The Diffusion of New Ideas and Practices." In *The Science of Human Communication,* edited by Wilbur Schramm. New York: Basic Books, 1963.

Kim, Young Hun. "Inter-Ethnic and Intra-Ethnic Communication: A Study of Korean Immigrants in Chicago." *International and Intercultural Communication Annual* 4 (1977): 53–68.

McDonald, Gordon. *Ordering your Private World.* Nashville: Thomas Nelson, 1985.

Minnick, Wayne. *Public Speaking.* Boston: Houghton Mifflin, 1979.

Norton, R. W. "Foundation of a Communication Style Construct." *Human Communication Research* 4 (1978): 99–111.

Ong, Walter J. "World as View and World as Event." in *Intercommunication among Nations and Peoples,* edited by Michael H. Prosser. New York: Harper and Row, 1973.

Perrin, L. J. *Second Person Rural.* New York: Doubleday, 1980.

Rich, Andrea. *Interracial Communication.* New York: Harper and Row, 1974.

Rodgers, Raymond. "Folklore Analysis and Subcultural Communication Research: Another View of World View." Paper presented to the Society for Intercultural Education, Training, and Research, Phoenix, February 25, 1978.

Rogers, Everett M. "Elements in the Subculture of Traditionalism." Paper presented to the Society for Applied Anthropology, Mexico City, April 9–16, 1969.

Sherif, Carolyn W., and Muzafer Sherif, eds. *Attitude, Ego-Involvement, and Change.* New York: John Wiley & Sons, 1967.

Sherif, M., C. Sherif, and R. Nebergall. *Attitude and Attitude Change: The Social Judgment-Involvement Approach.* Philadelphia: Saunders, 1965.

Smith, Alfred F. *Communication and Culture.* New York: Holt, Rinehart and Winston, 1966.

Smith, Arthur L. *Transracial Communication.* Englewood Cliffs, N.J.: Prentice-Hall, 1973.

Smith, Brewster M., Jerome S. Bruner, and Robert White. *Opinions and Personality.* New York: John Wiley & Sons, 1956.

Tichenor, Charla J. "An Examination of Cognitive Complexity and Its Relationship with Urban-Rural Locality." Master's thesis, Western Kentucky University, 1981.

Chapter 5

Intercultural Communication and Cognitive Culture

After completing this chapter, you should be able to:

1. Discuss the importance of cognitive culture for communication.

2. Understand cultural time orientations.

3. Differentiate between high-context cultures and low-context cultures.

4. Understand the elements inherent in world view and values.

5. Discuss concrete examples of how a culture's world view and values affect the attitude and behaviors of culture members.

6. List some basic cultural values.

The notion of cognitive culture is an important step in the development of a better understanding of intercultural communication. Communication theorists have known for a long time that cognitive orientations influence communicator style, approach-avoidance behaviors, and the nature of relationships. For instance, intensive research on cognitive complexity indicates that cognitively complex individuals have a richer, more diversified framework for making accurate judgments about others. They exhibit more tolerance for differences and offer a buffering quality to relationships that cognitively simple persons cannot. Personality variables also influence communication. For instance, highly dogmatic individuals display rigidity in communication style, take less risky positions on issues, and in general, respond with less communication and relationship openness than low dogmatics. Chapter 11 describes in greater detail a number of cognitive style variables that influence intercultural communication.

The point right now, though, is that cognitive orientations affect communication. Similarly, culture is more than custom. It is a shared perception about self and other people. Ideas, themes, world view, and values are all part of the cognitive system of a person. Culture has structure—systems, behaviors, norms, and organizational factors. But it also has its visions, beliefs, truths, and outlooks that together make up a mental framework that we call cognitive culture. So, cognitive culture is defined as the mind-set of a group of people that is related to their world view, themes, values, and methods of thought processing. It includes the mental organizing principles by which we operate our everyday lives. For example, in American macroculture, phrases that are cultural truisms, such as, "Haste is waste," and "A stitch in time saves nine," exemplify cognitive culture. Our cognitive culture guides our communication patterns. For instance, if we live in a culture that emphasizes efficiency of task above importance of time with people, then our communication performance will reflect that cognitive orientation.

This chapter examines the factors that pertain to how people think, how they see the structure of the universal order of things, and the values by which they judge themselves and others. Within these dimensions of how people think, believe, and evaluate are important principles of intercultural communication. My work in intercultural counseling has indicated that a large part of negative information processing, information overload, and stressful relationship interaction boils down to some fundamental differences in how people think, evaluate, and structure their world views.

Cultural Differences in Information Processing

Edward T. Hall's *Beyond Culture* (1977) expresses an important cognitive theory about the way cultures process time. Internal views of time have all kinds of implications about communication climates and consequent behaviors, including everything from irritation at being kept waiting to the very thought framework of time as cultural perception. According to Hall, the cognitive element of time structures our interaction. Indeed, there appears to be a continuum of time orientation, with monochronic time on one end and polychronic time on the other.

In the next sections, we discuss both monochronic and polychronic time orientation, as well as another variable of cultural information processing—high-context and low-context cultures.

Monochronic time-oriented people have a strong sense of doing one thing at a time. For them, time is like a long ribbon of highway that can be sliced into segments. Monochronics believe that accomplishments and tasks can and should be performed during each segment. Monochronics have a high need for closure—completing a task or coming to a conclusion in a relationship.

Monochronic Time Orientation

For example, I once counseled a couple from diverse regional cultures in the United States. The young man was operating from a polychronic orientation, trying to process many of the couple's future relationship decisions all at once. The young woman, on the other hand, was monochronic. She tended to focus on a single issue at a time and wanted closure, or completion, on each issue that the couple confronted in their dating relationship. Her need for closure was so high, in fact, that her demands for answers pressured the man into breaking up the relationship.

Monochronics are not all demanding, but they do need to see things finished. They are dissatisfied with dangling loose ends. Also, as a result, their tolerance for ambiguity is not high. As uncertainty rises, monochronics tend to articulate solutions and to work toward resolution, whether in conflicts or ordinary everyday decisions.

Monochronics usually think in a linear fashion. That is, they internally process information in a sequential, segmented, orderly fashion. For instance, monochronics schedule appointments linearly—arrival, meeting, conclusion, action—and they cycle through this same pattern all day long.

Being a monochronic is great if you are in a monochronic culture. But when a monochronic is placed in a polychronic situation, or worse yet, in a polychronic culture, stress and poor communication usually result. For instance, a colleague and I were in India a few years back and on one occasion waited for a transportation ticket. We got there early (like good Americans) and "secured" our place in front of the ticket window. Nobody else was around, so we felt confident that our waiting would be minimal once the window opened. However, when the ticket window opened, about one hundred people came out of nowhere and crowded around us, squeezing us out of what we thought was our place in line. After a half hour of standing in the same place while everyone else crowded in front, we finally realized that in this culture there was no such thing as a "line"—it was everyone for himself. Once we understood that, we soon had our tickets. We had cognitively structured our space just like our monochronic time orientation. But the Telegu people of India had a more polychronic view and apparently ordered their spatial relations accordingly.

If we examine situations in our lives that seem frustrating or nonproductive, we may find that all or part of the problem involves monochronic/polychronic conflicts. For example, many monochronic managers are faced with polychronic demands and must work with people who think polychronically.

An understanding of the differences of monochronic and polychronic time orientations may help to resolve some of the inherent problems in these situations.

Polychronic Time Orientation

Although monochronic individuals think in terms of linear sequential, time-ordered patterns (1, 2, 3, or *A, B, C*), there are cognitive cultures whose members think in terms of pictures or configurations. The configurational pattern of thought that follows a nonlinear order of attention to stimulus is called polychronic time orientation. Here, the stimulus items may follow an attention pattern unique to that culture, as for instance, 1, 16, 37, 2; or *A, M, Z, B*. The issue involves how we collect and process information and is being addressed in the psychiatric literature (Bandler 1985). The process of information processing, however, appears to be culturally dependent as well as individually derived. Thus, a significant part of understanding cultural differences involves examining methods of thought.

Polychronic individuals tend to think about and attempt to do a number of things simultaneously. In Latin America, for example, a businessperson may conduct business interviews by inviting a number of unrelated clients into his or her office at once, entertaining them for hours, and jumping from one to another and back again. Sounds unusual? Well, the one-at-a-time method seems unusual to polychronic cultures.

Actually, it appears more correct to talk about *individuals* who are monochronic or polychronic. While American, British, Canadian, and German cultures are largely monochronic (as evidenced by the school systems and the organizational patterns of most businesses and the military) and Latin American, African, Middle Eastern, and Southern European cultures tend toward polychronism, clearly, individuals tend one way or another.

Through some surveys conducted at my university, I have informally explained the concepts of monochronism and polychronism, given a few antecdotes about people who are one way or the other, and then asked the students in the survey which way they would say they lean, assuming they had to choose one or the other. With a sample of over six hundred, so far about 25 percent of the respondents report that they are polychronic. In actuality, we have discovered that we are probably monochronic or polychronic depending on certain situations. But everyone may have an overriding tendency, and that is what we are trying to explore.

Polychronic tendencies can become dysfunctional in situations that demand monochronic performance. Some organizational cultures, groups, systems, and families think, schedule, and operate in a monochronic fashion. Thus, a polychronic person can feel rather stressful, even depressed, in such a group.

Polychronics may experience high degrees of information overload. That is, they are trying to process so many things at once that they feel frustrated. They may also experience procrastination. And they seem to struggle harder to articulate abstractions without visualization. In fact, they seem to be very visually oriented people. These observations may in further research be found to correlate with the theories of left and right brain orientations, where it is asserted that right brain dominant people think creatively, visually, and artistically, while left brain dominant people think mathematically and linearly. In any case, there is a kind of cognition about how we process time that seems both cultural and personal, and this monochronic–polychronic continuum has an important influence on communication behavior.

Another way that cultures process information revolves around how much a culture expects its members to know already about situations and expectations compared with cultures that expect to explain these same situations. In other words, some cultures, by their norms, have built into their system an expectation that we are supposed to automatically know what to do and when and how to respond to certain situations. Other cultures do not make these assumptions. To put the idea another way, some cultures are not high in providing members with information about routines or rituals or about how to behave in common, everyday situations. Other cultures, however, provide information to equip members with procedures and practices in a number of situations.

High- and Low-Context Cultures

A culture in which information about procedure is rarely communicated is called a high-context culture (Hall 1977). Members are expected to know how to perform in various situations, but the rules of cultural performance remain implicit. The context is supposed to be the cue for behavior. Suppose, for example, a corporate executive says to you, "Here's the task—you have a college degree, so get started on this project." In situations like this, procedures are incompletely stated, if communicated at all.

In a low-context culture, on the other hand, information is abundant, procedures are explicitly explained, and expectations are discussed frequently. For instance, in a corporate culture where you are told, "Here is the task, and here is our procedure for accomplishing this task," information levels are adequate for cultural performance even if you don't have a lot of experience or background with that particular cultural group.

The intercultural communication breakdown that most frequently occurs, considering high- and low-context systems, is when one person assumes and operates out of a high-context mind-set, while the interpersonal other expects explanation, looking for a low-context condition. These assumptions are rarely understood, much less discussed between intercultural participants.

American culture is considered to be on the low-context side. In this culture, at least as compared with other cultures, a relatively hefty amount of information provides cues for how to respond. For instance, Americans tend to have a significant number of traffic indicators, signs, instruction lists, standard operating procedures, and the like. Interpersonally, Americans often provide cues for the conversation and expected behavior: "Wait a second—I'm not finished." "Come on in and help yourself." "Wait here while I talk to my supervisor, discuss the options, and then give you an answer, which will take about fifteen minutes." By contrast, the Japanese expect others to sense the

High-context cultures implicitly expect our understanding of cultural rules without formal explanation of those rules.

context and act in an expected manner, whether the situation calls for proper bowing, silence, nonverbal expression, or observance of conversational rules.

So not only can we contact groups and organizations that are high- or low-context cultures, but there are also the overriding norms of high- or low-context expectations, depending upon the larger culture. Although there are numerous exceptions, in general, Northern Europeans, Western Europeans, and North Americans tend toward the low-context factor; Middle Easterners, Africans, and Latin Americans tend toward the middle; and Japanese, Chinese, Southeast Asians, Indonesians, Micronesians, and Indians tend toward a high-context condition.

Cultural World View

A Nigerian student attending a major university spoke to his faculty advisor about a scene he had witnessed and had come to believe emphatically; the event had occurred in his home country. The situation revolved around soldiers' use of particular charms and amulets for special protection. Many on-lookers, including the Nigerian student, cheered individuals who demonstrated use of the charms. An awesome demonstration occurred in which one person allegedly brought a razor-sharp sword down upon the arm of another person wearing the special charm. In every case, the person wearing the amulet suffered no harm. The student then described his belief that the charm worked principally through the power of spirits, whose power was available to anyone who knew the secrets connected with this cultural phenomenon.

This student was reflecting one of the most fundamental concepts about the nature of culture, called cultural world view. World view is defined as a belief system about the nature of the universe and the effect of the operation of the universe on our social environment. Discovering a culture's world view involves finding out how the culture perceives the role of various forces in explaining why events occur as they do in a social setting. For instance, many tribal Kenyans believe that disease is the result of evil spirits. A number of Latin Americans accept the notion that wealth comes from a pact with the devil or possibly luck in finding buried treasure. The Nigerian discussed in the previous paragraph believed in what is called ju-ju in West Africa. Voodoo and the evil eye are well-known belief systems in Caribbean cultures.

World view is such a fundamental set of perceptual assumptions that it includes how a culture explains forces in the universe, the nature of mankind, the kind of impersonal spirits that can do harm or good, and so on. The notion of world view also encompasses the operation of forces like luck, fate, the power of significant others, the role of time, and the nature of our physical and natural resources. Because it is so fundamental, world view can affect communication. For example, a middle-school teacher working among a group of poverty students often faces communication patterns of fatalism, such as "Why try?" and "No one will let me."

Our interactions may be less than perfect for a number of reasons, but differences in world view can clearly be a cause of poor intercultural communication. We now explore some of the fundamental elements of cultural world view.

By examining some of the typical concepts by which cultures order their worlds, we develop a category system with which to assess some fundamental belief structures of a group of people. A knowledge of those belief structures can improve intercultural communication, a point reviewed by Garmon (1984).

Shame-guilt cultures. Some cultures can be characterized by their perceived sense of personal and group shame. This organizing feature of world view suggests that cultures can take on a strident sense of obligation for things that go wrong. In Asian cultures, for instance, shame is the worst thing that can happen to a person, next to losing one's group identity. In traditional Japanese culture, disgrace potential is an important decision-making characteristic. If a policy or a person has the potential for bringing about shame, then such risks are not likely to be sought. According to Marsella, Murray, and Golden (1976), Chinese and Japanese Americans both show tendencies to be more negatively sensitive to shame than Caucasian Americans. In fact, Japanese chief executive officers have been known to commit suicide if the organization experiences financial disaster.

Elements of Cultural World View

Shame-guilt cultures have a way of looking inwardly for obligation and responsibility. For if duty is overlooked, it could cause shame to someone else, which in fact would cause you yourself to be shamed. In Thai culture, for instance, it is especially important to not engage in any behavior that would show disrespect for parents or elders. To do so would bring shame.

Another facet of shame-guilt cultures is the emphasis of some cultures on the guilt aspect. It can be assumed that a sense of guilt is universal. However, some cultures express a need for that guilt reduction more than others. This results in a need for atonement, and purification rituals and systems of expiation arise to meet those guilt needs. Jimenez (1987) noticed this sense of guilt in his counseling practice with upwardly mobile Mexican Americans. His analysis revealed that economic mobility set in motion a number of guilt-provoking cognitions: "I don't deserve this; why am I so lucky and others so poor?" He based his analysis, in part, on his recognition that the culture in which his clients lived emphasized qualities that provoked guilt.

The general theme of "saving face" is significant in a considerable number of intercultural contacts. In general, Middle Eastern, African, and some Asian cultures engage in communication behaviors and communicator styles that enhance relationships in a way so as to avoid embarrassment to another person. While it is not certain that such face-saving communication strategies are rooted in shame-guilt cultural world view, some correlation is believed to exist. In any case, intercultural communication with individuals from face-saving cultures invites attention to our personal rhetorics. In public, at least, hard, personal attacks, unrelentless negative statements, and a lack of adequate listening would likely signal to a member of a face-saving culture that the one engaging in those behaviors is without wisdom.

Task versus people cultures. Some cultures emphasize accomplishment with tasks, while other cultures emphasize relationships with people. There is reason to believe that a fundamental belief system is part of the task-people dichotomy. Task cultures may well have an underlying world view structure of what makes a person good. For instance, one underlying cognitive structure is the notion that self-worth comes only from accomplishment and success. Therefore, working hard and successful task completion are means by which to prove oneself. Or, put another way, a task-oriented person may say, "I have to work hard to prove myself." Task accomplishment is fundamental to developmental stages of children, as developmental theories remind us.

Task-cultural people certainly have many friendships, and obviously, people are not totally pushed out of the way. But such organizing themes as "Get ahead," "No pain without gain," and "Move upward," are the surface structures of a deeper, underlying cognitive dimension of how people are viewed in comparison with tasks. Americans, for instance, are considered highly task oriented.

Sacred versus secular cultures. Another important continuum by which a culture can be evaluated for its cognitive structural world view involves whether or not the culture accepts a notion of a cosmos filled with spiritual beings and forces or whether it rejects a spiritual dimension. Francis Schaeffer

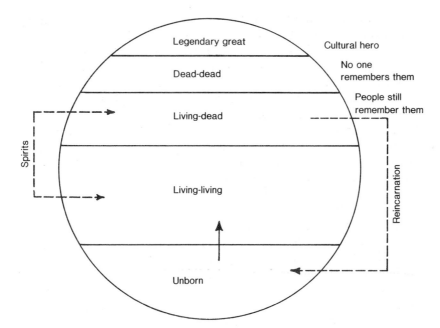

Figure 5.1
World view structure among Ashanti of Ghana, West Africa.

(Diagram labels: Legendary great, Cultural hero, Dead-dead, No one remembers them, Living-dead, People still remember them, Spirits, Reincarnation, Living-living, Unborn)

(1968), the well-known European philosopher, argued that a secular culture has an implicit faith in the presupposition of the uniformity of natural causes in a closed system. A sacred culture (which does not connote any kind of exceptional behavior) accepts the presupposition of an open system, implying the alternative of categories for God and spiritual dimensions. Essentially, a sacred culture places faith in the spiritual realm, which a secular culture does not accept.

Communication differences arising from this cognitive continuum can be sizable. With this cognitive position, members of a secular culture may label alternative cultures as untrustworthy, unintelligent, uninformed, and biased. Likewise, members from a sacred culture may view secular cultures in the same negative ways. A number of social philosophers, such as Schaeffer, believe that the presuppositions of the nature of the universe as open or closed to any force is the fundamental difference involved. Intercultural communication proceeds on the assumption that dialogue and friendship can transcend the secular-sacred continuum. There are clearly significant differences involved in these two cognitive schemas, but the differences need not be barriers for interpersonal relationships, task productivity, intercultural friendship, and group effectiveness.

The role of dead to living. Some cultures are characterized by their view of the relationship between living and dead. The well-known ancestor rituals in certain Asian and African cultures remind us that some people do not see death as an event that can be bridged with ceremony and ritual. The world view of the Ashanti of Ghana, for instance, is diagrammed in figure 5.1 and shows how ancestors are considered as a small part of an Ashanti's daily life.

Thus, at weddings and funerals, palm wine is poured on the ground to satisfy the thirst of the ancestor.

As we discuss later in this chapter in an examination of animism, there is an assumption here of a layered universe. Some of the powers available to a person are believed to come through ancestors, who can be called upon to perform certain things on behalf of the person asking. This same layered world view, however, may also involve impersonal spirits, magic, formulas, and rituals that perform services for the living.

Among the Yaruro of southern Venezuela, their gods and the dead are understood as being in a relationship with the living. The Yaruro visualize existence as having age levels divided into steps, something like a continuum, of which the dead and the gods are the two highest levels (Bock 1969).

Among the Navaho, the ghosts of the dead are greatly feared, and anything connected with death is carefully avoided. Not only do the Navaho have no desire to contact the dead, but they practice rituals to drive away the dead spirits and ghosts; certain illnesses are believed to be caused by contact with death. Navaho patients have even been known to flee a hospital upon learning that a death has occurred there (Bock 1969).

Some cultures hold assiduous beliefs about ancestors, though in a somewhat different way than beliefs about the afterlife in general. True *ancestor cults* remain in Oriental and African societies in which each major lineage honors its own set of founding ancestors. The Kai of New Guinea customarily "swindle" their ancestral ghosts, just as they try to swindle each other. In some cultures, the members try to outsmart the ancestral spirits by lying to them. Cajolery, bribery, and false pretense are common means of influencing the supernatural. In other cultures, ancestors are appeased in hopes that offerings and special ritual treatment will please the ancestors, who in turn will offer some benefit to the worshipper.

Another example deals with ancestor propitiation among the Mapuche or Araucanian Indians of Chile (Faron 1961). Ancestor worship or the belief in the spirits of the dead most clearly emerges in funeral activities of the Mapuche. The ceremony begins with the attempt to exorcise the dead person's spirit and other evil spirits that might be lurking. During the ceremony, the dead person's life history and ancestry are recounted in a loud voice, not for the benefit of the living, but to invoke the ancestors to accept, help, and protect the dead person's spirit from attack by the lurking evil spirits. Spirits are supposed to go to the spirit world and live tranquilly. However, if a spirit lingers on earth, it may be captured and put to a bad use by a sorcerer. Therefore, an unpropitiated spirit returns to earth to haunt relatives, not to do them harm, but to remind them of their obligation to him.

Nature of humankind. According to Kluckhohn and Strodtbeck (1961), cultures perceive humans in one of three ways. In one world view, human nature is considered good. The implications of this view are that people can handle responsibility and make their own decisions. For instance, managers, as Harris and Moran (1979) observed, may find that their primary organizational role is being a coordinator of information and as such must assume that people are inherently good. Or, as is noted in chapter 6 on organizational culture, McGregor's Theory Y makes the assumption of the goodness of humankind.

A second world view of the nature of humankind assumes a mixture of humans being good and evil. A third position assumed by some cultures is that humans are basically evil. With such an inherent nature presupposed, communication strategies gravitate toward such variables as control, regulation, protection of information, and a communication climate stressing upward and centralized communication. This cognitive world view position is similar to the Theory X approach noted in chapter 6.

Humans and nature. Another element of structural world view is the control a culture believes that it has with regard to nature. One cultural position is that humans are subject to nature (Kluckhohn and Strodtbeck 1961). Sarbaugh (1979) expounds well upon this point, stressing that, in this case, a person is considered a victim of nature, believing that nature was not meant to be controlled. A second cultural position is that humankind should be in harmony with nature—that we should preserve nature and work in coordination with natural conditions. A third cultural position is that humans should control nature in ways that benefit humankind, such as placing dams in rivers.

Interestingly enough, these cognitive cultural positions identify the controversies in the U.S. Department of the Interior for the past decade. One faction argues for total preservation of natural resources, while another faction argues for productivity and usage of many of the nation's natural resources.

Doing versus being cultures. Another structural world view difference between cultures is the doing-being duality. One cultural pattern is to prefer activity, productivity, measurable accomplishment, and the like. In fact, a doing culture often develops strategies to invoke guilt on its members for inactivity and loss of productivity. Such cultures emphasize goals, functional information giving and receiving, and less interpersonal communication time in its corporate cultures. Many of the world's technological cultures tend to characterize this type of culture.

Being cultures emphasize the meditative issues of a person's life space. These cultures stress the value of personal thought, discussion, interpersonal relationships, spontaneity, and harmony. Personal evaluation and guidance for self-help for the purpose of enhancing self-worth, knowledge, and good relationships are also emphasized. Consider, for example, a young couple where the man is a very meditative person, preferring quiet time in his life, and the woman enjoys going places and being constantly on the move. Their communication difficulties may relate partially to these cognitive differences stemming from their regional cultural differences on doing and being.

Life cycle. The examples noted thus far in this chapter imply that life can be viewed in two ways. One view suggests that life is linear—that birth, life, and death mark each person's existence. According to this view, there is no rebirth, only this life in which to accomplish. Therefore, time utilization is considered important. Individuals who maintain this linear view may or may not believe in an eternal existence after death.

A second view suggests that life is cyclical—that birth, life, death, and rebirth on earth mark each person's existence. This view also affects time utilization; since another earthly life follows, some cultures may believe that time pressures are not as important. Some analysts have argued, for example, that the United States was at an immediate disadvantage during the Vietnam war because of differences in these two time views. The North Vietnamese were prepared, reportedly, to fight for scores of years; the United States was accustomed to a quick end to war and thus grew weary when such an ending seemed illusive. These expectations may justifiably stem from each culture's view of time and life cycle.

Fatalism. Rogers with Svenning (1969) defined fatalism as "the degree to which an individual recognizes a lack of ability to control his future." A fatalistic outlook on life:

> results in a failure to see a relationship between work and one's economic condition. Having enough is thought to be almost entirely due to luck and is never believed to be brought about or furthered by personal initiative. (pp. 32–33)

Fatalism can produce two totally different outlooks. It can produce what has been generally characterized as so-called "failure" qualities, such as passivity, pessimism, acceptance, endurance, pliancy, and evasion. However, it can also be credited for success. For example, one Latin American stated that a successful individual has made a "pact with the devil" or perhaps has "found buried treasure."

Fatalism stems from a perception that something beyond our control causes our immediate circumstances. That cause may be random luck, manipulation of spiritual forces directed by someone else, the devil, juxtaposition of celestial bodies, and so on. The important point is that fatalism suggests a low degree of control over our environment.

Systems of Cultural World View

Not only can we identify the elements of cultural world view, but we can deal with and understand the systems of cultural world view that have been created in cultures. These systems function to enable cultural members to engage in various levels of control over their environments.

Mana. One system of control is mana, which is the existence of an impersonal supernatural force concentrated in objects or persons.* This force is sometimes inherited, sometimes acquired, or other times conferred. It is a power that is believed to reside in a person. In some cultures, this mana causes leadership; in other cases, the "high" mana individual is simply respected or asked for advice.

---

*Mana is a word of Melanesian and Polynesian origin and is akin to the Hawaiian and Maori *mana* (Webster's unabridged dictionary).

This altar in Central America was believed to represent a place where spirits could be appeased. The belief of impersonal power and its influence is prevalent in many parts of the world.

Mana can also characterize material objects. An amulet worn about some part of the body may serve in a special way to ward off evil in some Melanesian cultures. Among some North Americans, luck is considered to be a form of mana that can reside in a person or even in some material object.

Animism. Animism is closely associated with mana. It refers to the belief that impersonal spirits indwell every material form of reality, such as rocks, rivers, plants, and even thunderstorms and earthquakes in some cultures. These spirits are believed to be capable of producing either a benevolent or a malevolent influence. Among some Ghanians, it is believed that proper respect for animistically imbued objects can bring about certain benefits by the power of ju-ju. Voodoo and the evil eye in Caribbean cultures invoke similar forces. Sometimes, a special ambassador, called a shaman, is believed necessary to manipulate the spirit world.

In a study of the Mapuche Indians of Chile, Faron (1962) noted a dualistic world view most characteristically perceived by descriptions of phenomena as "left" or "right." Cultural aspects classified as "left" are evil, death, night, sickness, evil spirits, sorcerer, underworld, poverty, and hunger. In corresponding cultural classifications on the "right" are good, life, day, health, ancestral spirits, shaman, afterworld, abundance, and fullness. In this culture, for example, if anyone is startled by a bird's song near at hand, and the bird is on the right, it signifies good fortune. If the bird is on the left, it presages evil. As another example, when, in this culture, there is a dream of reaching a fork in the road and the person takes the left fork, he or she will have only bad fortune. If the person turns to the right, he or she will enjoy riches, huge quantities of food, and general good fortune.

Even natural elements and directions coincide with this dichotomous world view. On the left are west, north, winter, cold, moon, water, speech, ocean, below, blue, black, layman, and sin, while on the right in corresponding categories are east, south, summer, warm, sun, blood, ritual language, land, above, yellow, white, priest, and expiation. These, along with many more examples, led Faron to the conclusion that the Mapuche live in a dualistic or dichotomy-type society.

Shamanism. A shaman is an individual who acts as a diviner, curer, spirit medium, or magician for other people in return for gifts, fees, and prestige. The belief in a shaman's power is called shamanism. A long and hard training period may be demanded before a novice can attain the rights and privileges of the shaman position. Shamans are recognized by others as being different from the ordinary and usually take the lead in religious ceremonies, magical arts, or curing. It is believed that shamans' special abilities make it possible for them to enter into contact with spirit beings and to exercise some degree of control over supernatural forces. Shamans may enter a trance that augments their powers. Frequently, possession, the taking over of a human body by a spirit, is a part of a shaman's activities. While in this condition, the shaman may act as a medium, transmitting messages from the living to the dead and vice versa, predicting the future, finding lost objects, identifying the cause of illness, prescribing cures, or giving advice.

Other names frequently used in connection with shamans are magicians, seers, sorcerers, witch doctors, medicine men, and curers. Among the Tapirape Indians of Brazil, young people may be recognized as future shamans because of their tendency to dream, but the steps necessary to become a shaman are not easy (Bock 1969). Shamans differ from priests in that shamans derive their power or title from their connection with the spirit world through trances, while priests' authority comes from an organized church. Obviously, both shamans and priests are products of and influencers of the world view of their cultures.

Personal World View

Within a culture, individuals can, obviously, hold unique world views, particularly related to their communication environments. A relatively recent development in the field of intercultural communication is personal world view, defined as our belief about how much or how little control we have in our communication climate. We tend to organize information about ourselves and to utilize a communication style that reflects our fundamental view toward the amount of control we perceive. For example, one young college student stated that his reason for being reticent related to his feeling of helplessness with regard to changing his situation or his relationships, so why even bother to talk about things? A high school student realized that her lack of friendships was linked with her fatalistic feelings: "I can't alter my circumstances, so why even try?" Research in this area of personal world view has shown that around 25 percent of the Americans studied in various samples report high communication fatalism (Dodd and Garmon, in press).

A great deal more could be written here about personal world view. The important point, however, is that we become more aware of how cultural and personal world view contribute to communication relationships. This cognitive mind-set of world view can greatly condition us to respond only in certain ways. For example, if we believe that fate controls relationships, then our communication strategies in building relationships become jaundiced.

Values and Intercultural Communication

Values refer to long-enduring judgments appraising the worth of an idea, object, person, place, or practice. Many of our opinion statements and attitudes sometimes reflect deep-seated and fundamental values. While attitudes tend to be somewhat changeable, values tend to be long lasting. For example, you may prefer a political candidate for president of the United States because of that person's views on foreign aid, such as providing food for displaced Cambodians. Your attitude (evaluation of goodness or badness of something) may be positive toward the candidate because of a foreign policy stance, a position with which you may agree. But why do you have the positive attitude toward the candidate, as well as the favorable attitude toward foreign aid to Cambodians? Probably because you value altruism—you may think it is important to share wealth. Perhaps this value even relates to other values. Fundamentally, values relate to questions of whether something "ought" or "ought not" to be—when we finally get to the "why" of those questions, we have gotten to values.

Much work in the field of intercultural communication has centered on the role of values and their influence on communication. It stands to reason that values influence our perceptions, but more than that, they frame our fundamental assumptions of what is important. For example, a person may elevate the importance of extra effort and hard work, believing it produces success. Imagine the potential difficulty if this person were now teamed with an individual who devaluates hard work, believing that just getting by is enough so that there will be more time for enjoying life. Their communication may highlight these differences, and, once aware of their respective values, they may find their relationship strained until resolution occurs. An understanding of values, therefore, can pinpoint the differences between two individuals from separate cultures—and intercultural communication can proceed from an understanding of those differences. Let us now examine some of the more common values that the intercultural communicator is likely to encounter.*

A number of values center around evaluations concerning family and kin, especially values toward elders, parents, and ancestors.

Relationship with Family

Respect for elders. Almost every culture shows some degree of respect for its elders. In North America, we teach our young to use surnames in a formal manner when addressing older or respected persons. In some rural areas of the United States, the practice existed, not too many years ago, of addressing an older person as "Aunt" or "Uncle," even though no actual kinship

---

*Values are discussed extensively by Arensberg and Niehoff (1964), Kluckhohn and Strodtbeck (1961), Rokeach (1968), and, especially in the intercultural context by Condon and Yousef (1975).

was evident. Among North American family members, there is a degree of respect for age—up to a point. From retirement, or some point of less productivity, many North Americans seem to lose respect for their senior family members and senior citizens at large.

The respect North Americans hold for their elderly indeed is pale compared with the high value placed upon the elderly in other cultures. For many Asian and African cultures, age and its accompanying wisdom stand as a salient element—in some cases, a focal point—of culture. Many African men under twenty-five years of age will not make decisions without consulting older family members.

Respect for parents. Value of parental authority also varies culturally. North Americans typically stress individuality and making one's own decisions by the midteens. Accompanying this emphasis seems to be a disregard for parental authority and much less communication with parents—at least in a large number of cases. Such actions would be regarded as dishonoring parents in African and Middle Eastern cultures. In these cultures, to honor one's parents throughout life is considered one of the highest virtues.

Respect for ancestors. Although most North Americans typically do little more than occasionally remember a deceased relative, many people in other cultures pay deep homage to their ancestors. This value partially stems from some world view beliefs that ancestors can influence one's life and provide special benefits, as indicated earlier in this chapter. In some parts of Africa and among some subcultures in the United States, family members take out large newspaper ads, featuring a picture of a deceased family member and a personal letter addressing the deceased, as if that person were fully aware of the message. This form of communication with immediate ancestors or other deceased family members reflects not only an interesting communication form but also the importance of values. Respect for ancestors sometimes coincides with life cycles, illustrated in the ancestor-reincarnation view of the Ashanti (figure 5.1).

Relationships with Others

Another set of values focuses on interpersonal relationships. One's personal dealings with others is considered a sacred trust in some cultures but is treated casually in other cultures.

Equality of people. In the United States, people generally accept the norm of equality among people, at least philosophically. Among many other cultures, however, norms prevail concerning the rules of inequality. Members of these cultures accept status and role differences and in some cases espouse those differences as "natural" for orderly existence. Although in reality North Americans accept inequality in status, roles, and the like, the philosophical roots of equality and consequent personal freedom are deep—contradiction is likely to produce heated arguments. What appears to a North American, for example, as submission and loss of personal freedom among Asian villagers may in reality be their cultural response to values toward leadership.

Some cultures value emotional expression, but other cultures prefer less emotional display. Value differences toward emotion explain one reason for intercultural barriers.

Perhaps this one point illustrates an important communication principle: tolerance and understanding about the ways of a culture. North Americans may be particularly vulnerable to criticizing a culture for its appearing to have sacrificed personal freedom. In reality, we may have misunderstood that culture's values toward individuality and, instead, tried to superimpose our values where they do not belong and when we do not fully understand local customs.

Humanitarianism. Many cultures are surprised that people from the United States personally try to assist complete strangers. Although many North Americans typically value compassion, sympathy, and helping others, these "virtues" are not important to some other cultures.

Honesty. Most cultures have some taboo against dishonesty—under certain conditions. The middle easterner who values slyness and cleverness, for example, may be fully acceptable as long as he is considered sly in bargaining and not perceived as dishonest. Of course, one person's definition of honesty becomes another person's definition of cleverness—the United States businessperson who can cheat and not get caught is sometimes considered "shrewd." That person's foreign counterpart is considered "dishonest." In some cultures, a bribe is perceived as dishonest; other cultures view the same activity as a courtesy, as payment for a favor, or as an extended "tip."

Another set of values tells cultural members what they ought to think about societal behavior. Some of these values relate to personal behaviors, and some relate to group behaviors.

Morality and ethics. Morality and ethics seem highly personal to North Americans. But for many people around the world, morality is a group matter. Inappropriate premarital activity can cause a family to lose a certain bride price otherwise gained for a daughter. Incorrect use of property can become a grave societal offense among some African cultures.

Freedom. As noted earlier, personal freedom is not always valued in other cultures as it is esteemed in North America. Many cultures do not even have concepts to talk about personal choice in a way other than the individual's relationship to the group at large. One of the contrasting features that seems to surprise visitors from the United States to a host country is the sense of groupness. For instance, the Japanese sense of group relationship, loyalty, and hierarchy contrasts with the North Americans' sense of individuality (Doi 1976). Conformity to social norms exists practically universally. But within the boundaries of social norms, some cultures stress groupness while others stress individualism.

Emotions. Some cultures value emotional expression, but other cultures prefer reservation. While there are exceptions, Asian cultures generally practice reserve and emotional restraint. The idea of extreme emotion, such as loud sobs during a funeral or boisterous laughter on festive occasions, would be considered too emotional. To a lesser extent, some Scandinavian cultures appear publicly reserved. Britons and Germans appear more reserved than Italians, Greeks, and Czechs.

The use of emotion in communication, therefore, varies according to the relevant culture. For example, the speech one makes in Lagos, Nigeria, should differ from a speech in Denmark in terms of emotional elements of communication style. Similarly, we should not be surprised to find our intercultural communication colored by a high emotional pitch with some cultures or blanked by little enthusiasm with members of other cultures. To some cultures, we may appear "pushy" and too emotional; to other cultures, our same mannerisms may appear cold and unfeeling. An understanding of the importance of emotions should assist us in gearing our thinking to an intercultural context.

Work and play. Many people separate work and play. Work demands diligence, concentration, even tedium. Since play is considered frivolous, then combining work and play is unreasonable. Work and play do not mix! At least, that view predominates much North American thought. By contrast, other cultures blend work and play. For the North American to insist on the divorce of work from frivolity and to judge others negatively is to invite estrangement (Arensberg and Niehoff 1964).

Time. Time is valued more by some cultures than by others. For the U.S. businessperson, "Time is money." To the Ecuadorian storekeeper, time is relatively subservient to one's friendships and other social obligations. The values that cultures place upon time, however, cause numerous misunderstandings.

Another set of value variables deals with personal values toward success and material well-being. These values also relate to personal qualities of individualism.

Success. The idea behind "getting ahead," "winning," and generally being "above average" has deep taproots as a North American value. Competition also is valued, since it purportedly stimulates success. However, this notion of success and failure lacks correspondence in many other cultures. For many cultures, cooperation is fundamental.

Individualism. Success in North American values is linked with personal achievement and rugged individualism. Individualism pervades concepts of personal freedom in which each person has the right to individually pursue his or her choices. By contrast, many other cultures do not highly esteem individualism. Again, some Asian cultures emphasize group cohesion and loyalty. Many African cultural members thwart personal goals for the sake of the family, village, tribe, or larger cultural unit. In fact, some international observers have likened the North American's view of freedom to an adolescent who lacks self-restraint. The point of view, of course, depends upon the values one holds toward individualism, freedom, and other related concepts.

Material well-being. Many cultures value material accumulation of goods and wealth. Cattle herdsmen of East Africa, for example, prize their animals partially as a measure of status and wealth. In a similar way, North Americans accumulate goods as a measure of wealth and success. However, material well-being and accumulation of wealth can become ends valued in and of themselves—sometimes as the single-most important value. At any rate, a cultural value orientation toward material items can mark significant differences among cultures.

A special set of values centers around land. Farmland in China is related to a sense of security. It can be passed through generations; money may be used up, but not the land. Land values often center around kinship ties. This tie is reinforced by ancestor worship and creates a bond between a man and his land. It is not impossible for a man to sell his land, but to sell breaks the bonds of filial piety. Because these bonds are so rarely broken, from childhood onward, a man develops a sense of personal identity with his land; it becomes a part of his very personality.

Like the Chinese, the Maoris of New Zealand feel quite strongly about the inheritance of the land to develop an ancestral continuity. But these feelings have more immediate consequence for the Maoris than for the Chinese. Metge (1976) states the relationship as follows:

> It is the "land of our ancestors," a legacy bequeathed by a long line of forebears who loved and fought and died for it, and a tangible link with the heroes and happenings of a storied past. Often, it is associated with their own early life, kinsfolk, and friends. Even more important, inherited rights in Maori land are bound up with rights of precedence in Maori community life and on the *marae*

Relationship with Self

Relationship with Land

open space used as a gathering place. The older generation, in particular, recognize an almost mystical connection between land and personal standing. (p. 107)

Metge defined the aspects and consequences of the social standing and land relationship in the following passage:

In each local district, Maoris give a special status to those they call *tangata whenua* (literally "people of the land"). To qualify for this title and the privileges attached to it, a Maori must first of all be descended from a line of forebears who lived and owned "Maori land" in the district continuously over many generations. ("Maori land" is a technical term for land held by Maoris under special laws.) Many older Maoris hold that he should also own (or be heir to) shares inherited from these forbears in land in the district. They recognize those who have descent *and* land as *tangata whenua* under any circumstances, but express doubt about the status of those who have local descent without local land shares, though in practice I have never heard them deny the title to a claimant. (p. 107)

Metge also explains that even a person of local birth who has no ancestral connection or right to "Maori land" is considered an immigrant. Such "immigrants" are frequently barred from holding public office, and their voices never carry as much weight in any decision as the voice of a *tangata whenua*.

A North American Indian tribe, the Navajo, are agriculturally oriented. However, though a matrilineal kinship is established among these people, the concept of property is strictly individual. The woman may have her own plot of land, and the returns she reaps from it are strictly hers. The man does the same with his property. Even the children may be given designated pieces of land or a few animals and be expected to take care of these things themselves as soon as they are old enough (Leighton and Leighton 1944).

However, unlike the concepts of the whites around them, the land and its productivity are not a status symbol to the Navajo, even when they bring in a considerable amount of money. They have a high regard for possessions but feel that anyone who becomes extremely wealthy must have come by the wealth dishonorably. Therefore, they advocate that the wealth must be distributed among the wealthy's less fortunate friends and relatives.

The Kwakiutl Indians of Vancouver Island were not an agricultural culture, like those already mentioned. They subsisted through hunting, both on land and sea. Each tribe was divided into homogeneous groups called *numayms*. Each *numaym* had a group of hunters. The hunters of the different *numayms* would not hunt on the grounds of other *numaym* hunters, since encroachment usually produced a fight in which one or both groups were killed. This rule of ownership also applied to berry-picking grounds and to particular rivers where salmon fishing was done (Boas 1966).

Though the ownership of hunting grounds among the Kwakiutl Indians was specified, nature itself was believed to be controlled by a supernatural power. Animals, rocks, waterfalls, islands—all were approached by prayer, and a man could seek their help or offer thanks for their contribution. Some

The importance of one's land and of the earth is an important value among many Indians in the Western Hemisphere.

pieces of land had particular supernatural powers. For example, the soil from a land otter slide was believed to influence the weather.

The Plains Indians of North America were also hunters and gatherers, but their philosophy did not allow for a man's ownership of the land. To the Plains Indian, "All things are contained within the Medicine Wheel, and all things are equal within it. The Medicine Wheel is the Total Universe." A Blackfoot Chief explained the relation between the Indian and his earth as follows:

> Our land is more valuable than your money. It will last forever. It will not even perish by the flames of fire. As long as the sun shines and the waters flow, this land will be here to give life to men and animals. We cannot sell the lives of men and animals; therefore we cannot sell this land. It was put here for us by the Great Spirit, and we cannot sell it because it does not belong to us. You can count your money and burn it within the nod of a buffalo's head, but the Great Spirit can count the grains of sand and the blades of grass of these plains. As a present to you, we will give you anything we have that you can take with you; but the land, never. (Storm 1972, 5)

This concept of the land was not only related to the equality of all nature, but to the view of the earth as a mother. In most Indian literature, the earth is referred to as the Earth Mother. Her daily power and influence on the lives of the Indians is reflected in the following passage by Chief Luther Standing Bear, chief of the Lakota, a western band of the Sioux Indian tribe:

> The Lakota was a true naturist—a lover of nature. He loved the earth and all things of the earth, the attachment growing with age. The old people came literally to love the soil, and they sat or reclined on the ground with a feeling of being close to a mothering power. It was good for the skin to touch the earth, and the old people liked to remove their moccasins and walk with bare feet on the sacred earth. Their teepees were built upon the earth, and their altars were

made of earth. The birds that flew in the air came to rest upon the earth, and it was the final abiding place of all things that lived and grew. The soil was soothing, strengthening, cleansing, and healing.

That is why the old Indian still sits upon the earth instead of propping himself up and away from its life-giving forces. For him, to sit or lie upon the ground is to be able to think more deeply and to feel more keenly; he can see more clearly into the mysteries of life and come closer in kinship to other lives about him. . . .

The old Laḳota was wise. He knew that man's heart away from nature becomes hard; he knew that lack of respect for growing things soon led to lack of respect for humans, too. So he kept his youth close to its softening influence. (McLuhan 1972, 6)

This love and respect for the earth is in opposition to the agrarian societies, who would often clear and plow the ground for agricultural purposes. One Wintu Indian woman expressed these beliefs:

The White people plow up the ground, pull down the tree, kill everything. The tree says, "Don't. I am sore. Don't hurt me." But they chop it down and cut it up. The spirit of the land hates them. They blast out trees and stir it up to its depths. (McLuhan 1972, 15)

Relationship with Animals

Another set of values focuses on animals. The Hindu religion of India emphasizes the sacredness of all life. Harris (1974) commented:

Hindus venerate cows because cows are the symbol of everything that is alive. . . . So there is no greater sacrilege for a Hindu than killing a cow. Even the taking of human life lacks the symbolic meaning, the unutterable defilement, that is evoked by cow slaughter. (pp. 11–12)

In addition to the basic symbolism of the cow, the Hindu belief in reincarnation affects the cow and other animals. It is possible that a cow may be the reincarnation of a dead relative. The louse or tick on the cow also may not be killed for these may be the reincarnation of a great-aunt who has been condemned to penance and must be "purified" in this manner.

Love of cow affects the basic culture in many ways:

Government agencies maintain old-age homes for cows at which owners may board their dry and decrepit animals free of charge. In Madras, the police round up stray cattle that have fallen ill and nurse them back to health by letting them graze on small fields adjacent to the station house. Farmers regard their cows as members of the family, adorn them with garlands and tassels, pray for them when they get sick, and call in their neighbors and a priest to celebrate the birth of a new calf. Throughout India, Hindus hang on their walls calendars that portray beautiful, bejeweled young women who have the bodies of big, fat, white cows. (Harris 1974, 12–13)

Another animal highly revered in India, though not so much as the cow, is the elephant. To the Indian, the "elephant represents nobility, patience, grace, wisdom, and beneficence, no less than power or majesty" (Naravane 1965,

52). Any youth of noble descent must be knowledgeable in the ways of elephants. The Hastyayurveda, a treatise on the maintenance and medical care of elephants, emphasized their significance:

> If the high officials of the realm do not pay reverence to the elephant, the king and the kingdom, along with the armed forces, would be doomed to perish because a divinity had been disregarded. On the contrary, if the elephant is duly worshipped, crops will sprout in time; Indra, the Rain-god, will send plentiful showers; the country will be free from plague and drought; the earth will abound in treasures of precious metals and jewels. (Naravane 1965, 52–53)

This significance is furthered in the relationship of elephant and the universe, as Naravane continued: "Lakshmi is the personification of the Cosmic Lotus, which contains the seeds of creation; and the elephants carry the cosmos on their heads—they are the Diggajas, the 'Supports of the Directions' " (p. 59).

In some societies, however, all animals are not revered. The Jewish and Islamic peoples are sworn pig haters. This condemnation of pigs and pork stems from the denunciation of the pig in the Biblical books of Genesis and Leviticus. The first naturalistic explanation of the scriptures comes from a twelfth-century court physician in Cairo, Egypt—Moses Marmonides—who said that swine's flesh had a damaging effect on the body (Harris 1974).

Other societies revere the pig. The Maring, a remote group of tribesmen living in the Bismarck Mountains of New Guinea, hold a pig festival approximately every twelve years. During the festival, a massive number of pigs are sacrificed, and a battle is waged on enemy clans. Following the battle, a prayer is offered to assure the ancestors that the fighting is over and that the coming years will be spent replenishing the pig supply. The total concept of pig love is explained by Harris (1974):

> Pig love includes raising pigs to be a member of the family, sleeping next to them, talking to them, stroking and fondling them, calling them by name, leading them on a leash to the fields, weeping when they fall sick or are injured, and feeding them with choice morsels from the family table. But unlike the Hindu love of cow, pig love also includes obligatory sacrificing and eating of pigs on special occasions. Because of ritual slaughter and sacred feasting, pig love provides a broader prospect for communion between man and beast than is true of the Hindu farmer and his cow. The climax of pig love is the incorporation of the pig as flesh into the flesh of the human host and of the pig as spirit into the spirit of the ancestors. (p. 46)

Some cultures, such as the Bali, do not regard animals as being on the same level as humans and carry a revulsion of animal-like behavior within the culture:

> Babies are not allowed to crawl for that reason. Incest, though hardly approved, is a much less horrifying crime than bestiality. (The appropriate punishment for the second is death by drowning, for the first being forced to live like an animal.) Most demons are represented—in sculpture, dance, ritual, myth—in some real or fantastic animal form. The main puberty rite consists in filing the

child's teeth so they will not look like animal fangs. Not only defecation, but eating is regarded as a disgusting, almost obscene activity, to be conducted hurriedly and privately because of its association with animality. Even falling down or any form of clumsiness is considered to be bad for these reasons. Aside from cocks and a few domestic animals—oxen, ducks—of no emotional significance, the Balinese are aversive to animals and treat their large number of dogs not merely callously but with a phobic cruelty. (Geertz 1973, 419–20)

A blood sacrifice is offered to pacify the demons among the Bali people. No temple festival can be permitted until such a sacrifice has been performed, despite their hatred for many kinds of animals.

The Kwakiutl, on the other hand, claim animals as their ancestors, as Boas (1966) described:

According to Indian theory, the ancestor of a *numaya* appeared at a specific locality by coming down from the sky, out of the sea, or from underground, generally in the form of an animal, took off his animal mask, and became a person. The Thunderbird or his brother the gull, the Killer Whale, a sea monster, a grizzly bear, and a ghost chief appear in this role. (p. 42)

When the Kwakiutl hunted, an equality was established between the hunter and the actual and spiritual qualities of the animal they hunted. A certain ritual etiquette was observed by the hunters. The chiefs were the only real hunters of the tribe, because they embodied the spirits of the ancestors.

The Plains Indians of North America, because of their belief in the total harmony of the universe, also had a distinct respect for the animal. Any buffalo killed would have its heart left on the prairie as a sacrifice and as a symbol of the Indians' desire for the buffalo to prosper. Each person would receive a medicine animal at birth, a symbolic name of an animal that represented his or her character (Storm 1972).

Developing Skills in Dealing with Cognitive Cultures and Intercultural Communication

The following list of suggestions is intended to stimulate your continued thinking about world views and values and thus, in a way, to extend some of the principles we talked about into some further areas of application:

1. *Do as others do.* Whenever you are visiting another culture, try to observe the methods of respect toward symbols within the new culture. For example, if you are visiting a special shrine or some holy place, try to practice respect for the feelings of culture members toward their symbols.

2. *Develop self-awareness.* The ability to know yourself is truly helpful. Puzzling, demanding situations are the norm in intercultural communication. Understanding world view can provide tremendous insight into your own cultural background and the background of the host culture.

3. *Try to understand missing social cues.* When we go to another culture, familiar social cues are missing. In their absence, we can become confused, a disorientation especially augmented by extreme differences in world view. Realizing this principle and striving to keep ourselves learning new cues can be helpful.

4. *Do not assume that you know a world view.* This chapter may leave you with the impression that, because you know some of the categories of world view, you now know all there is to know about a particular culture. Cultural belief systems are very complex, so do not assume that you have a handle on a new culture's belief system. Instead, keep asking questions, observing, and listening.

5. *Discover when to use formal and informal modes.* Almost every culture has cues that relate to those times when, according to the belief systems, you are supposed to behave formally. Other times, it seems everyone is a lot different, somehow more relaxed. The difference may be one of formality and informality. After a while, you will find yourself easily conforming to the role-switching situations.

This Chapter in Perspective

World view is a significant element of culture and represents the means by which cultures organize their world and their place in the universe. This chapter discusses world view as an intercultural variable, since this is the way that culture members look at themselves in relation to the universe; world view compels many practices, rituals, attitudes, and communication behaviors.

The chapter also contains data on elements of cultural world view. Those elements include shame and guilt, task and people, sacred and secular cultures, role of dead to living, nature of humankind, humans and nature, doing and being cultures, life cycle, and fatalism. The chapter also describes systems of cultural world view and the concept of personal world view.

The chapter also discusses culture and values. Many values revolve around relationships with family, friends, and associates. Attitudes and values with respect to the elderly, parents, ancestors, others, self, society, the land, and animals are also examined in the chapter.

Exercises

1. Interview several people to assess more about world view. For instance, ask five people about their feelings about luck or owning personal property, or about their views of the past. There is certainly much more to world view than these items imply, but the responses you receive may help you to understand more of how people view themselves in relation to forces in the universe as we perceive them.

2. If you have seen *Star Wars* or any of its sequels, then do an analysis of the world view of some of the main characters. (Also, you can read a copy of the book if you have not seen the movie version.) For instance, what is Darth Vader's world view? Luke Skywalker? Han Solo? C3PO? Also, what are their respective values?

3. Try to secure a copy of precinct voting records in your area. Are the patterns of voting different or similar among various precincts? Are any patterns of voting related to residence? How? Do these suggest values?

Resources

Arensberg, Conrad M., and Arthur H. Niehoff. *Introducing Social Change.* Chicago: Aldine, 1964.

Bandler, Richard. *Using Your Brain for a Change: Neurolinguistic Programming.* Moab, Utah: Real People Press, 1985.

Beals, Ralph L., and Harry Hoijer. *An Introduction to Anthropology.* New York: Macmillan, 1971.

Boas, Franz. *General Anthropology.* New York: D. C. Heath, 1938.

Boas, Franz. *Kwakiutl Ethnography.* Chicago: University of Chicago Press, 1966.

Bock, Philip K. *Modern Cultural Anthropology.* New York: Alfred A. Knopf, 1969.

Brown, Dee. *Bury My Heart at Wounded Knee.* New York: Holt, Rinehart, and Winston, 1970.

Carter, William E. "Secular Reinforcement in Aymara Death Ritual." *American Anthropologist* 70 (1968): 238–61.

Condon, John C., and Fathi Yousef. *Introduction to Intercultural Communication.* New York: Bobbs-Merrill, 1975.

Dimen-Schein, Muriel. *The Anthropological Imagination.* New York: McGraw-Hill, 1977.

Dodd, Carley H., and Cecile W. Garmon. "The Measurement of Personal Report of World View as a Cognitive Communication Variable." In press.

Doi, L. Takeo. "The Japanese Patterns of Communication and the Concept of Amae." In *Intercultural Communication: A Reader,* 2d ed., edited by Larry Samovar and Richard Porter. Belmont, Calif.: Wadsworth, 1976.

Faron, Louis C. "On Ancestor Propitiation among the Mapuche of Central Chile." *American Anthropologist* 63 (1961): 824–49.

Faron, Louis C. "Symbolic Value and the Integration of Society among the Mapuche of Chile." *American Anthropologist* 64 (1962): 1151–63.

Garmon, Cecile W. "World View Differences among College and University Administrations and Faculty in the South." Ph.D. dissertation, Vanderbilt University, 1984.

Geertz, Clifford. *The Interpretation of Cultures.* New York: Basic Books, 1973.

Goldman, Irving. *The Mouth of Heaven: An Introduction to Kwakiutl Religious Thought.* New York: John Wiley and Sons, 1975.

Goodenough, Ward Hunt. *Property, Kin, and Community on Truk.* Hamden, Conn.: Archon Books, 1966.

Green, Margaret M. *Ibo Village Affairs.* New York: Frederick A. Praeger, 1964.

Hall, E. T. *Beyond Culture.* Garden City, N.Y.: Anchor, 1977.

Hammond, Peter B. *Cultural and Social Anthropology.* New York: Macmillan, 1970.

Harms, L. S. *Intercultural Communication.* New York: Harper and Row, 1973.

Harner, Michael J. "Jivaro Souls." *American Anthropologist* 64 (1962): 258–71.

Harris, Marvin. *Cows, Pigs, Wars and Witches*. New York: Random House, 1974.

Harris, Marvin. *Culture, People, Nature: An Introduction to General Anthropology*. New York: Harper and Row, 1975.

Harris, Philip, and Robert Moran. *Managing Cultural Differences*. Houston: Gulf, 1979.

Henderson, Richard N. *The King in Every Man: Evolutionary Trends in Onitsha Ibo Society and Culture*. New Haven: Yale University Press, 1972.

Hiebert, Paul G. *Cultural Anthropology*. Philadelphia: J. B. Lippincott, 1976.

Hill, L. Brooks, and Philip Lujan. "Rhetoric of Self Identity: The Case of the Mississippi Choctaw." Paper presented to the Rhetoric of the Contemporary South Conference, New Orleans, June 30, 1978.

Hockett, C. F. *Man's Place in Nature*. New York: McGraw-Hill, 1973.

Hoebel, E. Adamson, and Everett L. Frost. *Cultural and Social Anthropology*. New York: McGraw-Hill, 1976.

Jimenez, Robert. "Mythology of Life and Mexican-American Acculturation." In *Intercultural Skills for Multicultural Societies,* edited by Carley Dodd and Frank Montalvo. Washington, D.C.: SIETAR, 1987.

Kennan, William, and L. Brooks Hill. "Mythmaking as Social Process: Directions for Myth Analysis and Cross-Cultural Communication Research." Paper presented to SIETAR Conference, Phoenix, Arizona, February 25, 1978.

Kluckhohn, Florence, and Fred Strodtbeck. *Variations in Value Orientations*. Evanston, Ill.: Row and Petersen, 1961.

Kroeber, A. L. *Anthropology*. New York: Harcourt, Brace and World, 1948.

Leighton, Alexander, and Dorothea Leighton. *The Navajo Door*. New York: Russell and Russell, 1944.

Malinowski, Bronislaw. *A Scientific Theory of Culture*. New York: Oxford University Press, 1960.

Marsella, Anthony J., Michael D. Murray, and Charles Golden. "Ethnic Variations in the Phenomenology of Emotions." In *Intercultural Communication: A Reader,* 2d ed., edited by Larry Samovar and Richard Porter. Belmont, Calif.: Wadsworth, 1976.

McLuhan, T. C., ed. *Touch the Earth*. New York: Pocket Books, 1972.

Metge, Joan. *The Maoris of New Zealand: Rautahi*. London: Routledge and Kegan Paul Ltd., 1976.

Naravane, V. S. *The Elephant and the Lotus*. London: Asia Publishing House, 1965.

Nida, Eugene A. "Mariology in Latin America." In *Readings in Missionary Anthropology,* edited by William A. Smalley. Tarrytown, N.Y.: Practical Anthropology, 1967.

Ong, Walter J. *In the Human Grain.* New York: Macmillan, 1967.

Rogers, Everett M., with Lynn Svenning. *Modernization among Peasants.* New York: Holt, Rinehart and Winston, 1969.

Rokeach, Milton. *Beliefs, Attitudes, and Values.* San Francisco: Jossey-Bass, 1968.

Sanders, Irwin T., ed. *Societies around the World.* New York: Dryden Press, 1953.

Sarbaugh, Larry. *Intercultural Communication.* Rochelle Park, N.J.: Hayden, 1979.

Schaeffer, Francis. *The God Who Is There.* Downers Grove, Ill.: Inter-Varsity, 1968.

Schiller, Herbert I. *Communication and Cultural Domination.* White Plains, N.Y.: International Arts and Sciences Press, 1976.

Sitaram, K. S., and Roy T. Cogdell. *Foundations of Intercultural Communications.* Columbus, Ohio: Charles Merrill, 1976.

Spiro, Melford E. *Context and Meanings in Cultural Domination.* New York: Free Press, 1965.

Steen, William U. "Outstanding Contact and Cultural Stability in a Peruvian Highland Village." In *A Reader in Culture Change,* edited by Ivan A. Brady and Barry L. Isaac. Cambridge, Mass.: Schenkman, 1975.

Storm, Hyemeyohsts. *Seven Arrows.* New York: Ballantine Books, 1972.

Chapter 6

Intercultural Communication and Organizational Culture

After completing this chapter, you should be able to

Objectives

1. Define organizational culture.

2. Discuss approaches to communication leadership.

3. Critique various approaches to communication style in organizational cultures.

4. Define formal and informal organizational networks within organizational cultures.

5. Identify principles of intercultural communication within organizations.

6. Use a model of assessing leadership style in organizations.

7. Use an assessment instrument to survey the nature of organizational cultures.

Perhaps in our previous discussions of culture, it occurred to you that cultures also include organizations in which we work, as well as the many organizations to which we belong. Communication studies in recent years have concentrated on finding ways in which organizations are cultures. As cultures, organizations have features that, when understood, can help us better communicate with peers on the job, better relate to the community, and adjust effectively within the organizational culture. For instance, on one occasion, a middle manager in a Fortune 500 company documented a long list of office personnel problems and the perpetrators of those problems. His extensive notes indicated that his previous personal cultural background did not match the current corporate culture in which he found himself. In this example, organizational culture was not attractive to this particular manager, though others found the organization quite attractive.

There are times when organizational methods and norms clash with organizational norms of a person outside the corporate culture during interpersonal interaction. Here are a few other examples where organizations and culture blend:

— A top manager from ARAMCO in Houston goes to work in Saudi Arabia for a branch office.

— A high school teacher is promoted to an assistant superintendent position and must adjust to her new job and to the new norms of the central office.

— David received his M.A. from his native Michigan and has been hired by Delco to work in their regional office in Oklahoma.

— Deborah, a Canadian, works for the Canadian Development Office and has just been hired by Algoma Steel to work in their computer division.

— Samuel is joining a Japanese car sales force in his native Nigeria.

These are examples of people going from one cultural situation into another. But these situations also include adapting, one way or another, to corporate or organizational climates. The differences these people encounter and the communication demands in these cultures are the focus of intercultural communication principles. Of special importance is the organizational context of communication, which scholars now conclude can be analyzed as culture. Let us begin by defining organizational culture.

What Is Organizational Culture?

Elements of culture discussed in earlier chapters can be generally applied to organizations. The applications are often to traditional management concerns, but the cultural metaphor provides a rich set of insights to some traditional questions. We are trying to look at ways in which our cultural baggage links with the organizational cultures in which we function.

In this discussion, organizational culture refers to the communication climate rooted in a common set of norms and interpretive schemes about phenomena that occur as people work toward a predetermined goal. It includes how a group thinks about, interprets, and organizes its actions. In other words, we are dealing with how organizations get things done and how they think about what they do. However, organizational culture also includes the orga-

nization's structure—that is, its customs and rules. This structure and the mind-set of organization members profoundly influence the way people interact among themselves and how they communicate with people from other organizational cultures.

The study of corporate culture, as a particular type of organizational culture, for instance, has illuminated the need for looking at corporations in terms of how they can better improve their public image. Also, an organization that emphasizes task and performance above people factors will likely experience some frustration in communicating with an organization that emphasizes personal relationships even at the expense of time and productivity.

Again, the sense behind these conceptualizations is that organizations are themselves cultures. They stand as symbols of communication. But they also form the perceptual lens through which we organize and make sense out of that part of our lives touched by the organization. The idea is well summarized by Peters and Waterman's *In Search of Excellence* (1982), where they refer to organizational culture as the dominant idea behind the organization. Peters and Waterman cite Delta's "family feeling," Maytag's Iowa work ethic, Levi Strauss's predominantly people-oriented philosophy, and Texas Instrument's innovative culture. One of the themes in *In Search of Excellence* is that the most productive, successful corporate cultures have an underlying image and metaphor. With that image, each organization has its ways of doing things, its norms.

Organizational culture is an important metaphor to describe the norms, feelings, and shared interaction patterns of a group.

Let us begin examining organizational culture by looking first at management philosophies that significantly affect the norms of organizational culture. We also look at formal and informal organizational communication networks. We then discuss principles of organizational culture with regard to how organizational cultures work, how people communicate, and how people affect intercultural communication.

Patterns of Management That Affect Communication in Organizational Cultures

Leadership in organizational cultures tends to follow one of several communication patterns. These philosophies of management boil down to how a manager views people, productivity, and communication and what methods he or she uses to accomplish organizational goals. We examine several of the most well-known management patterns. The importance of these approaches, of course, lies in how such leadership approaches affect the organizational culture, especially communication.

The Classical Approach to Management

The classical management approach, especially popular after World War I, involved viewing workers in mechanistic terms. Taylor (1919) and others, for instance, reasoned that time and motion analysis could increase worker efficiency. For example, if a person could shovel more coal with a small shovel than a large shovel, efficiency engineers would find out how much more coal could be moved with what human movements for maximum output. Or, if a secretary could conduct an office procedure with fewer movements, then strategies would be introduced to improve the secretary's output.

Along with time and motion studies, this "scientific management" approach, as it was also called, viewed people as primarily economically driven. It was believed that, through the so-called carrot and stick approach, most workers could be rewarded into peak productivity. Other techniques included piecework, bonuses, and quotas.

The classical school of management was also known for its rigid adherence to the organizational structure, namely the formal organizational chart depicting who is responsible for whom. Communication in this system, however, was viewed chiefly as hierarchical, with the flow going from top to bottom and being mostly one-sided. Other concepts, like the maximum number of workers a person should supervise, called span of control, were also developed during this period.

In sum, this philosophy emphasized production rather than people. The structure of the organization was seen as the most efficient means by which to communicate. Time and motion studies resolved questions of how to help a worker to be more efficient. And workers were viewed economically, typically motivated by reward techniques.

The Human Relations Approach to Management

In sharp contrast to the classical approach, the human relations approach to management assumed that, if managers made workers feel good, productivity would increase. The evidence came from a series of studies in the late 1920s at the Western Electric Hawthorne plant in Cicero, Illinois. These now well-

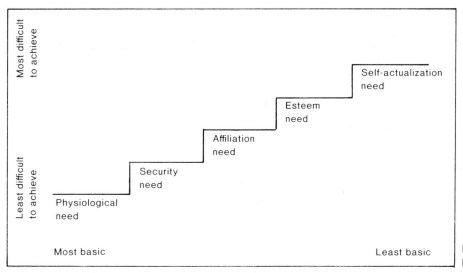

Figure 6.1
Maslow's hierarchy.

known experiments were designed to test the effect of lighting on worker output. Prior to the studies, the researchers believed that, as lighting was decreased, productivity would correspondingly decrease. To their amazement, decreases in lighting actually produced an increase in productivity! After some investigation, it was determined that management paying any attention to workers' needs was sufficient motivation for workers to increase production. In other words, attention increases productivity, a finding explained as the *Hawthorne effect.*

This finding created a dramatically different communication climate and a new communication style. Managers began looking for all kinds of gimmicks as well as sincere methods to make workers feel appreciated: company picnics, ball teams, bowling leagues, back-patting, and numerous other ideas all designed to promote "human relations."

Another management approach, begun in the 1950s, viewed workers as valuable assets or resources. This approach, generally referred to as the human resources school, argued that people have needs to grow and that good management should cultivate opportunities for that growth. People were viewed as having the potential to unleash personal change and organizational productivity.

The Human Resources Approach to Management

Maslow's hierarchy of needs. According to Abraham Maslow (1954), people have five universal needs (figure 6.1). The first need is physiological: Unless a person's hunger and basic drives are met, motivation is not likely, Maslow argued. The second need, continuing up the hierarchy, is the need for security or safety. After basic drives are satisfied, then people need to feel safe. The third need, once basic drives and safety are met, is the need to belong. Maslow suggested that people need groups to satisfy their social needs. He

Communication approaches in management vary from highly authoritarian to **very** open.

noted that, in these groups, a sense of affiliation is strong and can produce powerful effects in terms of personal fulfillment and group loyalty. After these first three needs are met, a fourth need is for self-esteem. Maslow argued that a person must feel that he or she is worthwhile or else motivation cannot be fully achieved. The fifth and final level of the hierarchy is self-actualization. At this level, individuals are fulfilling their greatest potential and have discovered their ultimate being.

Each successive level of the hierarchy is more difficult to achieve. That is, it is more difficult to achieve belonging than security, harder to attain self-esteem than belonging, and so forth. The Maslow philosophy assumes that people are need-motivated and that fulfillment of these needs stimulates individual progress that creates more self-motivation. Cultural management, then, according to Maslow, becomes a matter of creating systems and programs whereby individuals' needs are met, thus producing the motivating qualities that enhance working in the organizational culture.

Herzberg's job satisfaction and dissatisfaction. Frederick Herzberg (1968, 1971, 1974) surveyed several thousand workers and identified two factors leading to job satisfaction and job dissatisfaction. The *hygienic* factor includes company policy and administration, supervision, relationship with supervisor, work conditions, salary, relationship with peers, personal life, relationship with subordinates, status, and security. When the elements comprising this factor

Table 6.1 Hygienic and Motivating Factors in Producing Job Dissatisfaction and Job Satisfaction (Adapted from Herzberg, 1968)

Hygienic factor leading to extreme dissatisfaction in 1,844 events on the job		Motivating factor leading to extreme satisfaction in 1,753 events on the job	
Company policy and administration	36%	Achievement	42%
Supervision	19%	Recognition	31%
Relationship with supervisor	10%	Work itself	22%
Work conditions	10%	Responsibility	21%
Salary	8%	Advancement	12%
Relationship with peers	6%	Growth	8%
Personal life	5%		
Relationship with subordinates	5%		
Status	4%		
Security	3%		

are not met, workers feel extreme dissatisfaction. As we can see in table 6.1, hygienic elements have varying degrees of importance, but when taken together, Herzberg argued that these elements must be met to prevent dissatisfaction. However, the satisfaction of these elements does not necessarily produce job satisfaction.

Job satisfaction arises from what Herzberg called the *motivating* factor. This factor includes elements of achievement, recognition, the work itself, responsibility, advancement, and growth (table 6.1). Fulfillment of these elements leads to extreme satisfaction. Seeing workers in terms of their potential and tapping their inherent motivation was one of Herzberg's concerns.

One of the skills in intercultural management is to discover how different people and different cultural groups are motivated in terms of these factors. In the field of sales, Annas (1973) reported from his research on eighty sales and compensation arrangements that well-salaried, secure, and well-educated sales personnel react negatively to contests and gimmicky approaches to increase sale output. He found instead that the work itself and a desire for productivity were prime motivators. Black and Decker increased productivity 15 percent in its marketing and sales division by avoiding inducements as motivators. Instead, the company concentrated on job enrichment, salary, growth potential, self-development, training, communication, responsibilities, and recognition (Leahy 1973).

McGregor's Theory X and Theory Y. Another motivational and leadership theory was proposed by Douglas McGregor (1960). He basically compared and contrasted two philosophical positions about a manager's view of the nature of people. Theory X assumes a negative view of the nature of people. According to Theory X, people are lazy, they have to be driven, most people avoid work, external reward and security mostly motivate workers, and people have to be told what to do because they lack creativity. Theory Y, however, assumes a positive view of people. According to Theory Y, people like to work because it is inherently fulfilling, self-discipline plays a role in motivation, people want self-achievement that comes from taking responsibility, work itself can be rewarding, and people can iron out solutions to problems because each person has creativity.

In other words, how we view the nature of humankind predicts the communication style we choose in exercising leadership within organizational cultures. Furthermore, the kind of culture in which we work clearly alters how supervisory personnel view people. For instance, one American manager was shocked to learn that Greek office workers wanted the American to give direct orders, to coerce, and to otherwise highly control the office people. The American, on the other hand, wanted to work from a Theory Y perspective. His efforts were thwarted by the Greek cultural notion that humankind has inherent evil, which has led to a Theory X perspective for the Greeks. In this particular case, the conflict was enough for workers to quit and the American to suffer a diminished work productivity schedule.

Likert's systems 1–4. Rensis Likert and his associates saw managerial approaches on a continuum. At one end were systems 1 and 2—managerial styles similar to McGregor's view of Theory X, in which managers view workers with suspicion, and the congruent management style is somewhat authoritarian and coercive. Systems 3 and 4 at the other end of the continuum lean toward McGregor's description of Theory Y, where management operates out of trust and participates with workers in making various decisions. Obviously, the organizational climate of systems 1 and 2 emphasizes rigidity, while the organizational climate of systems 3 and 4 stresses the importance of creativity and innovation, preferring to enact a set of communication norms conducive to this climate (Likert 1967).

Likert also evaluated organizational settings in terms of six traditional management concerns: leadership, communication, motivation, goals, decisions, and control. His research led to an evaluation instrument that crossed his four systems styles with each of these six management concerns. For control, for instance, one of the questions on the evaluation instrument asks for the adequacy of the delegation of responsibility. Across the top of the scale, respondents can circle if the responsibility and authority is pushed two levels too high (system 1 response is indicated here), one level too high (indicates a system 2 response), adequate (system 3 choice), or just right (system 4 choice). By making choices that correlate for systems 1–4 crossed by questions for the six management concerns noted previously, a useful assessment results. The instrument allows the researcher to profile the nature of the organization, at least as viewed by the survey respondents. The common thread among many of the human resource type management approaches is their concern about two-way communication, employee participation in management decisions, and developing a personal communication style that helps workers as well as the total organization.

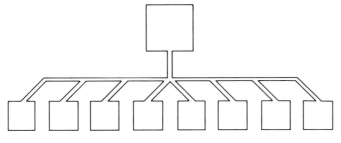

Flat organizational chart

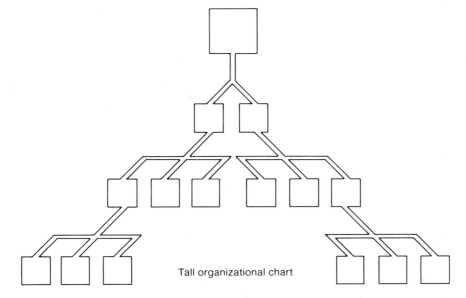

Tall organizational chart

Figure 6.2
Flat and tall
organizational
charts.

Like any other culture, people in organizations develop and maintain communication relationships. However, some of these relationships are by choice, and some are not. The organization maintains a set of authority roles in which we must operate. Let us take a look at both formal and informal networks within organizations to better understand the communication structures of organizational culture.

Formal organizational communication networks involve the organization's expected routes of information for authority and control, decision making, and goal analysis. Two basic patterns can develop.

One pattern is called the flat organizational chart (figure 6.2). In this case, one person supervises a large number of people, creating a system with what is known as a large span of control. The advantage to this type of organization is that there is one boss, and no management levels in between,

Networks within Organizational Cultures

Formal Organizational Networks

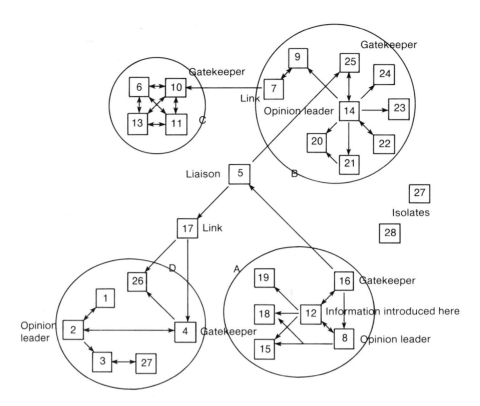

Figure 6.3
Sociogram of
informal
communication.

which often result in misunderstanding of authority. One disadvantage, however, is that the one person in authority can experience information overload
because the demand for communication exceeds his or her ability to handle
so many requests. Hence, requests can stack up and needs go unmet.

The second formal pattern of organizational communication is called the
tall organizational chart (figure 6.2). With the tall chart, authority is dele-
gated, and the span of control problem is alleviated. Thus, smaller organizational units can handle interpersonal communication and resolve problems more
quickly. A disadvantage of tall charts, however, is that information going up
the hierarchy to higher levels can be distorted more easily than in a flat chart.

**Informal
Organizational
Networks**

One of the most fascinating aspects of organizational culture is the social networks that inevitably develop. A communication network in an organizational
culture is the set of people who communicate with each other frequently enough
to be considered vital conduits of information. To conduct what researchers
call a network analysis involves discovering who talks with whom and with
what frequency. Once this is complete, the results can be diagrammed in what
is known as a sociogram, illustrated in figure 6.3.

To understand informal networks, it is important to know the terms used
to describe various information sources within the network. A *link* is a person
who passes information on to another person. A *clique* is a set of individuals

who communicate frequently and share information. A *liaison* is a person who interpersonally links two or more clique groups. A *gatekeeper* is a person who admits or closes off information to individuals within a clique. An *opinion leader* is a person to whom others go for information and advice, and who generally is similar in attitudes and social characteristics to the other people in the clique. An *isolate* is a person who does not necessarily receive information from an informal communication network and is somewhat removed psychologically from the informal social interaction patterns in the organization (McCroskey and Richmond 1976).

In figure 6.3, four cliques have developed. In clique A, number 8 is an opinion leader, although 12 has introduced information that is going to flow eventually to the other cliques. In a sense, 12 has some opinion leadership. Other opinion leaders are number 2 in clique D and number 14 in clique B. Numbers 16, 25, 10, and 4 serve as gatekeepers, letting information into their subsystems. Number 5 is a liaison, number 17 is a link, and numbers 27 and 28 are isolates.

Interpersonal, informal communication networks are also known for their rumor transmission. Sometimes, informal networks are referred to as the "grapevine." The rumor information that comes by way of the grapevine has been carefully studied. Surprisingly, grapevine information is 75 to 95 percent accurate (Davis 1973). Of course, that 5 to 25 percent error can often make the whole message unbelievable and inaccurate, as Davis illustrated:

> That 5 to 25 percent error can be vital to the truth of the story. I recall, for instance, one grapevine story about a welder marrying the general manager's daughter that was true with regard to his getting married, the date, the church, and other details. The one wrong fact in the report was that the girl was not the general manager's daughter but merely had the same last name. This one fact made the whole story erroneous—even though the rest of it was correct. (p. 45)

Grapevine information can be distorted in one of three ways. *Leveling* is the process of taking out certain facts and reducing the message in some way before it is passed on. *Assimilation* involves inserting extra details beyond the information originally in the story. *Sharpening* involves inflating certain features of the story far beyond their original significance.

The study of organizational culture reveals a number of principles affecting communication. Let us explore six of these principles.

Principles of Intercultural Communication within Organizations

The Principle of Filtering

Organizational cultures have physical and psychological boundaries; that is, each organization has a way of defining itself. That process of definition, however, builds a perceptual filter that screens inputs into the organization (Harris and Moran 1979). While there are many advantages in a culture having a clear view of itself, images and symbols of a corporate culture can also insulate the culture from outside influences. Ultimately, this privacy can reinforce negative features of intercultural communication, such as stereotyping and ethnocentrism.

One solution for preventing what we might call an organizational, cultural myopia is ongoing organizational development. In organizational development, there is continuous, planned change. The organization attempts to keep its members up-to-date. Where culture is involved, Harris and Moran (1979) point out that the most successful multinational corporations adapt themselves to the local culture while maintaining their unique and distinctive features as corporations.

The Principle of Organizational Adaptation to the Larger Culture

We just mentioned that successful corporate cultures adapt to the local context. However, that adaptation is not just public relations to project an image. The kind of organizational adaptation envisoned here involves orienting typical management functions to cultural formats and methods of operation. Some typical management functions include coordinating, leading, communicating, decision making, planning, goal setting, motivating, controlling, negotiating, training, evaluating, and selection. For example, if company policy calls for management by objectives (MBO)—where managers confer with employees, inviting their creative goals for, say, the coming six months—the corporate methods for MBO developed in the organization simply may not fit the existing culture. Some Mediterranean cultures, for instance, expect greater authoritarian communication and control—the idea of requesting worker input may be difficult to accept at first. Among other cultures, a six-month period for goal realization may be appropriate, while for others, three months or a year may be more suitable. Obviously, the need for corporate flexibility is a significant element of intercultural considerations in these matters.

Japanese corporate systems reveal some clear-cut methodologies and high levels of discipline and expectation. When Nissan came to Tennessee, it brought its corporate culture along. However, the company's success, as evidenced by low absenteeism and high performance, can be attributed to its cultural adaptation. Nissan melded its traditional corporate style of management into local culture in its attitudes toward friendliness, discipline, and listening.

The Principle of Cultural Symbolism

A fundamental finding in the organizational culture literature is that organizational cultures have significant communication systems (Gudykunst, Stewart, and Ting-Toomey 1985; Frost, Moore, Louis, Lundberg, and Martin 1985; McPhee and Tompkins 1985; Putnam and Pacanowsky 1983). Through the use of codes, values, heroes, storytelling, and other means of communication, an organizational culture develops a symbolic world. This communication and symbolism actually molds the organizational culture by shaping its norms. Through the stories that are told, workers sense how things are to be done. As Sypher, Applegate, and Sypher (1985) indicated, a strong organizational culture develops from implicit organizational communication. The metaphor of culture, therefore, indicates a significant role of symbolism and communication in the organizational culture. Some of the top performing companies, as Peters and Waterman (1982) explained, have "a rich network of legends and parables of all sort." A number of these stories surround the originators of the companies, such as J. C. Penney and his values toward business, honesty, and quality. J. C. Penney is still quoted in motivational business contexts, including today's J. C. Penney corporation.

Several cultural features result as a consequence of implicit organizational communication. First, a unique code system develops. Second, norms develop to clarify expectations within the organization. Third, the organizational culture maintains and creates a way for people to make sense and order out of what is going on around them. In other words, there is an organizational climate that allows cultural members to distinguish interpretations (Carbaugh 1985).

As explained in chapter 5, a low-context culture is one that makes meanings and information readily available and provides important explanations for what is expected. Information in these low-context cultures is explicit. Meanings are not in the context but in the verbal explanations provided. High-context cultures are the opposite. Expectations are inferred from the context. One is expected to know appropriate behaviors. Meanings are not explained but are implicit.

The Principle of Explicit and Implicit Information

Macrocultures exhibit a tendency toward low- and high-context information levels. In the same way, organizational cultures have a tendency to develop as either explicit or implicit. Consider the case of the young college graduate who was told by a major corporation, "You should know what to do within a couple of days. You have your accounting degree, and it should be no problem for you." While the manager in this case was intending to allow the new employee to be independent, the college graduate felt adrift. There was no orientation defining expectations or how the company typically engaged in certain procedures. Passing on corporate insights and defining the norms are functions of a low-context organizational culture. In this organization, however, the culture was high context—the accountant was expected to automatically know what to do and how to accomplish the task. So, a high-context organizational culture makes very little information available. A low-context organizational culture makes its procedures extremely clear—sometimes in large volumes of rules and procedures. (One problem is that such an enormous volume of explicit information can create information overload and lead to a dysfunctional organizational culture.)

In their book *In Search of Excellence* (1982), Peters and Waterman identified a number of factors that distinguish successful, excellent companies from less successful ones. One of their conclusions was that a strong corporate culture plus rich communication predicts an excellent company.

The Principle of Functional and Dysfunctional Organizational Cultures

Without cultural norms as guides, a corporation gets bogged down in decision making. The functional, excellent companies have a rich mythology and

Because of our filtering mechanisms, we can fail to listen, act, and respond adequately to each other, regardless of the organizational structures.

a set of norms. The organizational culture often shows itself in the cultural themes. Here are a few examples from Peters and Waterman:

Everyone at Hewlett-Packard knows that he or she is supposed to be innovative.

Procter and Gamble emphasizes quality over price, speaking of business integrity and fair treatment of employees without regard to cost.

Delta Airlines emphasizes a family feeling.

Texas Instruments is noted for a highly innovative attitude that permeates the organization.

Maytag claims its success in reliability is because of the strong Iowa work ethic where Maytags are made.

Levi-Strauss is highly people oriented with a no layoff philosophy that began after the San Francisco earthquake in 1906.

"IBM means service" is a company devotion to customer relations.

Dysfunctional organizations may have strong cultures, too, but they tend to focus on procedures. They also are highly concerned with costs and numbers. They tend not to realize that every person in the organization has meaning to the group, and most attention is concentrated on the top producers.

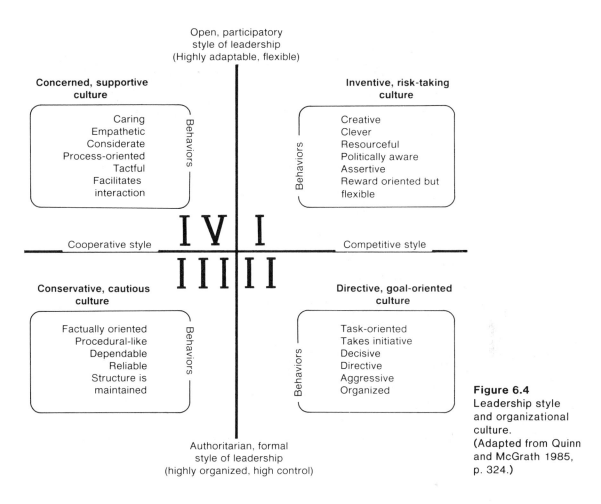

Figure 6.4
Leadership style and organizational culture.
(Adapted from Quinn and McGrath 1985, p. 324.)

Rogers (1983) cited evidence that innovative organizations could be discriminated from less innovative organizations based on the following variables: (1) positive attitudes toward change among leaders, (2) decentralized networks of ideas and decisions, (3) high expertise among members' range of talents and knowledge, (4) less formalization, (5) interconnectedness in the richness of interpersonal social networks, and (6) organizational resources.

The communication style of managerial leadership can have a tremendous effect on the kind of organizational culture that is perpetuated. Of course, it also is true that the kind of culture that exists influences the kind of leadership that emerges. But leadership style can be an important independent variable in the organizational cultures in which we operate. Some important pioneering work in this area by Quinn and McGrath (1985) showed that a combination of various communicator styles relates to predictable organizational cultures. An adaptation of their model in figure 6.4 reveals that styles of open versus authoritarian can be crossed with cooperative versus competitive styles. The

The Principle of Interpersonal Communication Leadership Style

resultant quadrants produce cultures that are inventive and risk-taking (I), directive and goal-oriented (II), conservative and cautious (III), and concerned and supportive (IV). Also, a number of predictable norms and behaviors are listed for each quadrant. This model can be useful in learning more about the communication patterns we could expect in certain cultures. The model also suggests that we can create change in organizational culture by changing the elements pictured.

Assessing Organizational Culture

One way of assessing the norms in various organizational cultures is shown in table 6.2. The method shown here takes selected cultural variables and theories from chapter 3 and asks respondents to evaluate the organization in terms of how each of these factors is perceived in relation to managerial style. Managerial style is conceived in terms of nonsupportive, closed, authoritarian style of leadership and communication (similar to Likert's systems 1 and 2) at one extreme and a supportive, open, and participative style (similar to Likert's systems 3 and 4) at the other extreme. Hopefully, the unique set of variables presented here, which do not appear in other organizational cultural models or scales, will be useful as you use this text and practice skills associated with intercultural communication. Other, interpretative methods are also available.

Developing Skills in Intercultural Communication within Organizational Cultures

The following suggestions may have practical applicability should you find yourself dealing with an organization:

1. *When you first go to work in an organization, give yourself time to ask questions and discover the norms.* A friendly co-worker who has been there longer than you may be able to provide insight.

2. *Do not make abrupt changes.* If you are in a position of leadership, try to operate within boundaries of change that can be absorbed. Abrupt change can lead to dysfunctional organizations. Pacing changes to fit into cultural norms is usually effective.

3. *Look for the subtle structure of communication networks.* The organizational chart may be only the tip of the communication iceberg within the organization. Try to look for the interpersonal and informal system structures. From there, you may discover a number of informal systems.

4. *Try to identify the organization's major symbols.* Logos, letterheads, architecture, and furniture arrangement can provide clues as to how organizations view themselves.

5. *Be flexible in your management philosophy.* Rigidly following only one managerial style of communication can limit your operational ability. Look for times and conditions under which a certain managerial style would be most functional. Don't engage in a style with which you are extremely

Table 6.2 Analysis of Organizational Culture

Selected Cultural Variables	Leadership and Communication Style		
	Authoritarian, Closed, Elite		Open, High Participation, Feedback Style
Social relationships	Unnecessary, only lines of authority and responsibility	1 2 3 4 5	Networking encouraged for morale and productivity
Ethnocentrism	Competitive toward other groups and thus egalitarian and ethnocentric	1 2 3 4 5	Cooperative and open to differences, shows respect for other groups
Thought patterns	Linear, sequential, highly structured, and organized categories	1 2 3 4 5	Configurations, process oriented, boundaries not always defined
Role behaviors	Roles highly defined by organization	1 2 3 4 5	Roles defined by individual
Cultural space	Tight control of territoriality, desk size, etc.	1 2 3 4 5	Status not determined by desk size, using psychological space not important
Cultural time	Task oriented, promptness and efficiency emphasized	1 2 3 4 5	People oriented, flexibility of task completion
Touch	Low touch	1 2 3 4 5	High touch
Dress	Insistence on proper dress, uniformity of dress	1 2 3 4 5	Little restriction on dress style
Rewards/recognition	Individual reward or recognition for performance	1 2 3 4 5	Group reward or recognition for performance
Decision making	Centralized	1 2 3 4 5	Decentralized
Political climate	High power, dominant, high intensity	1 2 3 4 5	Low power, low intensity
Values toward people	Theory X: Man is lazy	1 2 3 4 5	Theory Y: Man is capable
World view	High fatalism	1 2 3 4 5	Low fatalism
Themes	Success through hard work, control	1 2 3 4 5	Motivation and creativity lead to success
High/low context	Information implicit	1 2 3 4 5	Information explicit

unaccustomed or uncomfortable. Finding the blend between the communication style needed and your propensities is a delicate but important task.

6. *Try to identify the driving force behind the organization.* How does the organization see its overall purpose? That identification is important for better communication, especially upward communication. By understanding how the group sees itself and its goals, you can think and talk in ways that identify you with the group, within limits.

7. *Try to be more low context in your communication style.* Low-context cultures expect and give information. When you are first entering a new culture, your ability to explain yourself can help you succeed. Naturally, there are times when you can engage in high-context communication with individuals who share your experiences and codes. With others, however, the importance of explaining your meaning can seem awkward but be very helpful.

This Chapter in Perspective

This chapter identifies several major philosophical approaches to management. The classical scientific management school of thought underscored structure, organization, procedures, and formality as a means to achieve efficiency and productivity. Time and motion studies helped to determine how to increase worker efficiency. Taylor and others viewed workers as economically driven by rewards.

The human relations school of management sought to use morale and attention as means to greater productivity. The Hawthorne effect identified the attention-productivity hypothesis.

Proponents of the human resources management approach believed that workers can be responsible and that they chiefly want to work and succeed. Maslow, for instance, pointed out the motivational drives toward belonging, self-esteem, and self-actualization that can be achieved through the work environment. Herzberg identified the importance of satisfying hygienic and motivating factors to produce job satisfaction. McGregor contrasted two philosophical positions about a manager's view of the nature of people: Theory X assumes that people are lazy; Theory Y assumes that people like to work. Likert characterized management styles ranging from authoritarian to participatory. The common concern among many of the theorists in what is loosely called the human resources movement is their concern over two-way communication, employee participation in management decisions, and developing a personal communication style that is functional for workers as well as for the organization.

Formal and informal communication networks are also discussed in this chapter. These networks hold significance for understanding the internal messages and rumors of most organizations.

This chapter also examines principles of communication that can be applied within organizational cultures. The principle of filtering helps us see that organizations define themselves and then screen input that does not match their definition. Another important principle involves adaptation of organizational procedures to the larger culture in which the organization exists. The principle of cultural symbolism emphasizes how organizations use storytelling, heroes, and codes to mold organizational culture. The principle of explicit and implicit information describes the need to understand high- and low-context organizational cultures. Analysis of profiles of functional and dysfunctional organizations comprised another principle. Finally, the principle of interpersonal communication leadership styles describes how managerial communication style can affect organizational culture.

Exercises

1. With a small group from your class, identify the organizational symbols of your college or university. You may want to brainstorm, relying on your group's evaluation, or you may choose to conduct several outside interviews.

2. Pick two or three organizations in your area that have over fifty employees. Through phone or personal interviews, determine if the organizations are high- or low-context cultures in dealing with employees. Also determine the organizations' use of heroes, storytelling, and codes in daily interactions. For instance, does the management utilize stories to try to inspire workers? Do workers use stories to deal with their understanding of the organization? Of their jobs? Of management?

3. Choose a simple phrase with about four or five words. Whisper the phrase from one person to the next in your class, playing the gossip game. Usually, the phrase is distorted by the time it reaches the last person. Discuss why that occurs. How would you improve communication accuracy in that situation? Develop organizational strategies for ensuring communication fidelity.

Resources

Annas, John W. "Profiles of Motivation." *Personnel Journal* 13 (1973): 205–208.

Baird, John E. *The Dynamics of Organizational Communication.* New York: Harper and Row, 1977.

Blake, R., and J. Mouton. *The Managerial Grid.* Houston: Gulf, 1964.

Brady, Robert M. "Predictive Correlates of Adoption Behavior in a Social Context: A Multiple Discriminant Analysis." Master's thesis, Western Kentucky University, 1975.

Carbaugh, Donald. "Cultural Communication and Organizing." In *Communication, Culture, and Organizational Processes,* edited by William B. Gudykunst, Lea P. Stewart, and Stella Ting-Toomey. Beverly Hills, Calif.: Sage, 1985.

Capps, Randall, Carley H. Dodd, and Larry J. Winn. *Communication for the Business and Professional Speaker.* New York: Macmillan, 1981.

Davis, Keith. "The Care and Cultivation of the Corporate Grapevine." *Dun's* 12 (1973): 44–47.

Frost, Peter J., Larry F. Moore, Meryl R. Louis, Craig C. Lundberg, and Joanne Martin, eds. *Organizational Culture.* Beverly Hills, Calif.: Sage, 1985.

Gilbreth, L. M. *The Psychology of Management.* New York: Sturgis and Walton, 1914.

Goldhaber, Gerald M. *Organizational Communication*. 4th ed. Dubuque, Iowa: William C. Brown Company Publishers, 1986.

Gudykunst, William B., Lea P. Stewart, and Stella Ting-Toomey, eds. *Communication, Culture and Organizational Processes*. Beverly Hills, Calif.: Sage, 1985. (Volume 9 in the *International and Intercultural Communication Annual* series)

Harris, Philip R., and Robert T. Moran. *Managing Cultural Differences*. Houston: Gulf, 1979.

Herzberg, Frederick I. "One More Time: How Do You Motivate Employees?" *Harvard Business Review* 46 (1968): 53–62.

Herzberg, Frederick I. "Managers or Animal Trainers?" *Management Review* 16 (1971): 2–15.

Herzberg, Frederick I. "New Perspectives on the Will to Work." *Management Review* 18 (1974): 52–54.

Leahy, John I. "Total Motivation—Top Performance." *Sales Management* 21 (1973): 12–13.

Likert, R. *The Human Organization*. New York: McGraw-Hill, 1967.

Maslow, Abraham. *Motivation and Personality*. New York: Harper and Row, 1954.

McCroskey, James C., and Virginia P. Richmond. "The Effects of Communication Apprehension on the Perception of Peers." *Western Speech Communication Journal* 40 (1976): 14–21.

McGregor, Douglas. *Human Side of Enterprise*. New York: McGraw-Hill, 1960.

McGregor, Douglas. *Professional Manager*. New York: McGraw-Hill, 1967.

McPhee, Robert D., and Phillip K. Tompkins, eds. *Organizational Communication*. Beverly Hills, Calif.: Sage, 1985.

Peters, Thomas J., and Robert H. Waterman. *In Search of Excellence*. New York: Harper and Row, 1982.

Putnam, Linda L., and Michael E. Pacanowsky, eds. *Communication and Organizations: An Interpretive Approach*. Beverly Hills, Calif.: Sage, 1983.

Quinn, Robert E., and Michael R. McGrath. "The Transformation of Organizational Cultures: A Competing Values Perspective." In *Organizational Culture,* edited by Peter J. Frost. Beverly Hills, Calif.: Sage, 1985.

Rogers, Everett M., and Rekha Agarwala-Rogers. *Communication in Organizations*. New York: Free Press, 1976.

Sypher, Beverly D., James L. Applegate, and Howard E. Sypher. "Culture and Communication in Organizational Contexts." In *Communication, Culture, and Organizational Processes,* edited by William B. Gudykunst, Lea P. Stewart, and Stella Ting-Toomey. Beverly Hills, Calif.: Sage, 1985.

Taylor, F. *Principles of Scientific Management*. New York: Harper and Row, 1919.

Vroom, Victor H., and Bernd Pahl. "Relationship between Age and Risk-Taking among Managers." *Journal of Applied Psychology* 55 (1971): 399–405.

Chapter 7

Intercultural Communication and the Language of a Culture

After completing this chapter, you should be able to:

1. Give examples of the significance of language for understanding culture.

2. Describe the reciprocal influence of language on culture and culture on language.

3. Demonstrate the workings of the Whorf and Bernstein hypotheses.

4. Describe perceptual differences and attitudes people hold toward minorities and foreign speakers.

5. Identify theories of why certain dialects suggest prestige.

6. Identify the relationship between speech and employability.

The importance of language as an indicator of culture is well illustrated in the numerous occurrences of our creating unintended meanings through our usage of language. For instance, an insurance company discovered that fires inadvertently occurred because warehouse employees acted carelessly around "empty" barrels of gasoline, although they previously had exercised great caution around "full" drums of gasoline. The terms *full* and *empty* seem to mask the real danger in working with gasoline drums—empty drums are extremely combustible while full drums pose far less threat. Yet, empty drums seemed harmless, from the linguistic perception of that word to the workers. A story is told of a Christian Scientist who refused to take vitamins, since the recommender described them as "medicine." However, the same person gladly took the vitamins when he was told they were "food." Several years ago, Swedish citizens were embroiled in a controversy over the pronoun *ni*. This word was a term reserved for speaking to those of a lower social status. Apparently, some persons who were equal or superior in social status brought suit in court against those individuals who used *ni* toward them; the connotation of the word had evoked such strong images that it was almost literally a "fighting word" (Kluckhohn 1972).

Examples of linguistic misunderstanding could be dramatized by countless failures across cultural boundaries. During the 1976 presidential campaign, Jimmy Carter used the term *ethnic purity,* which evoked a round of strong criticism from the Black community in the United States, though applause from whites in South Africa. The actual meaning of words and phrases, as this example indicates, stems from our cultural experiences—in addition to the nuances of language. Blacks perceived the phrase as racist, an interpretation framed by that culture's experiences. South African whites perceived the phrase as supportive of their separatist policies that have dominated that culture from its conception. Candidate Carter apologized and interpreted the phrase to mean the need to uphold ethnic heritage and customs and to prevent their being swallowed up by a dominant culture. Cultural experience with and connotations of the word *purity* overshadowed the meaning Carter apparently intended.

The Interface of Language and Culture

Not only is language a part of culture; language shapes perceptions. Also, language usage is a function of the cultural context. The Whorf and Bernstein hypotheses suggest the active roles that language and social context play in determining our perceptions and also our behaviors.

Whorf Hypothesis

Many years ago, Benjamin Whorf wrote that language functions not only to report information but actually to shape our perceptions of reality, a point illustrated in figure 7.1. This idea revolutionized linguistic science—and intercultural communication specialists recognize today the continuing importance of language and culture on perceptions. One observer wrote that:

> language plays a large and significant role in the totality of culture. Far from being a technique of communication, it is itself a way of directing the

Whorf indicated that our linguistic categories influence our perception of reality.

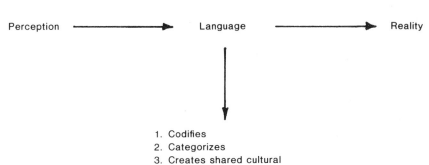

Perception ⟶ Language ⟶ Reality

1. Codifies
2. Categorizes
3. Creates shared cultural experiences that operate

Figure 7.1
Model of Whorf hypothesis.

perceptions of its speakers and it provides for them habitual modes of analyzing experience into significant categories. And to the extent that languages differ markedly from each other, so should we expect to find significant and formidable barriers to cross-cultural communication and understanding. (Hoijer 1976, 116)

The term *linguistic relativity* applies to language as the shaper of reality (Whorf 1956). Since languages differ, linguistic communities differ in their perceptual experiences of the world around them. Language acts like a filter, molding perception. A slightly different idea, *linguistic determinism,* refers to Whorf's assumption that language determines thought, which is to say that higher levels of thought hinge on language (Dale 1972). For the moment, let us focus on linguistic relativity.

Clearly, language categorizes our world. Just as the biologist uses a scientific taxonomy to classify organisms, so the normal speaker uses language to classify reality. For example, one word may stand for an entire cluster of things, as the word *animal,* which refers to an entire class. Or, you may already realize that colors are categorized differently in different languages. What you may not realize is that the native speaker's actual perception of the

Figure 7.2
Color spectrum for English, Shona, and Basa.

colors is influenced by this categorization process. For example, English contains seven basic colors on a type of color spectrum ranging from red on one end of the spectrum to violet at the other end. When this spectrum is laid end to end and compared linguistically with two American Indian languages—the Shona and the Basa—the result is that the Shona language has four words and the Basa language has only two words for the spectrum, as illustrated in figure 7.2 (Gleason 1961). Undoubtedly, few people would argue that the Basa tribe sees nothing but "hui" (the bluish end) and "ziza" (the reddish end). Of course, they can see the physical color (language does not change the retina), but Whorf's theory suggests that the language classification forces a category system that alters our perceptions where those differences become relatively unimportant.

Various anecdotal sources also underscore this point between language and cultural thought and activity. In English, the one word *snow* is a category for all types of snow, although we can use phrases to describe variations, such as "fluffy snow," "wet snow," and so on. In Eskimo languages, however, no one word is sufficient, and some claim that there are some twenty-five different words for snow. In Brazil, scores of words exist for coffee. Kluckhohn (1972) reported that Arabic contains more than six thousand different words for a camel and its parts. The languages of certain American Indians, such as the Sioux, do not have grammatical structure for past and future tenses.

These examples, and for that matter the entire Whorfian theory, do not unequivocally imply that people of one culture *cannot* think of objects for which another culture has plentiful vocabulary, like the camel parts. The fact is not that we cannot, but that we do not. That we do not think of such specificity may mean that such matters are unimportant or irrelevant to our life styles. As figure 7.1 illustrates, language categorizes our experiences, in a way almost without our full awareness. If we were to describe our experiences in linguistic terms, the very act of description would then reinforce the initial mental implant of the experience. For instance, how would you describe this text when you go to the library? Do you call it a book? a pamphlet? a text? a volume? Your perception of this "thing" is a perception partly influenced by your subculture—whether you are a college student or a professional person—by your experience with books, and by your language, which tells you what it is. You perceive the book partly by what you call it (a book is usually "better" than a pamphlet, for instance), and you name it based on how you perceive it. So, everytime you describe the book, you reinforce the very linguistic concept of book. Since other people in your culture also reinforce the use of the term *book*, then language and its perceived meanings become culturally shared. That is one reason why many cultural members share similar perceptions.

It is obvious that humans usually adapt their speech to the social context. For instance, as you pass a friend in a corridor, the constraints of the social situation act selectively on your speech with the friend. In fact your friendship, as a feature of this momentary social structure, may cause you to speak to each other in an almost telegraphic form. You use quips, phrases, single words, interrupted sentences in a pattern familiar to each of you because you know the other person and what he or she usually means by these things. An outsider listening to your conversation may not share your mutual experience and consequently may not understand the jargon and "shorthand" speech you can use with your friend. This common experience, though, has important scientific underpinnings, a relationship Basil Bernstein (1966) once described:

Bernstein Hypothesis

> Speech . . . is constrained by the circumstances of the moment, by the dictate of a local social relation, and so symbolizes not what can be done, but what *is* done with different degrees of frequency. Speech indicates which options at the structural and vocabulary level are taken up. Between language in the sense defined and speech is social structure. (p. 428)

Bernstein's conceptual explanation of dyadic social relations expands to include a broader social structure. Once we think of social structure as not only momentary social context but as a culture, subculture, or social system, then speech, communication behavior, or linguistic code results from the cultural contact. A graphic representation of Bernstein's hypothesis emphasizes the mediating nature of social structure. We actually convert a potential reservoir of language into speech behavior, or what is actually said, and the model that follows illustrates that principle:

Language⸻⟶*Social Structure*⸻⟶*Communication Behavior*

1. Lexicon (vocabulary)	1. Social context	1. Restricted code
2. Syntax (word relations)	2. Culture, subculture, social system	2. Elaborated code

In other words, what we say and how we say it comes directly from your perception of the cultural climate in which we find ourselves.*

Now let us examine what people say, given their perceptions of the immediate or larger cultural expectation. Speech, or what is said, emerges in one of two codes, restricted or elaborated. The *restricted code* involves message transmission through verbal, nonverbal, and paralinguistic (intonations, facial features, gestures, etc.) channels. Restricted codes refer to those messages that are highly predictable and thus approach redundancy. Both the vocabulary and the structure are drawn from a narrow range, or as Bernstein (1966) explained:

> The speech is played out against a backdrop of assumptions common to the speakers, against a set of closely shared interests and identifications, against a system of shared expectations; in short, it presupposes a local cultural identity, which reduces the need for the speakers to elaborate their intent verbally and to make it explicit. (pp. 433–34)

Restricted codes, then, are like jargon (Argot) or "shorthand speech" in which the speaker is almost telegraphic. For example, when you are with a close friend, you probably find yourself making brief references to something, and yet each of you is reminded of a wealth of experiences or concepts. An outsider would have difficulty understanding you because of your shared experiences; you know what your friend means sometimes even before he or she finishes speaking. Even special communication found among certain work groups represents a type of restricted code, such as CB radio speech, medical jargon, or engineering terminology employed by restrictive users. Bernstein (1966) observed that lower working class children in Britain tended to utilize only a restricted code while middle-class children utilized both elaborated and restricted codes. In his field research of a religious communal cult, Dodd (1975) found that a highly formalized restricted code played a major role in strengthening the group's norms and self-image. Restricted code communication also provided common ground for cult members from divergent backgrounds so that they could talk about the same things in meaningful ways. Restricted codes also arise in such closed communities as prisons, military units, gangs, clubs, families, and friendships.

Elaborated codes involve messages that are low in prediction. Hence, the speaker must employ verbal elaboration to communicate effectively. Since we cannot anticipate what is actually said, the verbal channel dominates. This dominance contrasts with restricted codes, where new information and

---

*In one way, we can view this relationship as follows. Communication behavior (CB) is a function of social structure (SS): $CB = f(SS)$. It seems reasonable to further assume that, since selected factors of social structure are a function of salient cultural features (SCF), $SS = f(SCF)$, then communication behavior is a function of salient features: $CB = f(SCF)$. In other words, things that are important to us will dominate our culture, and our culture (or social context), in turn, will cause our actual speech behavior at the moment.

uniqueness emerge primarily through nonverbal and paralinguistic channels. Bernstein (1966) further explained elaborated codes by contrasting them to restricted codes:

> Speakers using a restricted code are dependent upon these shared assumptions. The mutually held range of identifications defines the area of common intent and so the range of the code. The dependency underpinning the social relation generating an elaborated code is not of this order. With an elaboration code, the listener is dependent upon the verbal elaboration of meaning. (p. 437)

Field research efforts have demonstrated that class is a predictor of code behavior. Perhaps the imposing and reinforcing of salient cultural features may coordinate with communication behavior in future studies. We would certainly anticipate that the role of other variables interacting with social structure, such as age, education, sex, cognitive ability, socioeconomic status, ethnic background, and personality, would affect the use of one code over the other.

When we think of language and society, as the term *sociolinguistics* suggests, perhaps we are reminded of language and its almost elusive nature. In 1979, a United States Commission on Foreign Languages and International Studies noted that, in some foreign markets, cars with the interiors labeled "Body by Fisher" were advertised as having "Corpses by Fisher." When Pepsi was first

Where there is shared culture, individuals are more likely to use a restricted code, or jargon, appropriate for that culture and the situation.

Sociolinguistic Theories

introduced to Taiwan, the slogan "Come Alive" was translated into Chinese as a rather sacrilegious message: "Pepsi brings your ancestors back from the grave."

Such nuances of language, along with the numerous idiomatic phrases of most "foreign" languages, should lead us away from a simplistic view of language to the perception of language and culture as highly interrelated concepts. Language becomes a keyhole through which to understand culture, and culture is inextricably bound with language. However, that relationship extends beyond the confines of "language" and "a culture" to include dialectical differences within a spoken language and the relation of those differences to the structure of society. In fact, researchers have linked various dialectical differences with such social factors as social status, occupation, ethnicity, education, personality, and even appearance. Additionally, speech patterns serve as a cue, causing listeners to assign certain characteristics to a speaker with one dialect or another.

The term *dialect* refers to a *regional variation of a language used by a group of persons, called a linguistic community, and has unique features of pronunciation, vocabulary, and grammar distinguishing it from other varieties used by other groups.* Dialect includes "accented speech," distinguished by its phonological differences, but also includes word variations and grammatical differences. Many investigations have examined the existence of and effect of dialectical differences:

> Empirical research has clearly established that listeners form differential attitudes toward speakers on the basis of dialectical characteristics of speakers' linguistic presentations (Mulac and Rudd 1977).
>
> A large number of studies have now accrued suggesting that, in many cultures, there is a type of speech, peculiar to a given language community, that has more prestige than other varieties of that language (Giles, Bourhis, Trudgill, and Lewis 1974).
>
> Considerable data have been accumulated in recent years on the way in which a person's dialect affects others' attitudes and perceptions of him (Whitehead, Williams, Civikly, and Algino 1974).

Clearly, then, speech behavior is related to social groups and attitudes that others hold toward those groups. So, in the next sections, we focus on the attitudes that listeners develop toward a speaker with a dialect or an accent. We begin with some important theories of sociolinguistics before moving to ways that linguistic variations within a language create perceptions of positive or negative attitudes. Remember that the emphasis rests upon dialectical differences, how those differences are shared by a given linguistic community, and the effects of listeners' perceptions of that linguistic community.

Inherent Value of Linguistic Features Theory

One way people have explained attitudinal differences between two dialects has been to assess linguistic features of a particular dialect (such as its rate, melodic qualities, and other pronunciation characteristics) and attribute prestige or desirability because of its inherent pleasantness. For example, in Britain, speakers of the accented form of English known as Received Pronunciation are perceived as more competent and receive better attitudinal ratings than speakers with regional accented speech (Giles, Bourhis, Trudgill, and Lewis 1974). Listeners evaluate styles other than the Received Pronunciation style, as less standard and more unpleasant. Does this sort of rating imply that some dialects are inherently pleasant and others inherently unpleasant?

Empirical evidence for the inherent value hypothesis is intriguing. In one study, French Canadians rated speakers of European-style French as more intelligent, ambitious, and likeable than speakers of Canadian-style French; they also regarded their own French dialect as less aesthetically pleasing than European French. However, when a sample of Welsh respondents, totally unfamiliar with the language, listened to the two French dialects, they did not attribute more prestige or favorability to the European-style French speakers (Giles, Bourhis, Trudgill, and Lewis 1974). These neutral observers did not perceive inherently pleasing sounds between the dialects. Apparently, the linguistic cues provided in the two French dialects simply triggered perceptions of *status* differences based on cultural norms, not innate qualities of the dialects.

It seems that voice quality, as such, is not a universal gauge by which people judge dialects as pleasant or unpleasant, superior or inferior. For example, a nasal voice quality is associated with highly unpleasant Australian accents, although the same feature is considered pleasant to what is considered "nice" normal British English. In the same way, gutteral voice is a quality the working class Norwich people consider unpleasant, although this same feature marks high-status German and Arabic accents (Giles, Bourhis, Trudgill, and Lewis 1974).

One other study illustrates the point again as we put the question of inherent qualities to the test. Giles, Bourhis, Trudgill, and Lewis (1974) selected forty-six British undergraduates who had no knowledge of Greek to listen to two Greek dialects. The Athenian dialect is the prestigious form of Greek and is considered by native speakers to possess inherent pleasantness. The Cretan dialect of Greek produces stereotypic reactions among Greek respondents in that the Cretan speakers are perceived as less intelligent and sophisticated, but more amusing and tougher than Athenian speakers. Unknown to the respondents, the two audiotape versions of the two dialects were prose readings delivered by the same person, who simply performed bidialectically throughout the thirty-second recording. The results indicated that no significant differences between the two dialects occurred in terms of prestige, aesthetic quality, intelligence, toughness, amusement, and sophistication.

These linguistic studies cast doubt upon the inherent value hypothesis to explain prestige of one dialect over another. Apparently, dialectical differences produce stereotypic reactions—listeners judge speakers more by the associations of dialect with preconceived notions of what all dialectical speakers are like. The next section explains this point.

Sociolinguists have proposed another explanation for the judgments people make about dialectical differences or accented speech. The linguistic norms hypothesis argues that pleasantness and prestige are best accounted for by *cultural norms* toward accented speech. The cultural norms advocating favorability toward a particular accented speech pattern, furthermore, are often products of historical development. Thus, prestige is linked to the social group status from which the dialect originated. For example, "had the English Court in the Middle Ages been established in another region of the country rather than the southeast, then it could be suggested that the national news would now be broadcast and televised in what is considered today a nonstandard, regional accent" (Giles, Bourhis, Trudgill, and Lewis 1974, 406).

Proponents of the linguistic norms hypothesis argue that linguistic communities simply have notions of what they like and dislike—and the outcome is clearly linked to cultural norms forged through history and circumstance. Prior to the selections of two southern Presidents in the United States (Lyndon Johnson and Jimmy Carter), for example, it could have been argued that southern-accented speech was perceived less credibly by nonsoutherners. The elections, though, may have raised this region's linguistic acceptability, a possibility heightened by the addition of a southern-accented speaker on a national news network in the late 1970s in an industry that promotes general American speech patterns.

A related issue to the linguistic norms hypothesis concerns the norms of a given linguistic community where speakers of that linguistic community prefer one dialect over another. In fact, we can create a "we-they" subcultural attitude through the use of language. For example, Miller (1975) found that English-Canadian subjects responded more positively to a source described as English Canadian than to a source described as French Canadian. The attribution of these sources provided a cue strong enough to produce a feeling that English Canadians preferred one of their own dialect. In a field survey, Korinek (1976) asked southern listeners during the 1976 presidential campaign to evaluate such speakers as Jimmy Carter, Gerald Ford, Ronald Reagan, and Walter Cronkite. The results revealed a significant difference between Carter, who was evaluated as "similar in speech" and linguistically close, while the other three (Cronkite, Ford, and Reagan) were described as sounding very different in speech characteristics and were rated as less interesting. These examples provide some data to suggest that, sometimes, groups tend to evaluate speakers based upon their linguistic similarity or difference. One exception to this generalization, however, occurs when there is mobility away from one's regional association or some other reason to disassociate oneself from a region.

Attitudes toward Accented Speech

An individual from the South was overheard to say, "I don't care what other people think, I like Jimmy Carter. I don't know much about him or what he's doing for our country, but I like how he 'sounds' and I trust him." This example illustrates the influence of speech upon listeners' attitudes. Speech behavior, in the form of accented speech, establishes a cue (steeped in recall and experience with speakers of the dialect in question), which in turn triggers an attitude based on a listener's perception of the accented speech. Those perceptions encompass many varied aspects of listener-perceptions of speakers, the first of which is language and social status. So far, we have noted that norms and values, not necessarily inherent pleasantness of one dialect or accented speech pattern over another, can cause various attitudes toward accented speech. Let us now explore the attitudes themselves that people develop toward accented or dialectical speech.

During the 1960s, there were several major efforts undertaken in the United States to study the relationship between language and social stratification. The urban language research by William Labov (1966) in New York City and Roger Shuy and his colleagues (1967) in Detroit represented a working combination of sociological and linguistic research methods.

Language and Social Status

William Labov examined the relationship between language and social stratification in New York City, focusing upon frequently occurring linguistic patterns. After categorizing subjects from "lower class" to "upper middle class," the researcher then varied their speaking situations to elicit different styles of speech for each situation, including casual, formal, interview, reading, and overall word lists. The results indicated a relationship between the social class of speakers, the variations in the speech situation, and the performance difference on several linguistic variables. Among other things, higher social status respondents used fewer /d/-like sounds for the voiced "th" consonant as in "that," used more high vowels (generally /æ/) as in the words "bad," "bag," and "cash," and used fewer /t/-like sounds for the unvoiced "th" consonant as in "think" (see figure 7.3). The point is that Labov could detect social class from these specific linguistic variations (Williams 1972).

In another study, Roger Shuy used a random sample of approximately seven hundred residents in Detroit. Researchers attempted to evoke varying styles of speech, ranging from "careful" to "casual." The study provided a wide range of potential types of response data for the identification of linguistic variables. Results showed a correlation between social status of informants (index of occupation, education, and residence) and particular linguistic usages, particularly multiple negation ("He can't hit nobody"). Multiple negations increased dramatically from 1.7 for upper middle social status to 70.5 among the lower-class respondents, thus indicating that the percent usage of multiple negations is significantly more frequent in lower working class than in upper middle class respondents (figure 7.4). Once again, social class was linked with linguistic usage.

Often, students are asked to alter their pronunciation and conform to the practice of the "educated" members of the community. They are expected to change from substandard speech to socially acceptable speech. L. S. Harms (1961) questioned whether this process of "status dialect change" was a useful goal. Harms wanted to determine the degree of correlation between listener

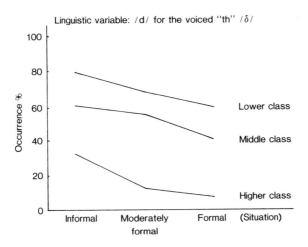

Linguistic variable: /d/ for the voiced "th" /ð/

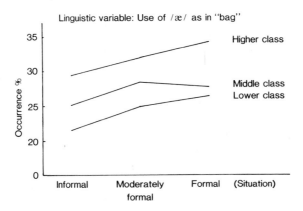

Linguistic variable: Use of /æ/ as in "bag"

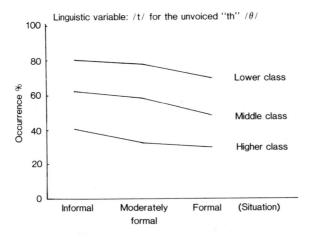

Linguistic variable: /t/ for the unvoiced "th" /θ/

Figure 7.3
Social class,
situation, and
linguistic variables.
(Adapted from
Labov 1966.)

Part 2   Cultural Systems Impacting on Intercultural Communication

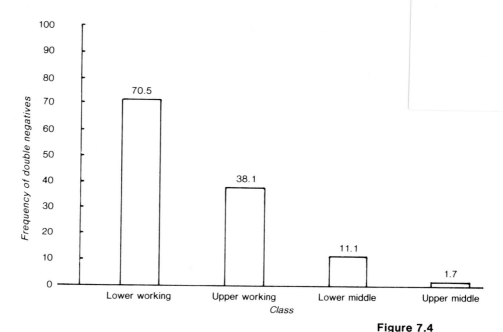

Figure 7.4
Social class
differences and
frequency of multiple
negations.
(Adapted from Shuy
1970.)

judgments of speaker status and speaker credibility. His study answered the question, "Is it possible to tell who a person is from the way he or she talks?" The experiment involved nine speakers of low status, middle status, and high status (on the basis of education) taping a forty- to sixty-second recording of "content free" speech. Listeners rated the speakers on status and credibility. There was a positive correlation between perceived status and credibility ratings. If a listener rated a speaker as high status, the listener also tended to rate the speaker as credible. This suggests that there are speech cues present that enable a listener to recognize the status of the speaker and to attribute credibility to the higher-status speakers (Harms 1961).

These studies suggest that, within intercultural communication, there are linguistic clues to actual social status. Perhaps tuning our ears to these linguistic variations can tell us something about our communication partners. Like any useful tool, however, such assessment must be processed carefully.

In a study of stereotypes, Delia (1972) invited student volunteers at the University of Illinois to listen to a taped speech delivered in three different American dialects: General American, Southern, and New England. After hearing the tapes, the students wrote their impressions of the speaker. Among other things, the results showed that, when these General American listeners heard the Southern or New England dialects (dialects usually different from their own), they not only correctly identified each region by its dialect but ascribed certain traits to the speaker, including their perception of the speaker's social role and status. With the General American dialect, the respondents were in a quandary about how to write impressions. Apparently, we use language as a cue to form impressions.

Language and Impression Formation

Another study examined listeners' expectations concerning two dialects speaking for and against George Wallace (Delia 1975). People who had General American accents (University of Illinois students) listened to tapes of a General American and a Southern speaker (actually one person varying his dialect), each giving a pro- and an anti-Wallace speech. Then the listeners rated the speaker on measures of credibility. In general, they thought that a speaker who advocated a position against what was perceived as the norms of that speaker's region was credible. These listeners were generally anti-Wallace. When they heard the pro-Wallace speech by a speaker with a General American dialect, these respondents did not care for the topic position, but they rated the speaker as having character. Similarly, they rated the southern anti-Wallace speaker to have high character. In other words, when speakers, perceived only by dialect, went against the norms stereotypically expected to be held by speakers in that region, they were considered more credible. Again, dialect provides a cue for attitude formation.

Bock and Pitts (1975) attempted to investigate the effects of three different black dialects on perceived speaker image by a black audience. The study measured the reactions to dialectical variations of a black speaker by a black audience. The three dialectical conditions were: (1) "jive" communication often used by blacks when talking to blacks, (2) uneducated Southern Black, and (3) common dialect used by blacks in black-white situations, similar to Standard American English. After listening to the speakers, listeners rated them on the basis of status and character. Subjects perceived the common dialect speaker as having expertise, high intelligence, and high status, but as an unreliable source of information. The uneducated Southern Black dialect speaker was rated as having low status. The jive condition produced the most favorable image, although subjects rated the speaker low in intelligence and experience. Despite that rating, listeners considered him to have high status and valued his opinion.

Still other studies focused on the effect of dialect differences in other cultures. Miller (1975) compared the effect of dialect and ethnicity on communicator effectiveness, using English Canadians and French Canadians as the focal ethnic groups. Each group was exposed to English speakers using French- and English-Canadian dialects, speaking on two topics, one relevant to each group. After listening to the tapes, subjects completed questionnaires concerning their perceptions of the communication and the author of the communication. On both messages, people agreed more with the English-Canadian dialect speaker. On the French topic, the English Canadian also was considered more competent, even though he was English. English Canadians tended to rate French Canadians in stereotypic fashion as poor, quiet, ignorant persons.

In another study, to explore language and impression formation further, Flores and Hopper (1975) studied the relationships between the degree of acculturation of Mexican Americans and their attitudes toward the language varieties that are common within the Mexican-American and Anglo-American cultures. In other words, how do people who speak good or bad Spanish rate others who speak good or bad Spanish? The people who considered themselves very much Mexican American perceived Standard Spanish as admirable. Those who spoke mostly Standard Spanish admired Standard English. The writers concluded that, in the Mexican-American culture, there is no indication that Mexican Americans rate their own language higher than others or their own particular brand of ethnic identification and accented speech as appropriate. That data also showed that Mexican Americans admire Standard Spanish, despite recent tendencies to tolerate nonstandard Spanish, for example, "Tex-Mex."

In another culture, Howard Giles (1973) was concerned with the question of prestigious accented speech in Britain. He used the four basic accented speeches of (1) Received Pronunciation (considered the "nicest" and thus most acceptable), (2) South Welsh, (3) Somerset, and (4) Birmingham in messages on capital punishment. Subjects heard four persuasive speeches, each using a different accented speech. The subjects had been pretested to determine their opinion on capital punishment. After the speeches, posttests determined any shifts. In rating the quality of the argument, subjects preferred the Received Pronunciation (the standard), but they were persuaded more by the nonstandard speech. Perhaps because the nonstandard speaker was associated with the lower class and was perceived as being more "informed" on crime, he was considered a more credible source. On another topic, Giles noted, the nonstandard speaker might not be as persuasive.

These studies suggest two major principles. First, a speaker's accented speech and dialect influence our attitudes toward the speaker. Second, speech forms outside the linguistic norms of the listener usually are evaluated negatively, except where the accented speech conveys the impression of experience with the topic or task at hand.

Several studies have assessed how teachers evaluate the speech of pupils, particularly in terms of the students "sounding disadvantaged." In one study, tapes of forty speech samples from fourth and fifth grade, black and white children, males and females, sampled from low- and middle-income homes, were evaluated. After listening to the children's responses to some questions, teachers rated the children's speech along two dimensions: confidence-eagerness and ethnicity-nonstandardness. The children who hesitated a lot were perceived as less confident-eager. The children who used some nonstandardizations in English were perceived as ethnic and nonstandard. Also, teachers associated "sounding disadvantaged" or "low class" with perceiving a child as reticent, even more so when the child sounded ethnic or nonstandard in his or her language usage (Williams 1970).

Williams, Whitehead, and Miller (1971) carried this research further to assess the effects of ethnic stereotyping. Four videotapes of fifth- and sixth-grade male children, one each of a black and a Mexican-American child, and

Language Attitudes and Perception of Children

two of white children, showed a side view of the child assembling a plastic car. As the child worked, he described what he was doing, but observers saw only slight lip movement. Groups of undergraduate education majors (University of Texas) viewed: (1) a black or Mexican-American child whose nonstandard speech, unknown to the respondents, had been replaced by dubbing in the speech of a Standard-English-speaking child; (2) a black or Mexican-American child speaking nonstandard English; and (3) a white child speaking Standard English. Findings indicated that the videotape image, showing the child's ethnicity, affected ratings of the child's language in the direction of racial stereotyping. Black children were expected to sound more nonstandard and ethnic. The same was true for Mexican-American children, and they were expected to be more reticent and nonconfident. It seems likely that this relationship also would affect teacher judgment of certain academic ability.

Williams and Naremore (1974) studied teachers' ratings of ethnic students. Data for the study consisted of teachers' ratings of videotaped samples of children's speech, teachers' stereotypic responses to ethnic labels, and teachers' indications of academic expectancies for three ethnic groups of children (black, Anglo, and Mexican American). Anglo teachers rated Anglo children as more confident and eager, but the others as nonstandard. The other teacher groups showed bias toward their particular minority groups as well. Anglo teachers also had higher expectations for Anglo children in language arts and lower expectations for black and Mexican-American students. Teachers' ratings in many ways seemed a product of their own ethnicity and the predominant student ethnicities at their schools.

In still another study by Whitehead and his colleagues (1974), the range of attitudes toward a student was examined. Their study showed Anglo children as standard, black children as confident and eager but low on standardness, and Mexican-American children as less confident and less standard.

One exception to these negative evaluations comes from the work of Piche and his colleagues (1977). These researchers had pre-service elementary teachers form a composite impression of individual children based on videotaped samples, selected social class information, and samples of children's written compositions. Black and white fourth-grade children, interviewed on videotape, used casual speech. These teachers viewed nonstandard English and white Standard English, and good and bad compositions allegedly written by the blacks and whites. Neither the dialect and ethnicity nor the quality of the written compositions caused major perceptual differences. Aside from other conditions, the authors concluded that dialect does not always exert a straightforward effect—it depends on the teacher's expectations.

Overall, however, research indicates that stereotypic impressions result primarily from perceived dialect (although in most studies even the same speaker merely switched accented speech in what is called bidialectical speech, using a matched guise technique). The effects toward the accented speaker may extend beyond an attitude toward the speaker, to what sociolinguists and others call the *Pygmalion effect*. Pygmalion, a Greek mythological character,

Accented speech creates impressions that often reinforce stereotypes toward the linguistic user.

sculptured a woman so beautiful that he fell in love with his creation. His wishes and expectations concerning the sculpture came true when Venus made the woman real. Similarly, the expectation of an event can actually create a self-fulfilling prophecy and cause the event to become reality. A teacher's stereotypes, based solely on linguistic dialect cues, may create negative impressions that become self-fulfilling prophecies; that is, the teacher expects the child to perform poorly, and the child obliges.

Hopper and Williams (1973) extended the previous studies on the effects of accented speech on person-perception into the world of business. They were interested in how people tend to evaluate prospective employees on the basis of their speech. For their research, they used four ninety-second tapes, each consisting of four different speech types, including (1) Standard English, (2) Black English, (3) Spanish-accented English, and (4) Southern English. Employers evaluated the tapes and then indicated which speakers they would hire and their attitudes toward them. Results showed that the following characteristics were potentially of primary concern to the employers: (1) intelligence and competence, (2) cooperative spirit and dependability, (3) self-assurance, and (4) Anglo or non-Anglo. Remember, these factors were assessed from the voices of four speaker types. Specific elements relating to specific jobs were: (1) competence and intelligence (these people were chosen as executives and supervisors) and (2) being relaxed and self-assured (chosen for clerical work). While cooperation and dependability did not appear as a major reason for hiring, ethnicity (perceived through the voice) had a slightly negative influence on hiring choices.

Language and Employability

Overall, the studies cited in this chapter tell us that how we speak does make a difference. When ethnicity is concerned, negative impressions often result. As an intercultural communicator, you should make a special effort to listen beyond mere dialectical differences. Hopefully, though, you now understand why accented speech affects interpersonal relations.

Developing Skills in Language and Culture

1. *Listen for unintentional meanings.* In intercultural contacts, users of a second language in this interaction may read unintended meanings into the word usages.

2. *Listen for emotional meanings.* A word understood denotatively by both parties nevertheless may carry strong emotional feelings that are culturally conditioned for one person but not for the other person. For example, the word *government* conjures images of political systems and institutions, power, and elections for North Americans. Yugoslavians view the same word as representing high position but, to a lesser extent, power, and few if any view the word with regard to elections or political systems or institutions (Szalay 1974). Thus, a word that appears equivocal may produce different images for the intercultural users of that word. We cannot assume that the word means the same thing to each person; we can only assume that words and phrases are culturally conditioned.

3. *Ask for clarification.* When someone speaks to you in a restricted code, ask for clarification. Invite the person to restate and amplify. The alternative, sometimes, is pretending you understood when, in fact, you did not.

4. *Offer clarification.* Our own cultural experiences make it unnecessary to elaborate in intracultural communication. Thus, we may unintentionally use a restricted code in intercultural contacts and produce confusion with conversational style and words that any of our intracultural friends might understand perfectly well. In intercultural communication, we should avoid slang, jargon, and personal references that exclude another person's experiences. Also, it may be helpful to avoid lavish words; try to be direct and straightforward.

5. *Give others the benefit of a perceptual doubt.* Remember that not only our cultural experiences but our language can shape how we see things. The foreign national in our country or the host country national when we travel may categorize his or her world differently. Try to understand that taxonomy and communicate as best you can within that person's framework.

6. *Meet people on their cognitive territory.* As the person who has studied intercultural communication, you must take the initiative in meeting people where they are cognitively. As you step into their cognitive territory, you will be more effective and broaden your self-insight.

7. *Learn greetings.* If you find yourself in a culture where the language difference suggests your learning a new language, then at least learn appropriate greetings. Of course, learn the entire language, but knowing how to greet others is imperative immediately.

8. *Realize that meanings are in people, not in words.* The dictionary does not really tell us everything about the meaning of words and phrases. The same word *bad* can mean something that is good or something that is awful, depending upon your cultural outlook and your use of language.

9. *Speak slowly.* If you are conversing with a person from another country, perhaps a visitor to this country, speak distinctly. Do not fall into the trap of compensating for the other person's broken English by speaking loudly. That only embarrasses you both.

10. *Do not give up.* When your attempts fail at language or at the larger considerations of intercultural communication, stay with the attempt.

11. *Learn when to be direct and indirect.* In Italy, you are expected to tell things to people in a straightforward manner; tell things as they seem to you. However, in Japan, people are concerned with saving face; you would rarely tell people something directly, especially if you know more than they about a particular matter. Rather, you would speak indirectly. In England or Scotland, one needs to be indirect also. One suggests but does not order or dictate (*Overseas Diplomacy* 1973).

Language shapes our views, just as experiences shape language. The following passage from the late Margaret Mead (cited by Kluckhohn 1972, 112–13) highlights the conceptual nature of language:

Reflections from Margaret Mead

> Americans tend to arrange objects on a single scale of value, from best to worst, biggest to smallest, cheapest to most expensive, etc., and are able to express a preference among very complex objects on such a single scale. The question, "What is your favorite color?", so intelligible to an American, is meaningless in Britain, and such a question is countered by: "Favorite color for what? A flower? A necktie?" Each object is thought of as having a most complete set of qualities, and color is merely a quality of an object, not something from a color chart on which one can make a choice which is transferable to a large number of different objects. The American reduction of complexities to single scales is entirely comprehensible in terms of the great diversity of value systems which different immigrant groups brought to the American scene. Some common denominator among the incommensurables was very much needed, and oversimplification was almost inevitable. But, as a result, Americans think in terms of qualities which have uni-dimensional scales, while the British, when they think of a complex object or event, even if they reduce it to parts, think of each part as retaining all of the complexities of the whole. Americans subdivide the scale; the British subdivide the object.

This Chapter in Perspective

The Whorf hypothesis suggests the mediating effect of language on reality. Implications of an adapted Bernstein hypothesis indicate that salient cultural features of a culture and social structure predict communication behavior. Communication behavior, or speech, is of two types: (1) restricted codes involve narrow, jargonlike messages understood by other members of the subculture; (2) elaborated codes include messages that necessitate verbal elaboration of meaning. Implications for intercultural communicators include feedback, clarification, renewed understanding, and initiative in encoding messages with the other person's cognitive framework in mind.

In view of the literature, we can conclude that: (1) people judge others by their speech, (2) upward mobility and social aspirations influence whether people change their speech to the accepted norms, (3) General American speech is most accepted by the majority of the American culture, and (4) people should be aware of these prejudices and attempt to "look beyond the surface."

In formal and informal speaking situations, we should not only realize our prejudices and try to understand more thoroughly various dialects, but also realize how our own dialect can affect others. This self-perception will help us to become better intercultural communicators. Also, through this knowledge of the effects of speech behavior, as teachers, researchers, or practitioners, our evaluations of others should become less narrow, and we should begin to see a total picture of others' communication behaviors.

Exercises

1. Can you think of other examples of language differences between you and English speakers from other countries? Scan the newspaper for examples of how language seems to affect culture and how culture affects language.

2. Interview someone from another English-speaking country (Canada, Nigeria, India, etc.). Make a list of familiar concepts and find the corresponding word in that person's use of English. Are different English words used for the same concept? Why?

3. Make a list of as many American English words for money as you can (for example, bread, greenbacks, change, skin, bucks, etc.). Do you think other cultures have as many words for money? Do Americans have many words for kinship, friendship, or other interpersonal relationships?

4. By talking to some of your professors and by looking at some relevant books in the library, try to ascertain which dialect or accent of English your region speaks. Try to find out what attitudes prevail toward that accented speech pattern. Why do such attitudes exist? How are those attitudes changed? Should those attitudes be changed?

5. Talk to several area employers—both in business and in universities. Are there any discernible attitudes toward employment that stem from linguistic usage? What about a person who uses bad grammar?

6. The chapter noted that sometimes teachers inadvertently rate their pupils on linguistic grounds rather than on competence. Discuss how this occurs and how it can be prevented.

Bernstein, Basil. "Elaborated and Restricted Codes: Their Social Origins and Some Consequences." In *Communication and Culture,* edited by Alfred G. Smith. New York: Holt, Rinehart and Winston, 1966.

Bock, E. Hope, and James H. Pitts. "The Effects of Three Levels of Black Dialect on Perceived Speaker Image." *Speech Teacher* 24 (1975): 218–25.

Burgoon, Michael, Stephen Jones, and Diane Stewart. "Toward a Message-Centered Theory of Persuasion." *Human Communication Research* 1 (1975): 240–56.

Chomsky, Noam. *Language and Mind.* New York: Harcourt and Brace, 1972.

Dale, Philip S. *Language Development.* Hinsdale, Ill.: Dryden, 1972.

Delia, J. G. "Dialects and the Effects of Stereotypes on Interpersonal Attraction and Cognitive Processes in Impression Formation." *Quarterly Journal of Speech* 58 (1972): 285–97.

Delia, J. G. "Regional Dialect, Message Acceptance, and Perceptions of the Speaker." *Central States Speech Journal* 26 (1975): 188–94.

Dodd, Carley H. "Social Structure and Communication Behavior among the Children of God." A Paper presented to the International Communication Association Convention, Chicago, April 26, 1975.

Flores, Nancy De La Zerda, and Robert Hopper. "Mexican Americans' Evaluations of Spoken Spanish and English." *Speech Monographs* 42 (1975): 91–98.

Giles, Howard. "Communicative Effectiveness as a Function of Accented Speech." *Speech Monographs* 40 (1973): 330–31.

Giles, Howard, and Richard Y. Bourhis. "Voice and Racial Categorization in Britain." *Communication Monographs* 43 (1976): 108–14.

Giles, Howard, Richard Bourhis, Peter Trudgill, and Alan Lewis. "The Imposed Norm Hypothesis: A Validation." *Quarterly Journal of Speech* 60 (1974): 405–10.

Gleason, H. A. *An Introduction to Descriptive Linguistics.* New York: Holt, Rinehart and Winston, 1961.

Greenberg, Joseph H. "The Linguistic Approach." In *Communication and Culture,* edited by Alfred G. Smith. New York: Holt, Rinehart and Winston, 1966.

Harms, L. S. "Listener Judgments of Status Cues in Speech." *Quarterly Journal of Speech* 47 (1961): 164–68.

Hoijer, Harry. "The Sapir-Whorf Hypothesis." In *Intercultural Communication: A Reader,* 2d ed., edited by Larry A. Samovar and Richard E. Porter. Belmont, Calif.: Wadsworth, 1976.

Hopper, Robert, and Frederick Williams. "Speech Characteristics and Employability." *Communication Monographs* 40 (1973): 296–302.

Kluckhohn, Clyde. "The Gift of Tongues." In *Intercultural Communication: A Reader,* edited by Larry A. Samovar and Richard E. Porter. Belmont, Calif.: Wadsworth, 1972.

Korinek, John. "Perceived Evaluation of Speech Characteristics of Jimmy Carter." Unpublished paper, Department of Communication and Theatre, Western Kentucky University, 1976.

LaBarre, Weston. "Paralinguistics, Kinesics, and Cultural Anthropology." In *Intercultural Communication: A Reader,* 2d ed., edited by Larry A. Samovar and Richard E. Porter. Belmont, Calif.: Wadsworth, 1976.

Labov, William. *The Social Stratification of English in New York City.* Washington, D.C.: Center for Applied Linguistics, 1966.

Lee, Richard R. "Preliminaries to Language Intervention." *Quarterly Journal of Speech* 56 (1970): 270–76.

McCroskey, James C. *An Introduction to Rhetorical Communication.* Englewood Cliffs, N.J.: Prentice-Hall, 1972.

Miller, Dale T. "The Effect of Dialect and Ethnicity on Communicator Effectiveness." *Speech Monographs* 42 (1975): 69–74.

Miller, Jack. "Black American Speech Patterns: Origins, Evidence, and Implications." Paper presented to Southern Speech Communication Association, Atlanta, April 4, 1978.

Mulac, Anthony, and Mary Jo Rudd. "Effects of Selected American Regional Dialects upon Regional Audience Members." *Communication Monographs* 44 (1977): 185–95.

Overseas Diplomacy. U.S. Navy, Bureau of Navy Personnel, 1973.

Piche, Gene L., Michael Michlin, Donald Rubin, and Allan Sullivan. "Effects of Dialect-Ethnicity, Social Class, and Quality of Written Compositions on Teachers' Subjective Evaluations of Children." *Communication Monographs* 44 (1977): 60–62.

Pulgram, Ernst. "Phoneme and Grapheme: A Parallel." In *Communication and Culture,* edited by Alfred G. Smith. New York: Holt, Rinehart and Winston, 1966.

Schramm, Wilbur. *The Science of Human Communication.* New York: Basic Books, 1963.

Sherif, Carolyn W., Muzafer Sherif, and Roger E. Nebergall. *Attitude and Attitude Change.* Philadelphia: Saunders, 1965.

Shuy, Roger. "The Sociolinguist and Urban Language Problems." In *Language and Poverty: Perspectives on a Theme,* edited by Frederick Williams. Chicago: Markham, 1970.

Shuy, Roger, and others. "Linguistic Correlates of Social Stratification in Detroit Speech." U.S.O.E. project 6-1347, Michigan State University, 1967.

Steward, Edward. *Outline of International Communication.* The BCIU Institute: American University, 1973.

Szalay, Lorand B. "Adapting Communication Research to the Needs of International and Intercultural Communication." *International and Intercultural Communication Annual* 1 (1974): 1–16.

Tomlinson, Delorese. "Bi-Dilectism: Solution for American Minority Members." *Speech Teacher* 24 (1975): 232–36.

Wheeler, Christopher, Judith Wilson, and Carol Tarantola. "An Investigation of Children's Social Perception of Child Speakers with Reference to Verbal Style." *Central States Speech Journal* 27 (1976): 31–35.

Whitehead, Jack L., Frederick Williams, Jean Civikly, and Judith Algino. "Latitude of Attitude in Ratings of Dialect Variations." *Communication Monographs* 41 (1974): 387–407.

Whorf, Benjamin Lee. *Language, Thought, and Reality: Selected Writings of Benjamin Lee Whorf,* edited by John B. Carroll. New York: Wiley, 1956.

Williams, Frederick. "Psychological Correlates of Speech Characteristics: On Sounding 'Disadvantaged'." *Journal of Speech and Hearing Research* 13 (1970): 472–88.

Williams, Frederick, and Rita C. Naremore. "Language Attitudes: An Analysis of Teacher Differences." *Communication Monographs* 41 (1974): 391–96.

Williams, Frederick, Jack L. Whitehead, and Leslie M. Miller. "Ethnic Stereotyping and Judgments of Children's Speech." *Speech Monographs* 38 (1971): 166–70.

Williams, Frederick. *Language and Speech.* Englewood Cliffs, N.J.: Prentice-Hall, 1972.

Chapter

Intercultural Communication and Mass Media as Cultural Influence

Objectives

After completing this chapter, you should be able to:

1. Identify ways in which the mass media aid a nation's development.

2. List the effects of mass media.

3. Demonstrate the relationship between mass media and culture.

The mass media's role in intercultural communication is complex. Some researchers verify the utility of mass media in producing modernization and national development. Other researchers focus on the global relationships of numerous variables that correlate with media presence and access across many world nations. A third group of researchers define the role of the mass media in persuading people to adopt new ideas intraculturally. This chapter surveys the role of the mass media and their place in intercultural communication. Those roles grow as governments and various cultural leaders utilize media for social, political, religious, and economic purposes.

The role of the mass media in national development is well-documented. Classic research by Lerner (1958) underscored the centrality of media; his well-known model suggests that urbanization produces individual participation. Schramm (1973) argued that the mass media serve as multipliers for information and learning and thus accelerate the rate of development within developing nations. He further noted that nations should invest capital into media development in a way similar to other capital investments. Rogers and Svenning (1969, 100–101) further outlined crucial reasons why national planners should invest in mass media: (1) interpersonal channels alone are inadequate for massive populations; (2) mass media technology (such as the transistor radio) has made the role of mass media in national development economically feasible; (3) mass media lend themselves to establishing a "climate for modernization," thus acting like an accelerator, multiplying change efforts.

Mass Media and National Development

Concern over national development has caused a number of scholars to attempt to discover how the media facilitate a nation's economic and social development. Research findings generally agree that media development seems to be linked with national development. For instance, Farace and Donohew (1965) developed regression equations in which they used some forty-two variables in various combinations to establish a link with press freedom, newspaper circulation, radio receivers, and number of cinema seats. They used data from UNESCO sources across 115 countries and found some strong links of demographic, social, and communication variables correlated with mass media development: press freedom (70 percent), newspaper circulation (86 percent), cinema seats (34 percent), and radio receivers (84 percent). This finding suggests that social changes like higher education and literacy may create a

Table 8.1 Correlations of Communication Variables with Gross National Product per Capita in Developing Nations

Communication Variable	GNP/pc
Daily newspaper circulation (per 1,000)	.80
Radios (per 1,000)	.85
Television sets (per 1,000)	.75
Cinema attendance per capita	.65
Percent literate (fifteen years and older)	.80
Domestic mail per capita	.89

Source: Frey 1973, 408.

"hunger" for the mass media to supply newly found information needs. In a subsequent article, Farace (1966) examined the role of fifty-four variables categorized into politics, agricultural productivity, population characteristics, cultural indicators, economic measures, and mass communication factors. Taken together, these categories jointly produced dimensions relating to national development. Studies like these are enormously valuable—they can help us see that the mass media work in concert with a number of other ingredients to assist in the process of national development.

Mass communication also has been linked to gross national product, which is one important measure of national development. For instance, Frey (1973) cited evidence that suggests that an increase in communication sources is linked with an increase in gross national product per capita (from various developing nations), as indicated in table 8.1. Although these data reveal communication variables associated with general development, Frey also demonstrated the relationship of communication development to socioeconomic development by noting the positive and high correlations of income per capita, literacy (percent population of two thousand or more), and industrialization (percent males employed outside agriculture) with media indices such as newsprint consumption, daily newspaper circulation, number of radio receivers, and number of cinema seats. In other words, an increase in these communication features coincided with increases in a developing nation's per capita income, literacy, and industrialization. Unfortunately, we cannot be sure that economic increases have not caused media increases instead of the other way around. Thus, we can only conclude a linking relationship, not a causal relationship.

In another paper, Jeffres (1975) underscored print media as a dependent variable—a result, not a cause. That he found literacy and per capita income the most significant variables, accounting for up to 95 percent variance, reflects again a growing concern and strong "hunch" that media usage is related to economic development of nations. Jeffres' review of previous research turned up several factors affecting newspaper development and availability, including literacy and language, presence of oral communication systems, cultural factors (that is, class, religion, education), political and legal factors, economic factors, and environmental factors. Not only do the mass media play a dominant role in a nation's economic development, but they alter its social and cultural awareness as well. For the media provide a means for a nation to communicate with its people.

In spite of their usefulness several criticisms concerning these international studies persist: (1) lack of sociopsychological variables (that is, empathy, aspirations, etc.); (2) lack of generalizability to smaller units within a country, such as a regional or subcultural unit; (3) disparity and "slippage" between elites and rural residents in a country; (4) the problem of deciphering causal relationships; and (5) a concern over accuracy of quality national data. The most striking problem with the aggregate level analysis approach hinges upon the assumption that media availability ensures exposure. Writing to that very point, Frey (1973) noted: Thus far, we have explored the general availability of various media of communication around the world, concentrating particularly on the contrasts and similarities between developed and underdeveloped nations. The obvious and necessary next step is to move from consideration of *access* to consideration of actual *exposure*. That radio is accessible, for example, does not mean that it is used. (p. 359)

We have already examined the impact of the mass media upon national development. This section briefly reviews mass media effects on culture.

As you may recall from an earlier chapter, opinion leaders are those individuals to whom people turn informally for information and advice. In addition to their other characteristics, opinion leaders are usually higher in mass media exposure. Mass media effects are therefore somewhat mediated by interpersonal contacts with respected opinion leaders. In early research on voting behavior in the 1940 United States presidential election, researchers discovered, unexpectedly, that the mass media accounted for little direct influence on voting behavior, while close to one-half of voting choices were determined by personal influences, ostensibly opinion leadership. Although the media are more important today, interpersonal influence still works in concert with the media to affect many of our choices in life.

DeFleur and Ball-Rokeach (1976) also testified to the mitigating influence of personal contacts upon mass media influence. Informational influence sometimes flows indirectly, often through a series of interpersonal relationships, where media information finally filters interpersonally to the "grass roots." We should point out, though, that the strength of the multistep flow probably lies among cultures that are not quite so monolithically inclined toward the mass media as the U.S. culture and in which interpersonal relationships are important.

How do the mass media work along with interpersonal sources? As we will see, the media are tremendously influential, increasing awareness of events and of salient information, but interpersonal contacts play an influential role as well. In a study of the 1972 Nixon-McGovern presidential election, Patterson and McClure (1976) found that personal influence accounted for 7 per-

Mass Media Effects on Culture
Mass Media and Interpersonal Communication

cent of the factors that influenced candidate choice, compared with 16 percent accounted for by political television advertising, and 42 percent of the choices influenced by events (for example, Vietnam peace talks, Watergate). Hirsch (1975) reported that 25 percent of his sample heard of the Martin Luther King assassination from personal contacts (though not necessarily opinion leaders), and 12.5 percent heard about the retirement of President Johnson by this means. This percentage is somewhat smaller than the Governor Wallace shooting interpersonal percentage (72 percent), but this difference can be explained because of the time of day when these events occurred, their salience, and the planned nature of LBJ's news conference. In his investigation of information sources concerning the swine flu inoculation program, Dodd (1979) reported that only 10 percent of the survey respondents learned of the vaccine from interpersonal sources as their initial information source, while 90 percent learned of the vaccine from the mass media. However, this research also revealed that 83 percent of the interviewed respondents sought additional information from interpersonal sources, and 95 percent utilized interpersonal sources for direct advice about their decision to accept or reject the inoculations after time passed following initial awareness. These findings were paralleled across a sample of elderly residents and a sample of college students.

In general, the effects of the mass media, it appears, are overshadowed by interpersonal contacts where decision making is concerned; however, less interpersonal influence is needed in conveying straightforward information and awareness about news events. In other words, the media tend to make us aware of information, but interpersonal sources help us to make decisions about that information.

| Mass Media and Persuasion | Early work examining the role of the mass media in persuasion basically agreed that the mass media are not all-powerful in effecting change. As we just indicated, the media accounted for only 16 percent of the votes in the 1972 presidential election. In the two decades before the mid-1940s, media specialists generally believed that the media could powerfully influence a somewhat passive audience (like the hypodermic needle model in figure 8.1). Then, from 1940 to 1960, researchers probed a number of other elements working coincidentally with the media and discovered that media effects were highly related to a complex set of other variables. Some of these other variables are the "causes" of several behaviors, with the mass media playing a smaller role than earlier expected. So, mass media effects are actually a function of the media *plus* the following "intervening" elements: |

1. Interpersonal networks

2. Cultural norms, values, and world view

3. Demographic categories (such as age, education, occupation, ethnicity, and so on) and group memberships

4. Motivation, needs, and salient means of gratifying those needs

5. Personality characteristics

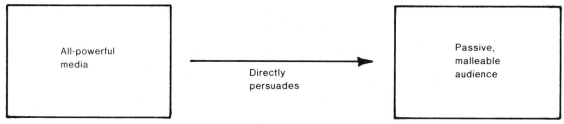

Figure 8.1
Hypodermic needle
theory of mass
media influence. This
early theory has
been replaced by a
better model of
mediating variables
of mass media
influence.

One example of how mediating effects work comes from the Surgeon General's report in the 1970s concerning the effects of television violence on children. This report revealed that the harmful effects on children partially depended on the child's state of social deprivation, motivation, contact with parents, and a host of other social and personality variables. This report, or any other report, does not imply that the mass media have no effect; rather that the mass media have some effect depending upon these other, intervening variables.*

What, then, are the persuasive effects of the mass media? Research studies have indicated that the mass media play varying roles. Joseph Klapper's (1960) classic work reported that mass media effects vary greatly. Sometimes, media messages accounted for direct behavioral and attitudinal effects of only 3 percent to 8 percent, though some media messages could be said to contribute up to 83 percent of change in individuals. Obviously, these effects depend upon the nature of the medium, the message content, psychological motivation, and mediating interpersonal contacts. Do recent studies provide any other clues that can tell us more about the persuasive effects of the mass media?

Patterson and McClure (1976) reported that only 16 percent of 1972 presidential voting choices were attributed to political television advertising. The media, then, served primarily to bring information to voters, not cause them to vote. In their study of the Illinois gubernatorial primary and general elections, Atwood and Sanders (1975) found that 73 percent of their respondents reported print and television media as their main sources of information for the primary election and 98 percent for the general election. Dodd's (1979) report of the swine flu inoculation program showed that vaccine adoption was highly correlated with newspaper exposure, with 80 percent of the daily newspaper readers being adopters. However, the same group of adopters also sought additional information (83 percent), which was primarily from interpersonal sources. Caillouet's (1978) extensive field analysis of a regionwide religious campaign and of a simultaneous Holiday-on-Ice campaign also revealed that

*This author wholeheartedly agrees with the deleterious effects on children of violence on television reported in a number of journals. The intended point here, though, is to introduce readers to the complex set of "mediating" variables that inevitably become other causes to the effects we observe. The exact "blend" and interaction of the media with other variables in producing some effect is a subject still under significant investigation.

The mass media play a dominant role in many cultures by providing information and entertainment.

the mass media worked in concert with interpersonal sources, largely crystallizing and reinforcing the attendance of people who already had learned of the event through interpersonal sources and who were largely partisans.

Overall, we can conclude that the media tend to make us aware of information, reinforce us, and persuade us indirectly, in concert with the persuasive influence of interpersonal sources. In sum, mass media persuasive effects can be described as follows:

1. The mass media serve an awareness function, creating interest in an event or an idea through direct information about its existence.

2. The mass media develop an *agenda;* that is, they call attention to what is salient. When news commentators say, "And that's the news," the subtle implication is that they have explained what is important and thereby call attention to that event exclusively. For the next few days, people then discuss that "agenda."

3. The mass media serve as "accelerators" for change, creating a climate in which change can more easily occur. For example, Johnny Carson on the "Tonight Show" created a toilet paper shortage with a comment that a toilet paper shortage might occur, and many people rushed to buy the product.

4. The mass media work in concert with and through interpersonal sources, depending upon the saliency, immediacy, and timing of the event. Special programs in India and Latin America, such as Telescuela, have enjoyed success in agricultural innovations when radio messages are listened to by an assembly of village family heads and leaders. Following the program, a village worker leads a discussion, and the villagers return home, often to implement new ideas for productivity. It seems apparent from such examples that the mass media and interpersonal contacts have a simultaneous influence.

5. The mass media, compared with interpersonal communication, are less influential in developing nations in accounting for persuasion since opinion leadership in those situations accounts for up to 75 percent of adoption decisions.

6. The mass media may stimulate rumors. The "short" nature of many electronic news broadcasts means that, by necessity, some details are omitted. This screening sometimes leaves ambiguity or vagueness, features that can heighten the possibility of rumor formation.

Since the 1960s, a substantial amount of information has described the mass media as a direct institution of culture and an influential shaper of culture. "The Medium is the Message," or massage, as McLuhan (1967) so tersely put it, has become the watchword of some media theorists. The clear implication is that a medium dominates our perceptions of an event, since it is precisely through some medium that we become aware of many events in our world. To put it loosely, we become the recipients of those scenes that the cameraperson and directors select, the reporter pens, and the gatekeeper for the news service allows to go through the "wire" to the nation. Should error exist, listeners have no way to check reality since the medium has, in a sense, become the reality.

Mass Media as a Shaper of Culture

However, in another way, we can note the ways that media and culture intertwine, more on the cultural and cognitive level. Picking up on McLuhan's suggestion that cultures might be examined in stages, let us posit a relationship about how people in a culture think and communicate. This connection is illustrated in figure 8.2. We call this relationship the *linear-nonlinear* nature of culture. Type I is a culture we might term "nonlinear." The thought-framework (or how people think) in this society is configurational (nonlinear), which implies that it has multiple themes, expressed in oral terms, and so on. Because of its configurational orientation, type I culture involves the simultaneous bombardment and processing of a variety of stimuli—and so, these people think in images, not just in words. Time orientation is less important than people and events, and time is not segmented.

Type II is a culture that has transformed auditory and oral communication into visual communication by means of written symbols, organized into

Cultural level:	Type I	Type II	Type III
Thought-framework:	Nonlinear	Linear	Nonlinear-linear

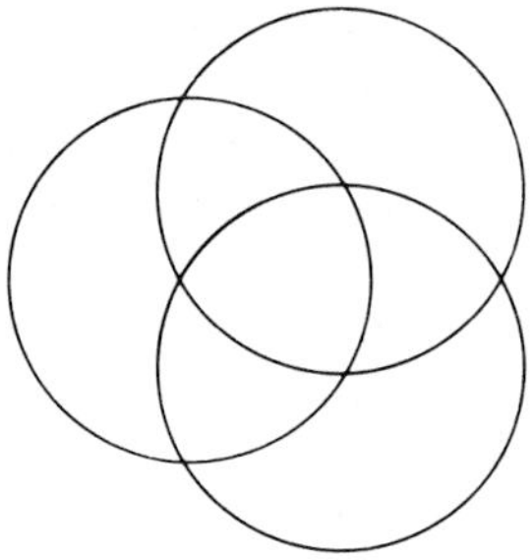

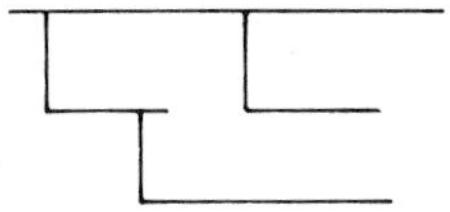

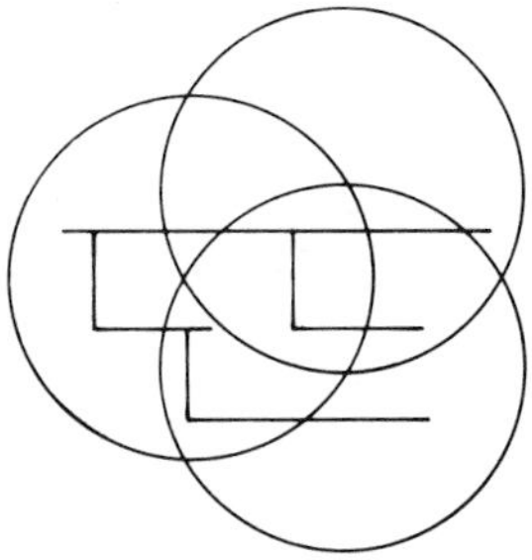

Communication behavior:	1. Does not necessarily have one theme.	1. Organized with beginning and ending points and subpoints.	1. Main central theme with numerous subthemes.
	2. Auditory in nature.	2. Consistently has one theme.	2. Definite time frame with precise beginning and end.
	3. Evidence stems from traditional wisdom themes and traditional authority.	3. Both visual and auditory, but superimposes visual thought pattern (spatial) on auditory communication.	3. Potentially numerous themes portrayed simultaneously.
	4. Heightened by nonverbal communication.	4. Usually occurs in relatively short amount of time.	4. Primarily visual.
	5. Lends itself to relationships and personal interaction (active communication).	5. Well suited for print media.	5. Evidence stems from experience, societal norms, and cultural themes.
	6. Event oriented (i.e., men returning home from the hunt, discussion ensues).	6. Evidence stems from logic and empiricism.	6. Passive in nature; little or no cultural themes.
	7. Events happen; little plot or planned movement occurs.	7. Object oriented (material technology heralded; machine is more important than person).	7. Events portrayed, objects viewed with wishful thinking.

Figure 8.2
The linear-nonlinear nature of culture through media: Type I, II, and III cultures.

linear thought patterns. This culture has beginnings and ends to its events, unitary themes throughout any one episode being described. It is object oriented rather than people or event oriented, and it is empirical in its use of evidence. Furthermore, its speech patterns superimpose a visual (usually outlined) structure upon the auditory speech process. That is, these people think from left to right (or right to left in some cultures) in a linear fashion.

Type III is an "electronic" culture that is simultaneously configurational and linear. Events can be portrayed with several themes running simultaneously, although evidence is based on experiences of receivers who remain passive while viewing events through the media of the culture. Television and film illustrate communication in a type III culture where linear and nonlinear sensory stimuli are focused on the viewer simultaneously. Often, a single, organized theme undergirds the nonlinear collage of filmed scenes.

Types I, II, and III have roots in cognitive culture, discussed in chapter 5 as monochronic and polychronic orientations. The point here is that the media may have some influence in shaping culture in these ways.

Up to this point, we have advanced the idea that the mass media increase our awareness of issues, although interpersonal sources serve to persuade us more directly. You undoubtedly recognize that the mass media have an unintended influence that is sometimes subtle, sometimes obvious, but nevertheless real. Several of Aronson's (1980) examples concerning these subtle influences are particularly insightful. For example, he pointed to the 1977 showing of Alex Haley's "Roots" on ABC television to over 130 million viewers, the largest television audience at that time to watch any one program in the United States. The film not only captured attention but seemed to inspire blacks to take an increased pride in their heritage and to guide a number of people in the United States to trace their geneaology, indicated by the increased geneaological enquiries after that showing. In 1978, NBC showed "Holocaust," a dramatization documenting the Nazis' execution of millions of Jews. When the same program was telecast in West Germany, it was credited with providing the motivation for the passage of a law stiffening Nazi prosecution. The 1974 showing of the NBC television movie "Cry Rape," in which a rape victim went through more hassle in trying to press charges than the horror of the rape itself, may account for the decreased number of rapes reported to the police in the weeks that followed. Perhaps victims identified with the movie and assumed that the police would be suspicious of them.

As already pointed out, mass media effects are mediated by a number of other effects, including social norms, the personalities of the viewers, the content of the mass media, and so on. But what the examples in the previous paragraph suggest is that media presentations that are not intentionally trying to persuade us or even inform us may actually have a greater effect than some media messages with such intents. Perhaps the emotional appeal coupled with the vivid imagery of the cinema and television productions make a subtle impact upon our conscious and subconscious minds. Thus, the media may be

Unintentional Effects of Mass Media

unwittingly influencing us in beliefs about things we see portrayed on the screen. If McDonald's advertises at intervals during a children's program that portrays violence, the child may unwittingly associate the "positive" image of Ronald McDonald with the violence. The reporter who selectively reports riots, murders, earthquakes, and international wars may inadvertently convey to viewers that all people behave violently and that the world is a pretty bad place to live.

Mass Media and Learning

The mass media also create the indirect effect of teaching and promoting social models. For instance, the negative stereotypes of blacks, Mexican Americans, and Asian Americans on television up through the mid-1970s harmed the images of those minorities. Efforts have been underway for years to eradicate sexism and negative female stereotypes from television and books. The opponents of stereotyping in the mass media generally object to the role models that the mass media, particularly television, inculcate by teaching through example.

The media can inadvertently perpetuate stereotypes regarding childbirth, old age, adolescent behavior, sexuality, war, parenthood, and a number of other topics. Serious news programs can help to erase misunderstandings on topics vulnerable to stereotypical perpetuation, but entertainment in movies, the theatre, and television may inadvertently foster perceptual error. Fortunately, socially conscious network efforts are attempting to eliminate media stereotyping.

Mass Media and Needs Gratification

Another theory of mass media effects holds that the mass media solve needs and stimulate individual motivation to acquire solutions to needs. That is, the mass media content can solve audience needs, and sometimes the attention to the medium itself can be gratifying, as, for example, science fiction or mystery stories that provide escapism and emotional release. In fact, it can be argued that the mass media create a motivation to buy new technology and other consumer products; unfortunately, a person in an economically deprived state senses a level of frustration that may erupt in social dissatisfaction.

The media, according to needs and gratification theory, may satisfy different social and emotional needs at different times in different ways. In fact, the media sometimes share in a division of labor. For instance, a person may want a radio on at work for entertainment, a newspaper for information, and a television for entertainment in the evening. A person who has interpersonal difficulties or problems with self-awareness may turn to various mass media sources (Katz, Blumer, and Gurevitch 1979). One is tempted to wonder, for instance, if some television talk shows and soap operas are not means of vicariously working out one's own problems or perhaps escaping from them. The rise in recent years of a number of magazines dealing with personal insight and self-help also may serve to gratify audience needs. Which media serve which cultures in which ways is a question still under scrutiny.

The media invent and portray cultural characters and types that may eventually influence personality and behavior.

Some evidence suggests that media satisfaction may be connected to a culture's overall satisfaction with its vital information sources (Palmgreen and Rayburn 1985). Ultimately, we may discover that media consumption and satisfaction links with a culture's stress among its members.

Developing skills in understanding media as culture involves a set of cognitive skills. By looking for examples of how media and culture interrelate, you can understand the importance of media in the intercultural climate.

Developing Skills in Understanding Media as Culture

1. *Stay tuned to current events.* Knowledge of current events can assist all of your intercultural communication relationships.

2. *Try to be conscious of ways in which the media may have personally affected your perceptions of some group.* The media can portray positive stereotypes or negative stereotypes. Understanding the source of your personal feelings can be enlightening.

3. *Be aware of the positive value of the media.* The mass media can open us to new ideas, current events, and explanations of certain dynamics that we previously did not know. These positive learning effects can improve our understanding of culture.

4. *Use media as a tool for understanding one view of culture.* Media sources can highlight for us a culture's agenda—things that are considered important for that culture. For example, you might be surprised by how much you can learn about certain American values by browsing through a Sears catalog.

This Chapter in Perspective

This chapter initially focuses on the ways in which the mass media shape national development—and ultimately cultural change. While some scholars argue for the momentous impact of the mass media in precipitating positive changes in a nation (such as higher gross national product and so on), others quietly ponder the harmful effects such rapid introduction of mass media systems make upon the culture at large. Too, observers question the validity of a mass media system that often does not reach the illiterate masses because it favors programming that serves primarily elite, urban populations.

This chapter also focuses on mass media effects on culture. Typically, the mass media serve to make people aware of new information and to reinforce previously held opinions. While a large body of research shows that the media serve as influential initiators of information, another body of literature demonstrates that mass media influence is mediated by a large number of factors, including culture and personal influence. This section also highlights an increasing concern about the mass media as a shaper of culture—an institution and a process that influences culture and yet is also sensitive to culture's reciprocal influence. Finally, this section calls attention to some unintentional, yet pervasive, media effects, as well as to the ways in which the media gratify audience needs.

Exercises

1. Clip a number of newspaper articles dealing with current events. The same day watch the evening news on one of the national networks. How are the same stories treated? What effect do you think the treatment of each story has, in the long run, on your culture?

2. Try to pick out some item of news or some current rumor that is traceable to a mass medium and then ask twenty people or so three questions: (1) From whom or from what source did you first hear this information (that is, the news, rumor, or whatever)? (2) If from a person, was this person a stranger, an acquaintance, a family member, or a close friend? (3) When did you *first* hear or discover the information? You can ask more questions if you want to, but these simple questions can provide abundant information about the comparison of mass media messages to interpersonal sources. How are the two the same? How do they differ?

3. In a newspaper article ("Popular Culture XV: Death of Mass Media?") that appeared May 14, 1978, one in a series of nationwide articles funded by the National Endowment for the Humanities and developed for the University of California Extension University, Alvin Toffler, the author, claimed that regionalism would take the place of the monolithic, centralized mass society. He called this process demassification and predicted that it would result in the death of the mass media as we know them. Do you agree or disagree? Why?

Aronson, Eliot. *The Social Animal.* 3d ed. San Francisco: W. H. Freeman, 1980.

Atwood, L. Erwin, and Keith R. Sanders. "A Longitudinal Analysis of Information Sources, Source Credibility, and Gubernatorial Vote." Paper presented to International Communication Association, Chicago, April 1975.

Barnlund, Dean C. *Interpersonal Communication.* Boston: Houghton Mifflin, 1968.

Caillouet, Larry. "Comparative Media Effectiveness in an Evangelistic Campaign." Dissertation, University of Illinois, Urbana, 1978.

DeFleur, Melvin L., and Sandra Ball-Rokeach. *Theories of Mass Communication.* 3d ed. New York: David McKay, 1976.

Dodd, Carley H. "Early and Late Converts: Bridges to Scientific Missiological Insight." *Mission Strategy Bulletin* 6 (1984): 1–4.

Dodd, Carley H. "Sources of Communication in the Adoption and Rejection of Swine Flu Inoculation among the Elderly." Paper presented to the Southern Speech Communication Association, Biloxi, Mississippi, April 14, 1979.

Farace, Vincent. "Identifying Regional Systems in National Development Research." *Journalism Quarterly* 43 (1966): 753–60.

Farace, Vincent, and Lewis Donohew. "Mass Communication in National Social Systems: A Study of 43 Variables in 115 Countries." *Journalism Quarterly* 42 (1965): 253–61.

Frey, Frederick W. "Communication and Development." In *Handbook of Communication,* edited by Ithiel de Sola Pool. Chicago: Rand McNally, 1973.

Gumpert, Gary, and Robert Cathcart. *Interpersonal Communication in a Media World.* New York: Oxford University Press, 1979.

Harms, L. S. *Intercultural Communication.* New York: Harper and Row, 1973.

Hirsch, Kenneth W. "Diffusion and Consistency of Media Source: The News of Lyndon Baines Johnson and Martin Luther King." Paper presented to the International Communication Association, April 1975.

Jeffres, Leo W. "Factors Affecting the Print Media: Media as Dependent Variables." Paper presented to the International Communication Association, Chicago, April 1975.

Katz, Elihu, Jay Blumer, and Michael Gurevitch. "Utilization of Mass Communication by the Individual." In *Inter/Media,* edited by Gary Gumpert and Robert Cathcart. New York: Oxford University Press, 1979.

Klapper, Joseph. *The Effects of Mass Communication.* New York: Free Press, 1960.

Lerner, Daniel. *The Passing of Traditional Society.* New York: Free Press, 1958.

McLuhan, Marshall. *Understanding Media: The Extensions of Man.* New York: McGraw-Hill, 1966.

McLuhan, Marshall. *The Medium is the Massage.* New York: Bantam, 1967.

Palmgreen, Philip, and J. D. Rayburn. "A Comparison of Gratification Models of Media Satisfaction." *Communication Monographs* 52 (1985): 334–46.

Patterson, Thomas E., and Robert D. McClure. "Political Campaigns: TV Power Is a Myth." *Psychology Today* 10 (1976): 61–64f.

Rogers, Everett M., with Lynne Svenning. *Modernization among Peasants.* New York: Holt, Rinehart and Winston, 1969.

Schramm, Wilbur. *Men, Messages, and Media.* New York: Harper and Row, 1973.

Smith, Ralph, and Wenmouth Williams. *Mass Communication.* Dubuque, Iowa: Kendall/Hunt, 1975.

Part 3

Interpersonal Communication Systems in Cultural Relationships

Chapter 9

Intercultural Communication and Nonverbal Messages

Objectives

After completing this chapter, you should be able to:

1. Describe categories of kinesics.

2. Identify oculesic movement and facial movement as indicators of emotion.

3. Discuss greeting behaviors most often as associated with nonverbal communication and their relation to cultures.

4. Identify kinesic, proxemic, chronemic, and sensoric differences among cultures.

5. Describe particular touching behaviors and their implication for intercultural communication.

6. Identify the role of paralanguage in structuring meaning and interpersonal understanding.

At a health clinic in downtown Los Angeles, a thin, stoop-shouldered, expectant mother made her way through the crowded waiting room to find the one remaining chair. Her obvious nervousness made the sound of her dropping a paper cup of coffee resound more like a cannon than a whoosh—at least to her overanxious ears—as the coffee blackened the tile floor. One of the other patients merely sighed and rolled her eyes, another mumbled something gruff under her breath, while a nurse standing by the counter released a rather loud "umph." Still others showed looks of disgust, amidst a mass of skewed mouths and arched eyebrows. Such scenes illustrate how actions can produce silent messages of approval or disapproval. The meanings we interpret from nonverbal behaviors are culturally conditioned.

The communication milieu of humans is not merely a world of word exchanges but a system of nonverbal messages. Our behavior often speaks louder than our words. And our interpretations of nonverbal cultural differences obviously prevail. Americans who travel in other countries typically feel the discomfort of smaller personal space, smell the contrasting odor of a different culture, experience the disappointment of schedules operating from a different time perspective, and puzzle over the "unusual" body movements and gestures of host nationals. This chapter examines the "language" of nonverbal communication. Nonverbal behaviors turn into unconsciously applied unspoken communication codes that are unconsciously understood by cultural members who share these codes.

Kinesics: Our Body Language

The term kinesics refers to gestures, facial expressions, eye contact, body positions, body movement, and forms of greeting and their relation to communication. Certain kinds of body movements are physiological, such as yawning, stretching, relaxing, and so on. Other kinesic patterns—such as staring, walking slumped over, raising a clenched fist, showing a victory sign, and the like—are personally and culturally conditioned. For instance, when you say "hello," you may use a greeting gesture such as the palm of your hand extended outward with the fingers pointed upward, in the manner of waving, moving the palm from side to side. As they say goodbye, North Americans place the palm of the right hand down, extend the fingers, and move the fingers up and down. In India, West Africa, and Central America, such a gesture would imply beckoning, as if we were calling a cab or asking someone to move toward us. The way we fold our arms, the direction of our body orientation (toward or away from the other person), the direction and manner of our eye contact, and our manner of walking and sitting in the presence of others are significant kinesic behaviors that differ culturally. Other people can quickly decide if we are angry or pleased with them, if they are members of our culture and share our nonverbal code.

In the intercultural setting, kinesic behaviors trigger totally unintended responses. In Indonesia, for instance, it is common to enjoy conversation with a person in his or her house while sitting on the floor. As you sit, however, great care must be taken not to "point" the soles of your shoes or feet toward the other person. Such a behavior is offensive, for the gesture, no matter how innocently intended, indicates that you consider that person beneath you. In certain parts of India, one does not point the toes or the soles of the shoes in the direction of hanging wall pictures of certain deities. This behavior is taboo in that culture. One of the first objectives in intercultural communication is to understand and observe the other culture's kinesics.

Misuse or misunderstanding of kinesic communication behavior has enormous consequences. In a well-known example, during the cold war days between the United States and Russia, Nikita Khrushchev visited the United States, and as he emerged from the airplane, officials, news reporters, and other visitors greeted him cordially. In response, Khrushchev clasped his hands together and raised them above his shoulder. To television viewers and U.S. observers, the gesture appeared like a boxer raising clasped hands signaling victory. However, Khrushchev intended the gesture to represent a clasping of hands in friendship. Or, consider the sometimes deleterious effects of unguarded kinesic behavior illustrated in the following example:

Several years ago, a popular American politician took a trip to Latin America. Upon his arrival at the airport, he emerged from the airplane, stood at the top of the loading ramp, and waved to the people awaiting his arrival. Someone shouted out, asking him how his trip was. He responded by flashing the common "OK" gesture. Shortly thereafter, he left the airplane and engaged in a short visit with a local political leader. Following that visit, he went to the major university in the area and delivered an address on behalf of the American people. During his talk, he emphasized that the United States was most interested in helping this neighboring country through economic aid that would help develop the economy and relieve the difficult economic surroundings of the poor. His speech, in fact his entire visit, was a disaster.

Why? Everything this gentleman did verbally was quite acceptable. But nearly everything he did nonverbally was wrong. To begin with, a photographer took a picture of our visitor just as he flashed the "OK" sign to the person who asked how his trip went. That picture appeared on the front page of the local newspaper. You may wonder, "What is so bad about that?" The gesture, which we use in the United States to signal "OK," is a most obscene gesture in this particular Latin American country.

After this "excellent start," our representative went to the university to give his speech, apparently unaware of the fact that this university had recently been a scene of violent protest against that government's policies. His choice of that place to speak was interpreted by the government as showing sympathy for the rioting students, but perceived by the students as an invasion of their territory by a friend of the government. Further, while our representative was presenting an excellent speech in English, concerning our interest in helping the poor people of that country, the speech was being translated for the audience by an interpreter in full military uniform. The interpreter was a clear symbol of the military dictatorship that was in control of the country at that time.

It is certainly not surprising that the intended goodwill visit of our representative had a contrary effect. This is an excellent example of what can happen when people are unaware of, or unconcerned with, their nonverbal behavior. (McCroskey 1972)*

Before we discuss other kinesic behaviors, let us turn for a moment to an overview of kinesic research. Some researchers classify kinesic research into three categories: prekinesics, microkinesics, and social kinesics. *Prekinesics* is concerned with the physiological aspects of bodily movements. Prekinesic research focuses on describing all bodily movements, regardless of their cultural meaning. This process of classification utilizes an elaborate taxonomy to accomplish this goal. (The fundamental unit of pure kinesic behavior, without any implication of attached meaning, is the kine.) In a sense, the value of prekinesic research is the same as any "pure" scientific investigation where the scientist examines something without specific regard to its application. Of course, some scientific discoveries were built on the foundations from pure research. Similarly, the immediate application of prekinesic findings may be reserved until later discoveries.

Microkinesics is concerned with the attribution of meaning to bodily motions, both intraculturally and interculturally. For instance, although prekinesic research indicates eleven discernible positions of the eyelid, microkinesic findings reveal that only a very few of these positions communicate distinct meanings for North Americans. The study of prekinesics sorts and classifies individual kines, while microkinesics sorts and classifies individual kinemes— bodily motions that represent different meanings.

A third area of kinesic research is that of *social kinesics,* which concerns the social role and meaning that different bodily movements convey. Consequently, this area usually includes comparing kinesics between two cultures. For example, LaBarre (1976) noted that spitting in most Western cultures is a sign of disgust and displeasure, but for the Masai people of Africa spitting is a sign of affection. Among the American Indians, spitting can represent an act of kindness; for example, the medicine man spitting on a sick person to cure him.

Most often, intercultural communication interests center on microkinesics and social kinesics. In those areas, codes and meanings for communication take on their greatest significance.

Gestures

Gestures, or hand and arm movements, fall into several categories. As we discuss these various aspects of gestures, determine which ones you frequently use and how you use them. In the process, you may learn a lot about how gestures interact in intercultural communication.

Adaptors. Some of our gesturing behavior occurs primarily out of a physical bodily activity we must perform at the moment. For example, holding our hand over our mouth as we cough or sneeze is a North American cultural

*Used by permission of the publisher.

Non-verbal behavior
stems from social
roles and from
personal feelings.

response to that bodily need. Shading our eyes with our hand in bright sunlight also represents an adapting type of gesture. Our hand and arm movements in opening a door also represent gestures that of necessity involve a set of arm and hand movements. In some ways, even these movements, which are physiological responses or that are skill oriented, have a trace of cultural influence: some African cultures do not cover the mouth when coughing, for instance.

Emblems. Nonverbal emblems are gestures that have a relatively precise, clear referent and thus are culturally assigned some meaning. For instance, holding your index and middle fingers upward in a "V" represented the victory emblem during World War II. During the peace movement in the United States during the 1960s, the "V" sign became culturally accepted as a peace symbol. During the 1976 Olympics, the black civil rights movement utilized the raised fist as an emblematic symbol of black power and thereby increased self-awareness of black culture.

Illustrators. Illustrative gestures serve to augment verbal meanings, to substitute occasionally for words or phrases, and to provide emphasis (Ekman and Friesen 1972). For instance, in pointing when we give directions to someone, we are illustrating the verbal message with a gesture, using perhaps the index finger to emphasize the direction. Sometimes, a person's hand slashes through the air to accent some word or phrase. A speaker who uses the hands to "draw" a picture in the air also applies an illustrator. For the moment, let us turn to some illustrative gestures utilized by Americans (Ekman and Friesen 1972):

1. *Batons.* Illustrators that emphasize or accent a word or phrase (example: bringing hand down on a key word)

2. *Directors.* Illustrators that point (example: pointing with a finger)

3. *Ideographs.* Illustrators that sketch a direction of thought (example: a speaker says, "I want to pursue this line of thought," and offers a sweeping arm gesture or raises a finger for a first point, second point, and so on)

4. *Kineographs.* Illustrators that depict bodily action (example: moving both arms as if you were jogging, thus depicting the idea of running as you converse)

5. *Pictograph.* Illustrators that "draw" a literal picture in the air (example: using your fingers, hands, and arms to illustrate the shape of a football)

6. *Rhythmic.* Illustrators that depict pacing a rhythm (example: snapping your fingers to coincide with a musical beat)

7. *Spatial.* Illustrators that depict spatial relationships (example: a speaker says, "Imagine three groups of people," and then gestures to the left for group one, the middle for group two, and the right for group three, as if to help the listener to spatially define three distinct groups)

Gestures become especially revealing in ongoing conversation (Wolff and Gustein 1972). For instance, illustrators tend to increase with a speaker's increasing enthusiasm, and they also increase if it seems the listener does not understand. How many times have you observed people talking with a foreign national resorting to using illustrators when language barriers appear?

Also, some studies show that, among North Americans, gestures reveal discrepancies in a speaker's words. When someone is lying, the hands and feet sometimes "leak" a message that tells us that something may be concealed. That mismatch between words and action also is evident in eye movement and facial expression (Ekman and Friesen 1972).

Kinesics add a significant "message" to our verbal communication.

Posture

Like gestures, posture is a significant aspect of kinesic behavior. Although many people can describe posture when asked, it is not by any means universal, since posture differs with culture, personality, religion, occupation, social class, gender, age, health, and status (Sheflen 1964). Despite these differences, we can examine three basic behaviors in posture: (1) inclusive postures, (2) interpersonal postures, and (3) reflective postures.

Inclusive postures involve using the body to block off or separate groups or individuals. One subtype is the "bookend" gesture, in which group members form a circle, or extend their legs or arms, to close off their group from outsiders. For example, while someone may extend his or her legs "simply to stretch," that person often will extend the legs in such a way that they form a barrier to any people outside the group. Another subtype of inclusiveness is intervention, in which someone intervenes between individuals who are disputing or being distractive. The third subtype is "spacing in," in which the individual becomes inclusive within the group and thus uses this posture to exclude outsiders while simultaneously enhancing a feeling of inclusion within the group.

Interpersonal postures involve seating arrangements where two people sit face to face. If two people sit side by side to view a common object, their interpersonal posture is parallel and focused away from the other person. Sometimes, a person can be both interpersonal and parallel by splitting the body in half (the upper torso turned parallel, the lower torso turned interpersonal) and in this way include more members in a group.

Reflective postures involve repetition of one's posture by another. For example, often when two people sit across from one another in a group, one person will begin to reflect the posture of the person opposite. Also, when one person in a group shifts postures, others often follow this shift.

Body movement can also be used to detect the beginning and end of discussions or statements. According to Knapp, Hart, Friedrich, and Shulmen (1973), group members give the following clues when they want to change topics or want to speak:

1. Leaning forward 40 degrees

2. Breaking eye contact

3. Smiling

4. Major nodding movements

5. Change of posture (trunk and/or legs)

6. Foot contact with the floor

These cues can effectively and subtly alter communication. Consider the person who stands with arms crossed, looks constantly at a clock, taps the foot repeatedly, and breaks eye contact frequently. These signals usually mean "It is time to go."

Another aspect of kinesics that affects intercultural communication is oculesics, or eye behavior, which may account for a good deal of our meanings in communication. According to Ellsworth and Ludwig (1972), eye contact varies with personality and sex but can greatly influence credibility. They reported that dominant and socially poised individuals seem to have more eye contact than do submissive, "socially anxious" persons. They also noted that, when people feel included in a social situation, they tend to have more eye contact. The study also indicated that females use more eye contact overall than do males. Finally, Ellsworth and Ludwig revealed that a speaker who uses more eye contact seems more informal, more relaxed, and yet more authoritative. In other words, credibility increases with the use of eye contact, at least in the United States (Beebe 1974).

Cultural differences in oculesics indicate why intercultural communication is sometimes ineffective. If a white teacher reprimands a young black male, for instance, and the student responds by maintaining a downward glance, rather than looking directly at the teacher, this behavior may anger the teacher (Yousef 1976). Members of certain segments of black culture reportedly cast their eyes downward as a sign of respect; in white culture, however, members expect direct eye contact as a sign of listening and showing respect for authority. Navaho Indians ascribe personal eye contact as a harsh way of indicating disapproval; thus, one does not meet the eyes.

Johnson (1976) observed that, among blacks, eye rolling expresses impudence and disapproval of a person in authority. Usually, the process begins by staring at the other person (though not an eye-to-eye stare) and moving the eyes quickly away from the other person. The eyelids are slightly lowered as the eyes move in a low arc. Furthermore, eye rolling occurs more frequently

Breaking eye contact in American is often perceived as distrust, boredom, or preoccupation.

among black females than males. Perhaps this oculesic behavior may explain the common black phrase, "Don't look at me in that tone of voice."

Other eye movements also hold culturally distinct meanings. For example, eye winking among North Americans means, "I'm teasing about this," or under some conditions connotes flirting, especially with the opposite sex. When Nigerians wink at their children, this eye behavior signals the child to leave the room. A "friendly" wink may be perceived as an insult in India (Smutkupt and Barna 1976).

Like other kinesic signals, oculesic behaviors are culturally dependent for their meaning. To illustrate, consider the various meanings of a widening of the eyes (Condon 1976):

Significance	Intention	Culture
Really!	Surprise, wonder	Dominant Anglo
I resent this	Anger	Chinese
I don't believe you	Challenge	French
I don't understand	Call for help	Hispanic
I'm innocent	Persuasion	Black American

Obviously, we can easily mistake a Hispanic child's plea for assistance, for example, as some other emotion, unless we understand cultural kinesics.

Cultures have unique greeting kinemes that are rich in diversity. The American handshake, or the hug and a pat for more intimate acquaintances, find parallels in various other cultural systems.* Several examples from LaBarre (1976) illustrate the diversity of greeting kinemes. For instance, Polynesian men greet by rubbing one another's back while embracing. An Ainu man, greeting his sister, "grasped her hands in his for a few seconds, suddenly released his hold, grasped her by both ears and gave the peculiar Ainu greeting cry; then they stroked one another down the face and shoulders" (LaBarre 1976, 221). In Matavai, a formal greeting after a long separation involves abrasively scratching the head and temples of the other person with a shark's tooth, to the point of bleeding.

Handshaking represents a common greeting in North America, although shaking hands is inappropriate as a greeting in some cultures. Many Asians bow the head slightly and put the hands in front of the chest to show respect. Vietnamese men, for instance, do not shake hands with women or with older people, unless the old people or women offer their hands first. Also, two Vietnamese women do not shake hands.

The practice of waving to someone as a greeting is as insulting as slapping someone on the back to signify friendship, at least to the Vietnamese. In the first place, waving motions are used by adults to call little children, but little children do not call adults in this fashion. Similarly, backslapping is considered rude and especially insulting to women.

One must also consider the relationship of the person one greets. In many parts of Asia, for example, bowing occurs at more precipitous levels, depending on the relationship and the status of the other person—in general, the more status, the lower the bow. The same type of principle holds true for the order of greeting. In North America, we greet persons in a group by convenience and proximity to each person. However, in many parts of Africa and Asia, one must greet the head of a family or older persons first, then the younger ones (Hong 1976).

Clearly, greeting kinemes involve intricate behaviors, for misusing them creates a negative intercultural first impression that may be difficult to erase. Perhaps these examples will remind you to observe, ask, and even experiment to learn this important element of kinesics—the nonverbal greeting.

The human face comes in many shapes and sizes. And sometimes, we make judgments about other people based on facial features. However, we also infer what people "really" mean by their facial expressions. Mehrabian (1981) claimed that 55 percent of our meanings are inferred from facial expression. Studies have indicated that we can detect emotions from facial expression.

*Among peoples of the United States, intricate patterns of greeting and leaving have developed, some of which are described in the late Eric Berne's works *Games People Play* and *What Do You Say After Hello*. Similar rhetorical modes are developed by Knapp, Hart, Friedrich, and Shulmen (1973).

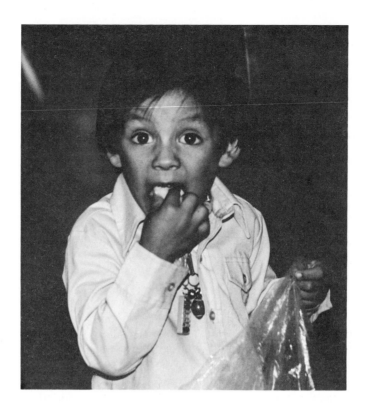

Through facial expressions, we convey our emotions, such as happiness and surprise.

The following emotions are somewhat universally conveyed by facial expressions, according to St. Martin (1976):

1. *Sadness*. With the corners of the mouth turned down, triangulation of the skin below the eyebrows, a "tightening" around the eyes, and the eyelids drooping, we have a representation of nonverbal facial behaviors referring to sadness. Research shows that white Americans and Latin Americans tend to feel similarly about "sadness," as they identified this emotion in videotape portrayals. Anecdotal sources indicate that some Asian people, such as the Japanese, hide sadness by wearing a smile; however, a wrinkled forehead and other nonverbal features may "leak" the actual emotion.

2. *Happiness*. When the corners of the mouth are up, the cheeks raised, the eyelids raised, and the eyes bright, the emotion is identified as happiness. In a comparison of white Americans, black Americans, Latin Americans, and Malaysians, St. Martin (1976) reported that all four groups perceive and identify this emotion similarly.

3. *Disgust*. Knapp (1980) described the emotion of disgust as involving a raised upper lip, wrinkled nose, raised cheeks, lines showing below the lower eyelid, and a lowering of the eyebrow. The display of this emotion is similar in a number of cultures.

The emotions that follow have a lot of diversity in their interpretation because of cultural differences:

1. *Anger.* Anger is revealed by drawing the lines of the eyebrow together, thinning and tensing the lips, and staring with the eyes. This emotion probably has the greatest amount of masking associated with it. It seems that anger is one emotion that can "fool" us culturally since not all cultures see anger alike.

2. *Surprise.* Surprise may be expressed by a raised eyebrow, the mouth opened either a little or a lot, and the eyes widened, among other things.

3. *Fear.* As Knapp (1980) indicated, fear is shown by the eyebrows raised and drawn together, the mouth opened slightly with the lips tensed, and the eyes opened widely. White Americans, Latin Americans, and Malaysians perceive this emotion similarly. Black Americans apparently differ highly from these other cultures in interpreting this emotion.

This discussion of facial expression reinforces something we already know—all cultures do not reveal or perceive emotions exactly alike. Perhaps this discussion sharpened your understanding, however, of several cultures that at least tend to perceive and identify emotions similarly. Many emotions are neurophysiological—for example, fear—and thus are universally and biologically shared. However, people learn "display rules" from their culture and learn how to manage emotions and display them in culturally appropriate ways (Boucher 1974). Display rule differences are a source of misinterpretation in intercultural communication.

Proxemics

Proxemics refers to the study of spatial relations. The study of proxemics includes not only fixed features of space (such as architecture and spacing of buildings), but semifixed features (such as seating arrangements and furniture arrangements) and dynamic space (use of personal space).

Fixed Features of Space

Visitors from parts of the southwestern United States, who are used to "wide open spaces," seem amazed at the "closeness" of residences in the Northeast. In the southwestern and western United States, for instance, a person can drive on a highway for miles and never see a sign of people or dwellings, a rare occurrence in more populated sections of the United States. North Americans from the United States visiting a foreign country sometimes express surprise about the proximity of individual dwellings and the "narrow" roads. There is probably some truth to the observation that Americans use more space than nationals of many other countries. Intercultural communicators need to realize that cultures have alternative approaches to space and ways of using it.

The shapes of our buildings affect individuals. An elaborately structured building may, in a sense, communicate modernity because of its architectural uniqueness. Other buildings may give a perception of power and strength. Obviously, values, economic factors, and even religion play roles in determining architecture, but a culture's values (or the architect's values) determine the use of space.

The size of rooms is also a subject of psychological impact. A large office in the United States communicates status and perhaps power. The smaller the office, the less status appears connected with the office occupant. In an office complex, office staff who share space are perceived to have less status, higher-status employees have their own corner or partitioned area, and the highest employees enjoy the most private, largest, "plushest" offices. This arrangement of status by space is expected in North America, but different cultures utilize and perceive room size differently. In some countries, high government officials may share an office with six or eight lesser employees in a fifteen-by-twenty-foot room. Within the United States, however, status differences among employees is often communicated by the structuring and use of the space provided for offices. This unspoken language of space is so strong that employment problems may arise when one person gets a larger office than someone else. For instance, in one large manufacturing firm in the United States, two corporate officers, on an equal level in the organization, received new offices. However, one office was six inches wider than the other, a fact that created a perception among office workers that management had sent a signal—the fellow with the larger office was being promoted. Although this message was inadvertently conveyed, this person actually was being chosen for a promotion; the space assignment told it all, even before any formal announcement.

The origin of fixed, semifixed, and personal features of space began with cultural needs over territoriality. That concern sometimes translates into geographical and political boundary questions between cultures and also converts to the ways cultures use buildings and fixed features of space in "screening behavior." Screening refers to our permanent and semipermanent use of our territory. For example, a fence marks a territory in much the same way we use hedges or survey posts. The message in these cases is clear, revealing private ownership and covertly saying, "Respect this boundary—this is mine."

Screening behavior is evident among Germans, who value privacy. In that culture, a closed door in an office, for instance, represents expected behavior. In North America, a closed door can indicate that the person behind the door is hiding something. A manager often attempts to maintain an aura of openness by leaving the door open. When an employee enters the office and closes the door, other employees receive a message that something is "secretive," depending upon how long the conference lasts, the facial expressions after the conference, and so on.

Semifixed Features of Space

Semifixed features of space refer to spatial arrangements of movable objects within a room, such as furniture, accessories, screens, file cabinets, and so on. In the United States, a small, cluttered desk implies low status; a larger desk usually indicates higher status. However, the position of the desk and the arrangement of the chairs in a business office are of communicative importance as well. If the chairs in an office are directly in front of the occupant's desk and if the occupant does not come from behind the desk, a nonverbal tone of impersonal behavior may be perceived. As we might expect, again, the use of space and material objects is culture-bound.

Semifixed features of space can be arranged to encourage face-to-face participation, called *sociopetal* arrangement. Living areas in personal dwellings in North America and meeting rooms of various sorts normally encourage interpersonal communication because of the furniture arrangement. *Sociofugal* arrangements tend to diffuse communication since the arrangements lead conversation away from interpersonal relations to impersonal relations.* Many lecture arrangements, waiting rooms, and libraries are sociofugal.

Semifixed features of space, of course, differ interculturally. For example, in the evenings, Syrian men converse sitting across a room from each other, with the furniture arranged to facilitate this pattern. Certain cultural groups, like the Chinese, seem to prefer furniture located in side-by-side seating arrangements for personal communication, rather than sitting with direct eye contact. The following example vividly illustrates the semifixed features of proxemics and the importance of this feature of nonverbal communication:

> In 1968, the majority of the American people were very concerned with getting peace talks started in Paris to seek a solution to the Vietnam war, but it seemed that it would take forever before the talks could begin. The problem centered around the seating of the various delegations for the peace conference and the shape of the table. The United States and South Vietnam each wanted two sides at the table; North Vietnam and the Viet Cong each wanted four sides. Four sides would put the Viet Cong on an equal status with the other three parties in the talks, something the North Vietnamese and Viet Cong insisted on, but that the United States and the South Vietnamese were unwilling to accept. After eight months and literally thousands of deaths and injuries on both sides, a compromise was reached whereby the North Vietnamese and the Viet Cong could interpret the table settled upon as four-sided while the United States and South Vietnam could interpret it as two-sided. Almost anyone not directly involved in those negotiations would agree that the behavior of these parties was absurd. Nevertheless, this extreme sensitivity to the nonverbal communication of the shape of the table resulted in months of delay and thousands of deaths. The importance of nonverbal communication in this setting could hardly be overestimated. (Note: The table selected was round.) (McCroskey 1972)†

At its root, spatial usage stems from a deep-seated concern over territoriality. For many years, scientists have explored how people feel about not only their cultural or national territory but also their personal territory, including personal space. Let us now discuss this aspect of proxemics.

Personal Space

Use of space often focuses upon dynamic space. Personal space refers to an individual's unconsciously structuring the microspace immediately surrounding the physical body. This space is not only culturally determined but

*E. T. Hall (1973) highlighted the terms *sociopetal* and *sociofugal*.
†Used by permission of the publisher.

Interpersonal space stems from a sense of cultural territoriality and expectations derived from cultural norms.

results from varying relationships. That is, among North Americans, friends usually stand closer than strangers. Furthermore, Hall (1973) observed that space communicates and thus affects our intercultural relationships:

> The flow and shift of distance between people as they interact with each other is part and parcel of the communication process. The normal conversational distance between strangers illustrates how important are the dynamics of space interaction. If a person gets too close, the reaction is instantaneous and automatic—the other person backs up. And if he gets too close again, back we go again. I have observed an American backing up the entire length of a long corridor while a foreigner whom he considers pushy tries to catch up with him. This scene has been enacted thousands and thousands of times—one person trying to increase the distance in order to be at ease, while the other tries to decrease it for the same reason; neither one being aware of what was going on. (p. 180)

In Middle Eastern countries, being close enough to breathe on another person is proper. In fact, the breath is like one's spirit and life itself, so sharing your breath in close conversation is like sharing your spirit (Yousef and Briggs 1975). That many cultures stand closely in conversation explains why some U.S. government officials, field workers, and visitors return from the Middle East, southern Europe, or Latin America and say things like, "It's all right if you don't mind garlic breath in your face," or "It's fine once you get used to having your eyeglasses fogged up in conversation." Their complaints center around the close interpersonal distances normally maintained in these cultures.

Research on personal space reveals several patterns of interpersonal distance. For example, Rosegrant and McCroskey (1975) analyzed American black and white contacts and found that (1) males established greater interpersonal distance from males than they did from females, than females did from males, or than females did from females; (2) whites established greater interpersonal distance from blacks than they did from whites or than blacks did from whites; and (3) female blacks established closer distances than female whites or either black or white males. Whitsett (1974) also examined spatial distances between blacks and whites under controlled conditions. The subjects in his experiment were asked to interact first with a stimulus person of their own race and then with a stimulus person of the opposite race. The stimulus person (one black and then, for the other condition, one white) were instructed by the experimenter to maintain a constant position. A one-way mirror enabled the experimenter to observe and record measures of dynamic space. His results showed that whites stood closest to the white stimulus person and blacks stood closest to the black stimulus person. Also, the blacks felt more comfortable in moving around, even changing their body orientation dramatically in conversing with other blacks, but not with whites. The subjects later explained that they "did not trust the whites" and thus felt uncomfortable in any personal space but head-on, face-to-face.

The reason for these phenomena relates to a smaller sense of territoriality—something like our personal body space, a kind of body "bubble." Although the idea of personal space has no particularly startling value, for it may seem commonplace knowledge, it has enormous consequences. Applbaum (1973) reminds us that, when others enter our personal bubble, we react with nervousness, discomfort, defensiveness, and uncooperativeness. At the same time, we use body space to convey personal attitudes toward those whom we address. In general, we establish shorter distances with people with whom we seek approval (Rosenfeld 1965) and maintain greater communication distances from those about whom we feel negatively (Mehrabian 1969).

Personal space is culturally related. For example, North Americans tend to prefer greater distances between themselves and others than do Latin Americans, Arabs, and Greeks (Hall 1973). As we have already indicated, when these proxemic expectations are violated, embarrassment or even hostility can result. Comparing intraethnic proxemic stability with interethnic stability, Erickson (1975) concluded that, at least among the blacks and Polish Americans whom he studied, the intracultural communication produced far more proxemic stability (black with black, Polish American with Polish American) than in interethnic communication (black with Polish American). It seems, therefore, that a comfort level exists intraculturally that lends itself to stability. So, when two persons with different ethnicity interact, they experience discomfort because they do not know the proxemic rules of the other person's subculture.

Sometimes, our problems in intercultural communication occur when one person's social zone is another person's personal or intimate zone.

Perhaps we can better understand why intercultural proxemic differences produce discomfort by discussing four zones of personal space. The *intimate* zone encompasses touching and a distance of up to eighteen inches and, for North Americans, is a zone reserved only for very close, intimate relationships and touching. The *personal* zone ranges from 1½ to 4½ feet and is used for confidentiality. The *social* zone is the normal conversational space for North Americans and includes space from four to twelve feet or so. The *public* zone is used for talking across a room and for public speaking and includes distances of twelve feet and larger.

Our difficulty in intercultural communication comes from conversing in unexpected and different zones. For instance, North Americans usually converse in the personal and social zones. Many Middle Eastern and Latin American individuals, however, converse in the intimate and personal zones. As a result, North Americans are perceived as "distant and cold," and these other cultures are perceived as "pushy."

We can express these unexpected spatial violations in terms of a model of interaction between personal space zones, as indicated in figure 9.1. As this model indicates, when a culture A person expects to communicate within the social zone, then appropriate distance and action is initiated. In response, that person expects social distance to be reciprocated. However, if a culture B person expects to communicate within, say, an intimate zone, then this second person in actual response moves closer to establish what he or she now considers the proper distance for communication. Now, the culture B person expects A to reciprocate, an action, of course, that does not occur. Instead A moves back, B moves forward, and so on. In terms of this model, the principle is simple: Interaction between parallel personal space zones is comfortable, but interaction between unparallel personal space zones is uncomfortable.

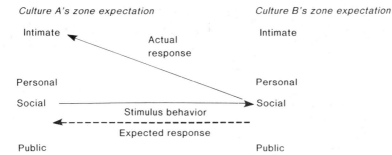

Culture A's zone expectation

Intimate

Actual response

Personal

Social —————————————→ Social
Stimulus behavior

←- -
Expected response

Public

Culture B's zone expectation

Intimate

Personal

Public

Figure 9.1
Model of interaction
between parallel and
unparallel personal
space zones.

Our understanding of and use of time falls under a class of nonverbal communication called chronemics and is influenced by culture and by chronological age. Time is a potent force, communicating as powerfully as verbal language. In North America, for instance, lateness for a business appointment communicates lack of interest. A recent news report indicated that certain U.S. workers can be docked half a day's wages for being as little as one minute late, according to one labor contract.

In intercultural communication encounters, ours and the other person's concepts of time may influence our communication behavior. It is not unusual for village meetings in Africa to begin when "everyone gets ready." A forty-five minute wait may not be unusual for a business appointment in Latin America, even though such a period seems insulting to a North American. The ensuing conversation between the Latin American and the United States businessperson is likely to be evaluated by a misunderstanding of the two cultural clocks.

In other research focusing on analysis of differential time conceptions, Horton (1976) noted that street time among blacks is mediated by culture, emotion, feeling, and situation. Cultural time differences are recognized by some blacks, who at one time used the term *CPT* (colored people's time) in reference to the different time conceptions between blacks and whites. In other words, culture affects our time perceptions. In some cases, researchers point to language as the cause of contrasting time conceptions, as in the case of the Sioux Indians, whose language lacks words dealing with time, such as *late* or *waiting* (Porter 1972). In other cases, differences may be a function of world view, economic motivation, outside contact with other cultures, need for achievement, or other factors.

Other researchers have focused on time conceptions among children. Studies in developmental dimensions of time concepts among children show that time sense is related to maturity. Time concepts appear around four years of age and seem to mature around thirteen. Apparently, children develop a clearer understanding of the past from the present around the ages of seven or eight (McAulay 1961). Some evidence suggests that time conceptions may be related to class and subculture. In comparing middle-class children with

**Chronemics:
Our Use of
Time**

children of a lower social class, Leshan (1952) found differences in their conception of future time. Subjects from less affluent surroundings appeared more responsive to immediate gratification than to promises of future reward. Also, Dodd and Payne (1976) found significant differences in concepts of past, present, and future time between five-year-old black and white children. In this study, the black children did not identify future events (such as placing the order of holidays in proper time sequence) or historical past events as well as white children, but the blacks scored significantly better than whites on past events that were personal.

North Americans tend to think of time as a road or long ribbon stretched out in a progressive linear path, having a beginning and an end. They also believe that this road has compartments, or segments, that should be kept discrete from one another. This compartmentalization of time is so distinct that the term *monochronic time* applies to many North Americans, a concept meaning that cultural members prefer doing one thing at a time. By contrast, many other cultures prefer operating with several people, ideas, or projects simultaneously, illustrating the concept of *polychronic time*. Observers sometimes condition us to mark Latin American differences with North Americans in terms of these categories, with the Latin Americans falling into the polychronic time category. Other observations lead us to believe that monochronic or polychronic time is not only cultural, but based on training, occupation, personality, and right or left brain orientation (see also chapter 5).

Time can also be viewed in terms of cultural synchrony (Hall 1966). Cultural synchrony means the rhythms, movement, and timing of a culture. For instance, when walking on the streets of New York, we have to move in a faster-paced manner than we would in a rural town in Montana. East Africans move with a methodology quite apart from Germans. The rhythms themselves have a time dimension to them. Part of effective intercultural communication involves getting "in sync" with those timed rhythms.

In general, North Americans feel that time is a commodity, something to be used, bought, wasted, saved, spent, and in other ways manipulated. By contrast, many cultures, including African, Latin American, and Southeast Asian cultures, view time more flexibly. A number of Southeast Asian cultures view time cyclically rather than linearly, a contrast that may explain the North Vietnamese attitude during the United States conflict in Vietnam of, "We will wear you down." The Americans were used to a "quick" end to war because of their history and their attitudes toward time, but the "enemy" was accustomed to waiting scores of years, even centuries, for desired results.

One reason for these differing views of time is the difference that cultures maintain concerning *types* of times (Hall 1973). *Informal* time refers to loose calculations of time, such as "after a while," "later," "some time ago," and so on. *Formal* time refers to exact points in time, such as "by 2:00 today," and "yesterday at 5:00"; in other words, more of a clock time. *Scientific* time refers to ultraprecise designations of time, such as laboratory timing of experiments and so forth. One of the most frequent intercultural communication breakdowns occurs when one cultural member operates on formal time and a member of a different culture operates from an informal time orientation. So, the one person shows up for a meeting at 2:00 P.M., and the other person arrives sometime in the afternoon, whenever circumstances allow, if at all. Our understanding of these different perceptual expectations can reduce enormously our stress level in intercultural communication.

Sensorics: Sensory Perception in Intercultural Communication

Sensorics indicate the communicative and perceptual functions of the human senses. Our senses can be considered instruments of functional nonverbal communication. For example, some people are often "turned off" to another culture because of the *smell* of foreign situations; one cultural group thinks the other has a somewhat obnoxious odor. Highlanders of New Guinea saturate their bodies with mud and pig grease and hardly ever bathe. Compare that situation with a Ghanaian, who typically bathes once or twice a day, and imagine the intercultural barriers between these two engendered by the one variable, smell. Scholars such as E. T. Hall increasingly consider the olfactory sense a highly significant feature of cultural transactions.

The sense of *taste* differs culturally, as any international traveler knows. *Color* and *texture* preferences are likewise visual features that are culturally appreciated. (Perhaps some of the initial conflicts during the 1960s "generation gap" arose because of the color schemes in the clothing of a subculture.) *Auditory* preferences are also culturally influenced. Consider, for instance, widely divergent musical preferences in various countries. The notion of *thermal* sensory communication, in which we perceive others' body heat, may also be considered sensory perception. Some people actually seem to radiate more heat than others, and Hall (1966) has suggested that this factor may account for our descriptions of others as "warm" or "cold" personalities.

Obviously, our sensoric perceptions work together, interacting with the cultural context, to shape a total view of a culture and our intercultural contacts. One way to describe our intercultural reactions comes from the following formula:

$$\text{Degree of sensory difference} = \frac{\text{Importance} \times \text{Number of disliked sensory experiences}}{\text{Importance} \times \text{Number of liked sensory experiences}}$$

This formula illustrates that, if our "disliked" sensory experiences outweigh the "liked" ones, then the ratio of our feelings, weighted and added according to their importance, is high. The resulting ratio is the sense ratio difference. The higher the number, the greater the degree of sense ratio differences.

All of these contrasting differences bombard the senses simultaneously and account for some of the reasons why people experience culture shock. Overcoming sensoric nonverbal differences is an important part of intercultural adjustment.

Haptics: Our Use of Touch

Intercultural communication also involves cultural touching and its effects. Let us examine the nature and importance of our use of touch, called haptics.

| Factors Related to Haptics | A number of factors have been linked with haptic behavior. Some of these are outlined in the sections that follow. |

Haptics and communication apprehension. Research studies have linked a person's apprehension about communicating in a number of different settings, such as public speaking and interpersonal and small group settings, with touch avoidance. The more a person demonstrates communication apprehension, the more likely that that person will avoid touching, since communication apprehensives avoid some kinds of communication.

Touch and verbal expression. The connection between verbal and tactile expression is not too surprising, especially in light of Montagu's (1971) report that mothers' vocal intonation and dynamism correlate with the frequency of touching their babies. Other studies indicate that touching actually increases verbal interaction under conditions where nurses touched patients more than they touched patients in a control group. Touch has even been positively linked with a therapeutic relationship, such that touch may increase verbal interaction among some people.

Haptics and self-disclosure. Basically, research studies agree that the more a person engages in self-disclosure, the more likely that person is to touch. While touching clearly depends upon the sex of the other person in whom one is confiding, a moderate correlation may exist, so that as self-disclosure increases, touch also may increase.

Haptics and sex. Observations of touching during communication show that males avoid touching other males, but females express themselves in touching other females during conversation. It can also be demonstrated that females tend to avoid touching males, more than males avoid touching females. If there is a link between haptic behavior and the sex of the communicators, its roots lie in cultural roles. Males are inhibited from touching other males because of cultural taboos against homosexuality, though females are allowed flexibility in touching other females. However, cultural roles restrict females touching of males, though males are often permitted greater flexibility in male-female communication.

| Intercultural Differences in Haptics | A body of observations suggests that some cultures are highly touch oriented, while others are nontouching cultures. For example, Arab, Jewish, Eastern European, and Mediterranean cultures have been characterized as touching cultures, while Germans, English, and other white Anglo-Saxons are characterized as infrequent touchers (Mehrabian 1981; Sheflen 1972; and Montagu 1971). However, these observations should be coupled with other findings. For instance, one empirical study compared German, Italian, and North American tactile displays in an extensive field survey utilizing trained observations in natural settings (Shuter 1977). Shuter's findings partially deny national stereotypes in that generalizations about contact and noncontact cultures partly depend on several factors, such as the sex of the interactants. For instance, males interacted farther apart and touched less in both Germany and the United States than in Italy. But Italian males stood closer and touched |

Touch is a fundamental, universal need by which we communicate many of our interpersonal feelings and attitudes.

significantly more than Italian females. It also appears that Italian males interact nonverbally in ways considered appropriate for German and American women. However, Shuter found that German females were more tactile than Italian women and that U.S. women showed as much tactility as Italian women.

When we find ourselves in a contrasting culture, we should initially observe, ask, and probe—and avoid operating on stereotypical information only. It is imperative that we become observers of nonverbal behaviors in a host country to avoid the barriers that only nonverbal behaviors can erect. Obviously, a toucher in a nontouching culture can be just as uncomfortable as a nontoucher in a touching culture. Keep in mind that the dimension of touching is determined by a number of factors.

Paralinguistics: How We Say Things

Paralanguage is that set of audible sounds that accompany oral language to augment its meaning. In other words, speech carries symbolic cues, not only through verbal and nonverbal cues, but also through vocal qualities to which various linguistic systems ascribe meaning. In a now classic experiment, Mehrabian (1981) reported that, under a situation of induced disagreement, where Americans communicated feelings, words accounted for 7 percent of the messages, paralanguage for 38 percent, and facial expressions for 55 percent of the total feelings communicated.

The following examples may clarify the importance of paralinguistic cues in intercultural communication (Taylor 1976, 36):

1. I'll see you tomorrow. (declarative statement of fact)

2. I'll see you tomorrow? (question)

3. I'll see you tomorrow! (excitement)

4. *I'll* see you tomorrow; I'll *see* you tomorrow; I'll see *you* tomorrow; I'll see you *tomorrow*. (contrast)

In this statement, the words alone do not carry the meaning. Rather, we interpret the feelings and emotions of the speaker by perceiving the variations of vocal quality. Furthermore, a number of variations in vocal quality, intensity, tone, and pitch height can alter the simple declarative statement of fact as illustrated in the examples that follow:

5. (matter-of-factly) I'll see you tomorrow.

6. (demandingly) I'll see you tomorrow.

7. (resignedly) I'll see you tomorrow.

8. (conspiratorially) I'll see you tomorrow.

9. (invitingly) I'll see you tomorrow.

For good or ill, it is precisely the paralinguistic features of language of which many learners of English remain unaware. Also, mistakes in paralinguistic features cue native speakers to develop negative attitudes toward a speaking style used by many learners of English as illustrated in the following example:

10. (evenly segmented, flat intonation, incomplete terminal contour) I will see you tomorrow.

Native speakers react defensively to this last utterance "since the foreign speaker sounds insistent and demanding" (Taylor 1976, 36).

In another way, perceptions we create about ourselves to listeners clearly develop from paralanguage. We noted earlier that dynamism in credibility largely stems from vocal expressiveness. Many people understand our emotional involvement and sensitivity from vocal and facial cues. In this way, our vocalics may reveal our feelings to others. For example, Thai people use silence to show respect, agreement, or even disagreement, depending upon how the silence is used (Smutkupt and Barna 1976). Also, speaking softly shows good manners and education. Consequently, many Thai feel that the people in the United States are angry because Americans speak more loudly than Thais.

Throughout the chapter, we have discussed cultural differences, nonverbal examples, and even suggestions of what to do. In closing this chapter, you may find some of the following skill suggestions helpful in improving nonverbal communication:

1. *Observe and discover specific kinesic behaviors for any one culture.* When people do things that puzzle you, ask them why they are acting in that manner.

2. *Avoid letting your emotions get the best of you.* In many cultures, people will touch you and bump you, and you may feel emotionally insecure or angry. Remember, some cultures simply do not think of private, personal body space. Sometimes, fifty Africans can crowd into the same amount of space that holds only twenty North Americans. The reason is that the Africans' personal space suffers no intrusion from crowding and touching.

3. *Notice spatial positions.* To figure out the appropriate interpersonal distance in an intercultural contact, plant yourself and avoid backing away. The other person will then stop at the culturally relevant distance.

4. *In practicing eye contact, observe what is appropriate within different contexts.* In some cultures, you may observe males maintaining eye contact, but a male and a female avoiding eye contact. Thus, you can learn how to respond.

5. *If you think you acted incorrectly, ask people, if it seems appropriate, what you did wrong.* Only by asking will you learn, because a host national normally will not volunteer information.

6. *Certain sensoric differences can be frustrating because our old social cues are removed.* To counteract this tendency, remind yourself that differences do not have a "wrongness" about them. By enthusiastically trying new foods and enjoying new sounds, for instance, you can create a pleasant feeling for yourself. In a word, be positive!

Clearly, a significant element of intercultural communication is the "silent" language of nonverbal communication. Kinesics refers to gestures, posture, body movement, eye contact, facial expression, and greeting behaviors and their effects on communication.

Dimensions of space emit silent messages, especially as cultural members structure their interpersonal body space according to cultural norms. The study of proxemic behavior, particularly because of its obviousness and frequency, may be one of the most significant aspects of nonverbal communication.

Another element of nonverbal communication involves chronemics—our understanding of and use of time. Perceptual misunderstandings with regard to time create frequent intercultural communication breakdowns.

Understanding the relationship of familiar "senses" to unfamiliar sights, sounds, tastes, smells, and touches of a host culture leads the intercultural communicator to try to avoid overreaction and to probe deeper meanings of a new culture. The most evident way that the effects of a large "sense ratio" can be overcome is by further understanding of predictable stages of psychological intercultural distress in the process of culture shock.

This chapter also discusses cultural touching behaviors and their effects. Finally, the chapter briefly describes the nature of paralanguage.

In reality, nonverbal communication operates under incredibly complex rules. Hopefully, the basic concepts introduced in this chapter will be enough to prepare you for the dynamics of intercultural communication.

Exercises

1. Spend some time in the student center or some public place and make a list of the nonverbal communication behaviors you observe. What do these behaviors mean? When are they used?

2. With your list of nonverbal behaviors from exercise 1, go back another time and look at nonverbal communication in terms of interpersonal relationships. What type of oculesic patterns do you observe? What kind of relationships produce what types of proxemic behavior? What is the role of sex on nonverbal behaviors that you observe?

3. Interview some international students about haptics in their culture. What cultural practices differ from your own cultural practices? Ask the international students to describe their feelings when they first came to the United States and attempted to interact meaningfully in nonverbal ways. What did they do to adapt to the new culture? What principles does this suggest for you in adapting to intercultural acculturation?

Resources

Applbaum, Ronald. *Fundamental Concepts in Human Communication.* San Francisco: Canfield, 1973.

Argyle, M., and J. Dean. "Eye Contact, Distance and Affiliation." *Sociometry* 28 (1965): 289–304.

Arnold, William E. "The Effect of Nonverbal Cues on Source Credibility." *Central States Speech Journal* 23 (1973): 227–30.

Baird, John E. "Some Nonverbal Elements of Leadership Emergence." *Southern Speech Communication Journal* 42 (1977): 352–61.

Becker, F., and C. Mayo. "Delineating Personal Distance and Territory." *Environment and Behavior* 6 (1974): 212–32.

Beebe, Steven A. "Eye Contact: A Nonverbal Determinant of Speaker Credibility." *Speech Teacher* 23 (1974): 21–25.

Boucher, Jerry D. "Culture and the Expression of Emotion." *International and Intercultural Communication Annual* 1 (1974): 82–86.

Condon, E. C. "Cross-Cultural Interferences Affecting Teacher-Pupil Communication in American Schools." *International and Intercultural Communication Annual* 3 (1976): 108–20.

Dodd, Carley H., and Kay E. Payne. "The Effects of Culture and Sex on Time Concepts between Black and White Children." Paper presented to Southern Speech Communication Association, San Antonio, Texas, April 9, 1976.

Ekman, Paul, and Wallace V. Friesen. "Hand Movements." *Journal of Communication* 22 (1972): 353–74.

Ellsworth, Phoebe C., and Linda M. Ludwig. "Visual Behavior in Social Interaction." *Journal of Communication* 22 (1972): 379–81.

Erickson, Frederick. "One Function of Proxemic Shifts in Face-to-Face Interaction." In *Organization of Behavior in Face-to-Face Interaction,* edited by Adam Kendon, Richard M. Harris, and Mary R. Key. Paris: Mouton, 1975.

Felipe, N. J., and R. Sommer. "Invasions of Personal Space." *Social Problems* 14 (1966): 206–14.

Hall, E. T. *The Hidden Dimension.* Garden City, N.Y.: Doubleday, 1966.

Hall, E. T. "Proxemics." *Current Anthropology* 9 (1969): 83–108.

Hall, E. T. "Environmental Communication." In *Behavior and Environment: The Use of Space by Animals and Men,* edited by A. H. Esser. New York: Plenum, 1971.

Hall, E. T. *The Silent Language.* New York: Anchor, 1973.

Heston, Judee K. "Effects of Personal Space Invasion and Anomic or Anxiety, Nonperson Orientation and Source Credibility." *Central States Speech Journal* 25 (1974): 19–27.

Hong, Nguyen Kim. "Vietnamese Themes." Paper presented to Regional Indo-Chinese Task Force, City of New York Board of Education, New York, January 19–21, 1976.

Horton, John. "Time and Cool People." In *Intercultural Communication: A Reader,* 2d ed., edited by Larry A. Samovar and Richard E. Porter. Belmont, Calif.: Wadsworth, 1976.

Johnson, Kenneth R. "Black Kinesics: Some Non-Verbal Communication Patterns in the Black Culture." In *Intercultural Communication: A Reader,* 2d ed., edited by Larry A. Samovar and Richard E. Porter. Belmont, Calif.: Wadsworth, 1976.

Kahn, A., and T. McGaughey. "Distance and Liking: When Moving Close Produces Increased Liking." *Sociometry* 40 (1977): 138–44.

Knapp, Mark L. *Essentials of Nonverbal Communication.* New York: Holt, Rinehart and Winston, 1980.

Knapp, Mark L., Roderick P. Hart, Gustav W. Friedrich, and Gary M. Shulmen. "The Rhetoric of Goodbye: Verbal and Nonverbal Correlates of Human Leave Taking." *Speech Monographs* 40 (1973): 198.

Krail, K., and G. Leventhal. "The Sex Variable in the Instruction of Personal Space." *Sociometry* 39 (1976): 170–73.

LaBarre, Weston. "Paralinguistics, Kinesics and Cultural Anthropology." In *Intercultural Communication: A Reader,* 2d ed., edited by Larry A. Samovar and Richard E. Porter. Belmont, Calif.: Wadsworth, 1976.

Leshan, L. "Time Orientation and Social Class." *Journal of Abnormal and Social Psychology* 47 (1952): 589–92.

Lin, Nan. *The Study of Human Communication.* Indianapolis: Bobbs-Merrill, 1973.

McAulay, J. D. "What Understandings Do Second-Grade Children Have of Time Relationships?" *Journal of Educational Research* 54 (1961): 312–14.

McCroskey, James C. *Introduction in Rhetorical Communication.* Englewood Cliffs, N.J.: Prentice-Hall, 1972.

Malandro, Loretta A., and Larry Barker. *Nonverbal Communication.* New York: Random House, 1983.

Mehrabian, Albert. "Relationship of Attitude to Seated Posture, Orientation and Distance." *Journal of Personality and Social Psychology* 10 (1968): 26–31.

Mehrabian, Albert. "Significance of Posture and Position in the Communication of Attitude and Status Relationship." *Psychological Bulletin* 71 (1969): 359–72.

Mehrabian, Albert. *Silent Messages.* 2d ed. Belmont, Calif.: Wadsworth, 1981.

Mehrabian, Albert, and J. T. Friar. "Encoding of Attitudes by a Seated Communicator via Posture and Position Cues." *Journal of Consulting and Clinical Psychology* 33 (1969): 339–46.

Montagu, M. F. A. *Touching: The Human Significance of Skin.* New York: Columbia University Press, 1971.

Porter, Richard. "An Overview of Intercultural Communication." In *Intercultural Communication: A Reader,* edited by Larry A. Samovar and Richard E. Porter. Belmont, Calif.: Wadsworth, 1972.

Rosegrant, Teresa J., and James C. McCroskey. "The Effects of Race and Sex on Proxemic Behavior in an Interview Setting." *Southern Speech Communication Journal* 40 (1975): 408–20.

Rosenfeld, H. M. "Effect of an Approval-Seeking Induction on Interpersonal Proximity." *Psychological Reports* 17 (1965): 120–22.

St. Martin, Gail M. "Intercultural Differential Decoding of Nonverbal Affective Communication." *International and Intercultural Communication Annual* 3 (1976): 44–57.

Shaw, Marvin E. *Group Dynamics: The Psychology of Small Group Behavior.* 2d ed. New York: McGraw-Hill, 1976.

Sheflen, Albert E. "The Significance of Posture in Communication Systems." *Psychiatry* 27 (1964): 27–36.

Sheflen, Albert E. *Body Language and Social Order.* Englewood Cliffs, N.J.: Prentice-Hall, 1972.

Shuter, Robert. "A Field Study of Nonverbal Communication in Germany, Italy, and the United States." *Communication Monographs* 44 (1977): 298–305.

Smutkupt, Suriya, and La Ray Barna. "Impact of Nonverbal Communication in an Intercultural Setting: Thailand." *International and Intercultural Communication Annual* 3 (1976): 130–38.

Sommer, R. "Sociofugal Space." *American Journal of Sociology* 72 (1967): 654–60.

Taylor, Harvey M. "Non-Verbal Communication and Cross-Cultural Communication Problems." *ESL Papers,* 1976–1977.

Watson, Michael. "Conflicts and Directions in Proxemic Research." *Journal of Communication* 22 (1972): 442–43.

Whitsett, Gavin. "An Examination of Eye Contact, Body Orientation, and Proxemics in Black-White Interviews." Unpublished paper, Western Kentucky University, 1974.

Wolff, Peter, and Joyce Gustein. "Effects of Induced Motor Gestures on Vocal Output." *Journal of Communication* 22 (1972): 227.

Yousef, Fathi. "Nonverbal Communication: Some Intricate and Diverse Dimensions in Intercultural Communication." In *Intercultural Communication: A Reader,* 2d ed., edited by Larry A. Samovar and Richard E. Porter. Belmont, Calif.: Wadsworth, 1976.

Yousef, Fathi, and Nancy Briggs. "The Multinational Business Organization: A Schema for the Training of Overseas Personnel in Communication." *International and Intercultural Communication Annual* 2 (1975): 74–85.

Chapter 10

Intercultural Communication and Culture Stress

Objectives

After completing this chapter, you should be able to:

1. Cope with anxiety upon entering a culture.

2. Understand the stages of culture shock and adjust accordingly.

3. Describe the process of acculturation and adaptation of a person into another culture.

4. Understand why some people acculturate and others do not.

5. Describe reverse culture shock.

6. Develop skills for cultural reentry.

When we enter a different culture, a "natural" anxiety emerges within us. This normal tendency to feel somewhat worried about the new culture and your response to it, however, can become an overwhelming fear, turn to inordinate mistrust, and lead to an eventual return from the culture earlier than we expected. We do not have to leave the United States to enter a second culture—sometimes another culture is only a few miles away. This chapter focuses on the process of adapting to the new culture and the related process of learning its ways.

The problem of culture shock is well illustrated by the following statements from people who entered a new culture:

"At first, I felt as if this country was the best place in the world. But after a while, I began to feel as if they were all crooks."

"I don't know what happened to me. I hadn't been in this place for more than three months when I had a compelling urge to return home. It wasn't just homesickness which I expected to feel, but it was a kind of compulsion."

"My anxiety about the country did not really have to do with the food. I developed what I now guess was a phobia about the place and my interaction with people. Back home, I was always outgoing, but in the new country, I hardly felt like leaving the compound. I was almost scared to death."

These statements typify people's feelings, which fall rather predictably into a pattern we call culture shock. Culture shock refers to the special transition period and the accompanying feelings after entering a new culture. Culture shock is similar to stress and anxiety, but the concept particularly fits the unique feelings a person experiences during the first weeks to over a year after entering a new culture.

There is no right or wrong to experiencing culture shock—it happens to almost everyone, though it occurs in varying degrees. After all, your nervous system is working overtime, and your surroundings are very new. So, it is normal to experience some level of culture shock. However, just like anxiety in your own culture, culture shock can become overwhelming. Knowing what to expect and knowing how to cope with culture shock should assist you in handling these feelings. When you experience this phenomenon, you may even feel temporary physical symptoms, such as a slight headache, an upset stomach, and sleeplessness. The following general symptoms also can surface (Oberg 1960; Adler 1975; Bennett 1977):

1. Excessive concern over cleanliness and health
2. Feelings of helplessness and withdrawal
3. Irritability
4. Fear of being cheated, robbed, or injured
5. A glazed stare
6. Desire for home and friends
7. Physiological stress reactions
8. Anxiety, frustrations, and paranoia
9. Loneliness and disorientation
10. Defensive communication

Because of its disorienting qualities, culture shock blocks effective intercultural communication and can present personal problems. Cultural shock is really symptomatic of almost any transition, such as entering college, moving to a new house, taking a new job, moving to another city, or losing a loved one. For those reasons, we can experience transition shock, job shock, role shock, and, according to Alvin Toffler (1970), shock related to rapid cultural and technological change, called future shock.

The good news is that we can control culture shock. This chapter reveals the culture shock phases that people go through and ways of combating the debilitating effects of this process. The chapter also explains what long-term residents in a new culture can do in living and working in the new culture through the process of acculturation. The chapter concludes with a discussion of the stress involved with cultural reentry.

Stages of Culture Shock

A number of writers have explored the causes and symptoms of culture shock and have outlined the phases that people enter and leave throughout the transition process (Oberg 1960; Adler 1975; Bennett 1977; Stewart 1977). In addition to these works, the United States Navy manual *Overseas Diplomacy* (1973) outlines a number of phases and subphases that commonly occur. We define four stages here.

Eager Expectation Stage

In this stage, you plan to enter the second culture. The planning and development of the trip and the purposes of the entry make you simultaneously excited and wary. You may be looking forward to new food and yet remain apprehensive. You may be enjoying the new language and yet remain concerned about using it properly. You anticipate how new people will respond to you and yet worry that they might reject you. However, you face the future with optimism, and the planning continues.

Everything Is Beautiful Stage

When you arrive in the new culture, you feel a sense of excitement, pleasure, and self-satisfaction for making the decision to come to this "beautiful" place. During this phase, nearly everything appears wonderful. The food is exciting; the people seem friendly. Although you may experience some of the symptoms mentioned earlier, such as sleeplessness and mild anxiety, your enthusiasm and curiosity quickly overcome these minor discomforts. The sense of euphoria is so great that some writers call this stage the "honeymoon" stage. You should have come long ago—you think to yourself—to this piece of "heaven." The people are polite and gracious, unlike some people you know back home, and so you may come to feel that you have discovered utopia.

Studies indicate that this stage lasts anywhere from a couple of weeks to six months. However, this stage of ecstasy is soon lost to a period of depression.

Everything Is Awful Stage

The honeymoon is over! Now, things have gone sour. After a while, you begin to feel more anxious, restless, impatient, and disappointed. It seems you have a more difficult time saying what you mean. You are meeting more people who do not speak English, and yet your foreign language knowledge has not improved dramatically. Perhaps you begin to realize that the eager expectations were just a fantasy, colored by the honeymoon stage, reinforced by your euphoria when you first arrived. Now you feel that you were wrong.

There is increasing difficulty with transportation. Shopping seems to come too often, and you are getting a little tired of having to bargain for almost everything you purchase. Even with these surmounting problems, no one seems to care. The host country seems indifferent. Today, you learn that devaluation of the dollar has shrunk your purchasing power in the new culture. Besides that, your wallet or purse was stolen last week.

This period of culture shock is marked by a loss of social cues and a time of inconvenience that you had not experienced earlier. The confusion heightens with the unfamiliar smells, sounds, food, and cultural customs. Not only do some of the physical symptoms set in at this stage, but depression, feelings of loneliness, and fear pervade your attitudes and feelings. The reaction is predictable.

The "everything is awful" stage can last from a few weeks up to several months. Some people never experience this stage at all, though others experience it more seriously. The goal, of course, is to work toward a balanced view of the people, the customs, and self.

Most people in the "everything is awful" stage cope with the frustration in one of the four ways that follow (*Overseas Diplomacy* 1973).

Fight. Some people in the "everything is awful" stage of culture shock scoff at the host country. They may also reject the nationals of that country, thinking that the people in that culture have inferior ways—in short, they look

Culture shock can leave the person entering the host country with a feeling of alienation and can result in decreased intercultural contact.

down on the culture of the host country and act ethnocentrically. Other people in this situation actually destroy property, which only fuels the guilt and makes the situation worse. For example, one teenage boy, whose father served as a change agent in a foreign country, reacted not only with insolence to his classmates at the international school but also destroyed personal property of some of his father's friends in the new culture. To say the least, the fight reaction during the "everything is awful" stage can lead to legal difficulty in the host culture.

Flight. Other people in the "everything is awful" stage of culture shock remove themselves from the culture. The most obvious examples are the people who leave for home shortly after arriving in the host culture. Even if these people do not leave, other symptoms accompany this coping behavior. For example, they may withdraw from all contact with the new culture. Not only do they avoid speaking or trying to learn the new language, but they avoid contact with the host nationals. During this episode, they may develop nervousness, depression, alcoholism, and even mental illness. Or, they may experience excessive homesickness.

Filter. Some people in the "everything is awful" stage of culture shock can experience three kinds of filtering behavior. The filtering behavior refers to a denial of reality, and it occurs in several ways. For one thing, these people can deny any differences between themselves and people in the host culture or between their hometowns and a city in the new culture. Some people in this condition go to great lengths to argue the harmony and similarity between, say, North Americans and the people of the culture. One international student in a North American university, for example, spent a great deal of time in his conversations with North Americans trying to convince them of how few differences he had noticed and "how wonderful America is." He, like all of us at times, was denying differences.

A second way in which these people filter is by glorifying their home country. For example, a North American from the United States may forget all about the problems back home and remember only the good things. This process is something like the old statement about looking at things through rose-colored glasses. Only in this case, the tinted glasses are framed by a need for security. This distortion of perceptions extends into views toward the host nationals of the host culture. Not only do these people glorify the United States, for example, but they may view the people in the new culture with disgust and contempt.

Still a third reaction within this filtering behavior is to "go native." Sometimes, people totally reject their old culture and enthusiastically adopt the host nation's culture. Of course, the problem is that these people are never accepted in the new culture for anything but what they actually are, so this behavior really does not work.

Flex. A final behavior within the "everything is awful" stage is flexing. Now the visitors or new residents observe, try new things, and reflect on events, trying to sort out the frustrations and understand them. During this situation, they begin to look at life in the new culture, to reflect on why the people act in a certain way. Then, they go out and try some new food, habits, and customs. Eventually, this process leads into the final stage of culture shock—the "everything is OK" stage.

Everything Is OK Stage

After several months in the new culture, you may find that you view both the negative and the positive in a balanced manner. You finally have learned a lot more about the culture, and while you still do not like some things, you now like more things than a few months ago. Not everyone is a crook, you think to yourself, and, in fact, there are some good folks along with some bad. By now, you have become more accustomed to the foods, sights, sounds, smells, and nonverbal behaviors of the new culture. Also, you have fewer headaches and upset stomach problems and less confusion, uncertainty, and loneliness. Your physical health and mental health have improved. Normal contacts with host nationals are increasing, and you do not feel that you must defend yourself. You can accept yourself and others around you. Congratulations! You have just made it through the worst of culture shock.

As you read a moment ago, some people experience culture shock in varying degrees. Also, because culture shock occurs over a period of time, you may not always realize that its stages are temporary. The best thing to do is to admit that you are experiencing culture shock, to try to identify your stage

Working through culture shock involves balancing the good and the bad things one perceives about the new culture and then adapting to the culture through intercultural contacts.

of culture shock, and to work toward becoming more familiar with the new culture. Feeling good about yourself before you go into the new culture is also helpful (Steward 1977; Bennett 1977). A positive self-concept alleviates self-doubt and allows you to experience new things with less stress.

The Process of Adaptation

How would you feel if you moved to a new town, changed schools, or undertook a new job? As you can guess from the previous discussion, there would probably be some degree of culture shock. But what if you were an immigrant coming to a new country, an international student entering the United States, or an American Indian moving to Chicago? The process would be more difficult. Beyond culture shock lies the process of acculturation. Acculturation refers to the process of learning and adapting to new cultural behaviors that are different from one's primary learned culture. Although a number of observers are interested especially in how acculturation works with relatively new immigrants, such as the influx of Cubans, Vietnamese, and Koreans into the United States, the principles of acculturation apply broadly to moving to a new location, changing jobs, ethnic relations, and so on. To understand acculturation is to discover interpersonal relations, the effects of prolonged culture contact, and how a person changes to adapt to a new culture. Let us now turn to some of the principles that frame this discussion of acculturation.

The Nature of Cultural Adaptation

What happens when one culture comes into contact with another? Beyond the culture shock stages are the important concerns that follow.

Survival skills. Part of the process of acculturation is learning survival skills—how to cook, eat, work, rest, do banking, seek transportation, and the scores of other things that bombard the new person who plans to live permanently in the new culture. The daily press of living becomes the dominant concern, leading to a kind of "surface level" thinking (Stewart 1977). Thus, the issues relate to a person's physiological needs. From our discussion of Maslow's hierarchy of needs in chapter 6, you may also recognize that, once these physiological needs are met, then a person seeks more psychological assurances, such as security, self esteem, and acceptance. If the survival skills are not adequately dealt with, a person may suffer more severe culture shock than otherwise would be the case.

Attitude change. Culture contact can also produce attitude change. Gudykunst (1977), for example, writes that intercultural contact generally leads to attitude change toward individuals from the contact culture. However, this "contact hypothesis" works in different ways, depending on the following conditions:

1. If one member has a negative stereotype of the other member, positive attitudes do not necessarily result.

2. Equality of status is important for positive attitudes to result.

3. The contact must be rewarding for positive attitudes to emerge.

4. Previous contact reduces significant change in current contact.

5. Contact in a conflict situation does not necessarily produce positive attitudes and can reinforce negative attitudes toward the other cultural groups.

Cultural borrowing. Culture contact also produces acceptance of the new culture's ideas and technologies. For example, the documented study of Eskimo borrowing of snowmobiles is a classic example of culture contact that results in borrowing. Of course, the process of social change, discussed in chapter 15, explains the diffusion and communication variables used to spread ideas and technologies, once contact with a new culture has occurred.

Symbiosis. Another feature of culture contact extends to more permanent relationships that become rooted and established between two cultures. In this case, two or more cultures have mutual needs. To satisfy those needs, they establish expected lines of communication and economic and social relationships, such as trading. For example, culture A may have computers that culture B needs, but culture B may have wheat that culture A needs. By establishing a more or less long-term symbiotic relationship, the two cultures come to depend on one another. In the process of this more formalized culture contact, the cultures learn from one another in ways that may result in some changes.

A number of variables have been examined in an attempt to identify the communication and participation activities of individuals arriving to live permanently in a new culture. Although most of these studies are very specific, dealing with particular minorities, the following principles emerging from these studies apply to our discussion of acculturation.

Ethnic identification. Whenever a minority culture is faced with learning the new ways of a contrast culture and surviving in that culture, there is a

Communication and Adaptation

The process of acculturation often involves adaption to the host culture.

strong ethnic identification. By that we mean that the minority person or immigrant seeks identification with familiar people, customs, and even language. Thus, the barrios of New York mark almost precise boundaries of numerous immigrant and minority groups. In recent years within the United States, these groups have been encouraged to maintain their ethnic ties, in what is termed "cultural pluralism." Such a view conflicts with an earlier notion in the United States that this country was a "melting pot" where all become one culture, so to speak. The reality of minority pockets in the United States testifies to the fact that cultural pluralism has existed historically and probably will continue. Young Kim's (1977) study of Korean immigrants in Chicago indicates that ethnic identification is high, especially in the early years of acculturation. Interpersonal and organizational involvement among this group remains stronger than ties with the host nation, although the number of intercultural contacts increases over a period of time. Jin Kim (1980) found that a strong network of ethnic relationships in the early stages of acculturation tends to reduce rather than facilitate acculturation.

Friendships. Although ethnic identification remains higher than identification with persons in cultural groups other than the minority, studies indicate that, as time passes, intercultural friendships develop. For example, Kim (1977) reported that, among her Korean respondents, the number of casual friends who are Americans increases significantly after the Korean immigrant has been in the United States about five years. After a few more years, the number of Korean casual friends decreases but always remains greater than the number of American friends. The same principle works for intimate friends: After about nine years, the number of American friends rises dramatically, and the number of Korean friends decreases somewhat. In other words, as the immigrants first begin the new country, they attach themselves to friends who are also Korean immigrants. Although they maintain ties with

Koreans, the new immigrants learn to "branch out" and develop American friends after a number of years. Jin Kim's (1980) analysis of Korean immigrants reported that communication with nonethnic sources (that is, intercultural communication) significantly facilitates the acculturation process. Kim's data also pointed out that occupational status facilitates the acculturation process. See also studies by Kim (1979), Inglis and Gudykunst (1982), and Baldassini and Flaherty (1982).

Cultural involvement. The longer a person lives in a new culture, the more that person tends to become more culturally involved, at least under the following conditions.

1. If a person is highly motivated to be acculturated, he or she usually becomes more culturally involved with group memberships in the host culture and develops more friends from the host culture than a person who is not motivated to acculturate.

2. Kim (1977) also found that English competence is important for explaining why some people acculturate faster and better than other people.

3. Education also affects acculturation and cultural involvement, since more highly educated persons entering the host culture seem to develop more friendships and join more groups than less educated people.

4. Kim (1977) reported that people involved in the minority culture, through group memberships and friendships, also tend to be involved in the host culture. Just as the centripetal effect in mass communication occurs when exposure to one medium is highly related to exposure to another medium, then this dual cultural involvement effect can be called the "centripetal acculturation effect." Only in this case, the data suggest that acculturation and involvement in one's own culture seem to predict involvement in a host culture—involvement breeds involvement.

As we can see, then, acculturation does not occur in everyone's life in the same way. Some people are motivated to acculturate, while others are not. At least for first-generation immigrants and for immediate culture contact, total integration is gradual and depends upon several factors. Even then, however, perhaps we are recognizing the reality that cultural pluralism is a fact for the future. The challenge for intercultural communicators is to recognize the dynamics of the culture contact hypothesis, the acculturation principles, and culture shock and to apply these principles to meaningful relationships.

Intercultural Reentry

A body of literature has been evolving that documents the process of reentry into one's home culture after a stay in another culture. The research in this area reveals staggering information about what Austin (1987) cited as a "conspiracy of silence." No one wants to admit that he or she is having difficulty readjusting to the home culture, so the reentry process has often involved people suffering a quiet stress. Austin, a leading researcher in reentry, having surveyed and counseled in his psychological practice hundreds of returned gov-

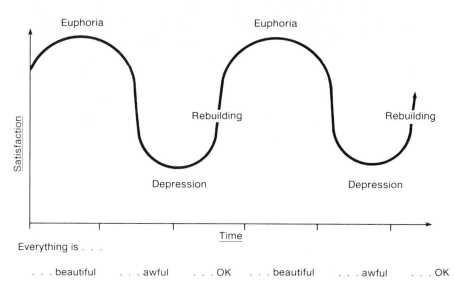

Figure 10.1
Entry and reentry
stress curve: W-
curve.

Entry to host culture   Reentry to home culture

Euphoria   Euphoria

Satisfaction

Rebuilding   Rebuilding

Depression   Depression

Time

Everything is . . .

. . . beautiful   . . . awful   . . . OK   . . . beautiful   . . . awful   . . . OK

ernment, missionary, and business personnel, noted that a slight majority of people returning face stress in reentry and that in some cases the need for counseling is severe. Among children, 10 percent are reported to need psychological counseling. Data also suggest that returning children may experience a delayed adolescence by as much as ten years.

The cycle of reentry stress is similar to the cycle of entry stress experienced upon first arrival in a new culture. Thus, a W-curve best represents a model for understanding the entry/reentry cycle (figure 10.1). Upon first returning home, there is a sense of relief and excitement about being in familiar surroundings, seeing old friends, and so on. However, to the surprise of everyone, especially the returning expatriate, a sense of depression and negative outlook follows the initial reentry honeymoon. Symptoms described earlier in the chapter may result.

Research in reentry has revealed some special factors that contribute to this second, somewhat down stage. First, self-concept takes a nosedive. There is a feeling of nonacceptance of the self and a general search for identity (Austin 1987). In fact, evidence suggests that returning Vietnam veterans especially experienced this loss of self because they came home to a U.S. culture that rejected their role. A second factor that can lead to reentry depression is a homesickness and nostalgia for the country the person just left (Moore 1981). The home culture looks so negative at times that the reentering person longs for the "good old days" in the country where he or she lived for the past several years. A third reason for reentry depression, according to Austin (1987), is that persons facing reentry may experience a value change. One of the most obvious areas of value change is a kind of disgust with American materialism and feeling an "embarrassment of riches." Finally, other changes that contribute to a depression stage following reentry include the returned person's dissatisfaction with the fast-paced way of life, a desire for a simpler life, a desire for deeper friendships and relationships, a heightened concern over ecology and politics, and an astonishment at racial prejudice.

Practically speaking, reverse culture shock, or cultural reentry, is a "cultural vertigo" because of the dizzy feeling persons experience when returning from overseas to find that the home culture is no longer the same. The snapshot they took when leaving is now out of focus and blurred. Reactions to cultural vertigo have been documented by Schmidt's (1986) interview research and include the following observations:

1. You're not the same person upon returning, and you have a new outlook on the country.

2. It's difficult to use your experience from overseas, and people can't deal with you—it's hard to fit in.

3. You find that you're two years behind the times in clothing, slang, etc.

4. You don't have a network to help you, as you had overseas, which makes it difficult to break in and hard to make friends.

5. Preparing for reentry is a little like preparing for old age. It doesn't begin at age seventy.

6. Find a friend or mentor before going overseas who can keep you abreast of things at home and see that your name is brought into conversations.

7. Keep in communication with people back home and keep them up-to-date with you but also ask what changes they're going through. Don't flaunt your foreign experience. Some suggest writing two letters a week—one to work associates and another to family/friends.

8. Indicate new skills being developed and how they might be used back home.

9. Make preparations (information gathering) before returning and be prepared for changes—home will be new.

10. Distill the essence of your overseas experience because people won't want to sit for hours listening to you and seeing slides. Don't assume that you are the person who has had the exciting time—listen to others.

Overall, adapting to new cultures involves first working through culture shock. The following suggestions should assist you not only in culture shock but also in longer-range adaptation.

1. *Do not become overreactionary.* This advice stems from the tendency to become overly frustrated during various stages of culture shock. Patience goes a long way; if you control your emotions, you can more easily see yourself and others.

Developing Skills in Intercultural Communication and Culture Stress

2. *Meet new people.* Force yourself to go out of your way to meet others. By engaging in these new friendships, you gradually gain personal confidence and ultimately learn a lot more about the culture than by your personal sheer determination. A new friend can tell you things that you may spend months learning otherwise.

3. *Try new things.* Being creative and trying new foods, clothes, and so on can assist you in meeting the stress of the new culture. Trying new things is not easy, but if you can try them gradually yet persistently, you will enjoy the new culture quickly.

4. *Give yourself periods of rest and thought.* Adapting to a new culture is like being in school for several hours a day—it is hard, mental work. And like any other serious learning endeavor, you need time to rest properly. Also, you need time to reflect and put your thoughts together. Do not be a recluse, but a little time to yourself can prove beneficial.

5. *Work on your self-concept.* The mind can be directed toward positive or negative thoughts. While this idea may seem oversimplified at first, try "feeding" yourself a diet of positive thoughts. Of course, you can go overboard and distort reality, but positive thinking can help you. Tell yourself that you are really not so bad and that most other people go through the same experiences that you face during culture shock.

6. *Write.* Sometimes writing in a diary or some other medium can release tension and frustration. Also, reflecting at a later time on what you have written can prove insightful to personal growth.

7. *Observe body language.* As we note in chapter 9, body language and nonverbal communication in general are subtle but persuasive. Part of the frustration of culture shock is not knowing the culture's system of body language. People bump into you without apology, and people may not smile at you the way they do back home, and so you miss the cues once so familiar. By learning the nonverbal rules, you may discover that the behavior of the people of the new culture does not indicate anger or any other dissatisfaction with you personally.

8. *Learn the verbal language.* Take time to learn as much of the host culture's language as possible. Not only does using the native language compliment people in the host culture, but it obviously aids your survival skills.

This Chapter in Perspective

This chapter describes physical and psychological symptoms of transition into a new culture, called culture shock. Some of those symptoms include upset stomach, slight headache, obsession with health and with material things, irritability, homesickness, and defensiveness.

The chapter also outlines four stages of culture shock: (1) the eager expectation stage refers to the planning stage and the accompanying excitement; (2) the "everything is beautiful" stage involves a sense of euphoria and pleasure with the new culture; (3) the "everything is awful" stage is typified by a flurry of negativism in which one fights, flees, filters, or flexes; and (4) the "everything is OK" stage is characterized by a balanced view of the new culture.

During and after culture shock, however, people who plan to be permanent residents of a host culture face the long-term stress of adapting to the new people and customs. Culture contact, an obvious part of acculturation, means we first have to learn survival skills. We typically change our attitudes toward host nationals following culture contact, but only under a number of conditions. Long-term acculturation includes borrowing technologies and ideas and also includes formalized symbiotic relationships, such as economic and social relationships. The chapter discussion of adaptation also highlights the importance of ethnic identity during the early acculturation years for an immigrant, the importance of making friends from the host culture as soon as possible, and the importance of group membership in producing cultural involvement.

This chapter also documents processes and suggestions for meeting the demands of cultural reentry. The psychological stresses underlying reentry can be understood and dealt with. A number of useful suggestions are provided.

Exercises

1. Interview a business or professional person who has been working overseas for a while. Ask for impressions of his or her psychological states during the earlier and then during the later period of this person's stay in the host country. What patterns emerge? Why?

2. Discuss with some ethnic leaders in your community the problems of acculturation of minorities in your locale. Ask them for their advice as to how ethnic groups or other minorities can acculturate in ways mutually beneficial to ethnic group members and the dominant culture.

3. Do some research in the library or in some of your other university or college courses about the theory of cognitive dissonance. What parallels do you see between that theory and the patterns of culture shock discussed in this chapter? How can dissonance theory reduction techniques be utilized in reducing culture shock?

Resources

Adler, Peter S. "The Transitional Experience: An Alternative View of Culture Shock." *Journal of Humanistic Psychology* 15 (1975): 10–14.

Austin, Clyde N. "Cross-Cultural Reentry." In *Intercultural Skills for Multicultural Societies,* edited by Carley Dodd and Frank Montalvo. Washington, D.C.: SIETAR, 1987.

Baldassini, José G., and Vincent F. Flaherty. "Acculturation Process of Colombian Immigrants into the American Culture in Bergen County, New Jersey." *International Journal of Intercultural Relations* 6 (1982): 127–35.

Bennett, Janet. "Transition Shock: Putting Culture Shock in Perspective." *International and Intercultural Communication Annual* 4 (1977): 45–52.

Communication Yearbook. Published by the International Communication Association, Austin, Texas. See volumes 1–7.

Gudykunst, William B. "Intercultural Contact and Attitude Change: A Review of Literature and Suggestions for Future Research." *International and Intercultural Communication Annual* 4 (1977): 1–16.

Hoopes, David S., ed. *Readings in Intercultural Communication.* Washington, D.C.: SIETAR. See volumes 1–5.

Inglis, Margaret, and William B. Gudykunst. "Institutional Completeness and Communication-Acculturation." *International Journal of Intercultural Relations* 6 (1982): 251–72.

International Journal of Intercultural Relations. See volumes 1978 to present.

Kim, Jin K. "Explaining Acculturation in a Communication Framework: An Empirical Test." *Communication Monographs* 47 (1980): 155–79.

Kim, Young Yun. "Inter-Ethnic and Intra-Ethnic Communication: A Study of Korean Immigrants in Chicago." *International and Intercultural Communication Annual* (1977): 53–68.

Kim, Young Yun. "Toward an Interactive Theory of Communication-Acculturation." *Communication Yearbook* 3 (1979): 436–53.

Moore, Leslie. "A Study of Reentry Stress of Returned Missionaries from Churches of Christ." Master's thesis, Abilene Christian University, Abilene, Texas, 1981.

Oberg, Calvero. "Cultural Shock: Adjustment to New Cultural Environments." *Practical Anthropology* 7 (1960): 170–79.

Overseas Diplomacy. U.S. Navy, Bureau of Navy Personnel, 1973.

Roper, Cynthia S. "The Effects of Communication Apprehension, World View, Innovativeness, and Communication Style on Culture Shock." Master's thesis, Abilene Christian University, Abilene, Texas, 1986.

Ruben, Brent D. "Human Communication and Cross-Cultural Effectiveness." *International and Intercultural Communication Annual* 4 (1977): 95–105.

Schmidt, Wallace. Personal Correspondence. 1986.

Stewart, Edward C. "The Survival Stage of Intercultural Communication." *International and Intercultural Communication Annual* 4 (1977): 17–31.

Toffler, Alvin. *Future Shock.* New York: Random House, 1970.

Chapter 11

Intercultural Communication Effectiveness

After completing this chapter, you should be able to:

1. Identify the importance of interpersonal relationships in intercultural communication effectiveness.

2. Understand and identify personality characteristics that mediate and influence intercultural communication.

3. Describe how perceived relationships and certain verbal behaviors, such as self-disclosure, affect communication effectiveness.

4. Cope with interpersonal conflict and gain personal awareness of intrapersonal conflicts.

5. Understand assumptions behind intercultural communication effectiveness.

6. Identify predictors of intercultural communication effectiveness.

7. Improve skills at intercultural interaction.

Recently, a midsize city in the midsouthern portion of the United States received a number of Cambodian, Laotian, and Vietnamese refugees. Some of these people were once "boat people," and the community was sincerely interested in the refugees and their plight. Church, civic, and governmental groups combined their efforts with the local mass media to encourage participation in various relocation efforts. Despite the encouragement and dedicated efforts of many people, a number of minor frustrations gradually arose among the townspeople. Finally, a seminar was conducted to assist not only community personnel, but educators and other interested persons. During the seminar, it became clear that one of the struggles in working with the refugee group was in the area of understanding the cultural differences involved. Other minor frustrations involved some basic needs to understand interpersonal communication between persons from different cultures.

This particular situation is not unique, for it has been enacted thousands of times throughout the world wherever people from two cultures meet. Beyond the language differences, there are numerous other factors that enter into the relationships we establish in intercultural communication. This chapter explains the perceived relationships between two people, personal orientations that people bring to interpersonal-intercultural interactions, and the interpersonal dynamics involved when intrapersonal and interpersonal conflicts occur. This chapter also examines assumptions and variables related to intercultural communication effectiveness.

Almost daily we confront intercultural differences, though sometimes the differences are subtle. During a newscast, for example, we may discover that the Italian actress Sophia Loren has been communicating interpersonally with legal advisors about a recent stay in her home country. We also may learn that a Middle Eastern culture has heavy investments in land holdings in the midwestern section of the United States and that interpersonal negotiations are underway for more property acquisition. Or a new international student may become a classmate. In the student center, we can observe and talk with other American students whose racial backgrounds differ from ours. Perhaps on Friday night, you have a date with a person from a different region of the country than your place of origin. What these examples indicate is that interpersonal communication in an intercultural context is almost inevitable—and part of our understanding of intercultural communication involves our exploring the nature of interpersonal-intercultural communication.

When we speak of interpersonal communication, we refer to two or more persons involved in direct verbal and nonverbal communication, and when we add the cultural differences dimension, we, of course, refer to intercultural communication. So, in actuality, intercultural communication is interpersonal communication in which we take cultural factors into account. However, the relationships with and perceptions of other people in our interpersonal encounters have a lot to do with our being effective communicators.

As we already noted, intercultural communication is in a large measure highly related to our perceptions of another person and the consequent nature of our relationship with that person. For instance, if we perceive someone to share our values, then we may be more attracted to this person. Or we may discover that a person is friendly and knowledgeable about some topic of interest to us, so our interpersonal communication is heightened and a communication relationship grows by these perceptions. By the same token, when we perceive certain attributes or characteristics in another person, that perception affects our relationship. Let us turn for a moment to some interpersonal relationships that are especially helpful in intercultural communication.

Effectiveness in Communication Relationship Climates

One variable in the interpersonal communication interface is the degree of similarity, or homophily, between individuals engaged in an interpersonal interaction. Most of us realize that we listen more to our friends than to strangers, but perhaps we never realized the subtle reasons why. You may have had the experience of making a new acquaintance and feeling an immediate sense of commonality, as though the two of you were on the same "wavelength." One reason for this phenomenon is the perception of identification, a kind of one-to-one correspondence called homophily.

Similarity Relationships

Homophily includes similarity in appearance. A person who dresses like us is a person with whom we may feel more comfortable. Likewise, when there is perceived similarity in background (age, education, ethnicity, residence or geographical region), we usually feel a more immediate sense of heightened interpersonal communication. When two communicators share attitudes and values on a moral or political question, they initially find themselves on a deep level of interpersonal communication with a significant degree of satisfaction (McCroskey, Richmond, and Daly 1975). Personality similarity is still another factor (Berscheid and Walster 1969).

Research demonstrates that interpersonal communication between members of two different cultures is more effective when homophily exists. For instance, in Colombia, informal interaction among traditional farmers occurs mostly between farmers of similar background. When Colombian farmers discuss new farm ideas, they usually do not discuss the innovations with very large landowners. Rather, lines of communication flow horizontally—small farmers converse with other small farmers (Rogers and Svenning 1969).

As we discussed in chapter 1, credibility also is important for intercultural communication. In general, when credibility is high, a listener places more attention and importance on the communication. For example, suppose an employer is anticipating hiring a minority person whose credentials look highly promising on paper. Perhaps the prospective employee has experience, superb educational background, and outstanding recommendations. By credentials and reputation, therefore, this person's credibility is high. When the employer subsequently interviews this person, the previously established credibility may influence the employer in such a way that every aspect of the interview is

Credibility Relationships

perceived positively. In some ways, high credibility is like a halo hovering over the communicator, causing us to perceive almost everything about that person positively.

On the other hand, credibility is also a phenomenon developed and maintained throughout the course of the interpersonal relationship. Consider, for a moment, the same person with high credentials and reputation. Suppose that, for the job interview, this person dressed sloppily, spoke with no enthusiasm, demonstrated negative attitudes, or performed in ways that reinforced negative stereotypes of his or her culture. This person could fail to receive the job. Why? Credibility hinges not only on person A's reputation but also on person B's perception of A.

Another credibility possibility in a relationship is that a person may have excellent reputational credibility, evidenced by letters of recommendation, high grades, and so on. However, during a job interview, a prospective employer may be influenced by the interviewee's race or cultural background. During the Iranian crisis of 1980, some excellent prospects for jobs in the United States were turned down, once it was discovered that they were from any part of the Middle East. Minority membership has long influenced hiring practices in the United States, sometimes working for and sometimes working against the prospective employee.

Self-Disclosure Relationships

Self-disclosure refers to information that a person conveys about himself or herself to another person. Self-disclosure is viewed as intimate or objective. Intimate levels involve carefully guarded information about oneself. Objective levels include factual, nonthreatening information (Jourard 1964). Research reveals a strong relationship between self-disclosure and trust, liking, and joint self-disclosure. As interpersonal trust increases, self-disclosure increases. Furthermore, in the presence of sufficient self-disclosure, the chances are greater that a fondness for the other person will occur (Brooks and Emmert 1976; Jourard 1964). Of course, just telling about yourself indiscriminately does not necessarily produce positive effects, but a climate of self-disclosure can produce trust, just as trust can produce self-disclosure. Unless two people share or disclose at some level, they remain strangers, dwarfed in a never-growing relationship and seldom aware of the other's needs. Also, self-disclosure in one person tends to encourage self-disclosure from the other person in a dyad.

Researchers have reported differences in self-disclosure between males and females in the United States. The results of one study indicated that females tend toward more self-disclosure than males and that females demonstrate even greater self-disclosure toward persons they know well. Also, research shows that females reveal more negative and honest information through less guarded control over the depth of the self-disclosure (Wheeless and Grotz 1975). By contrast, perhaps males have unknowingly adopted a "strong and silent" image in their interpersonal communication. It should be stressed, however, that lines of communication need to remain open for increased sharing and liking. Without such sharing, interpersonal communication is likely to remain superficial.

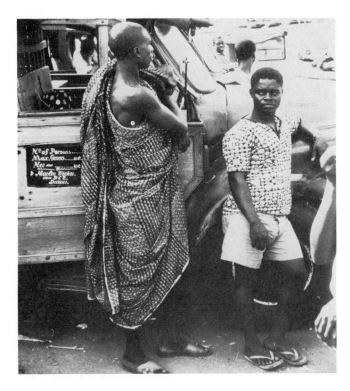

Without self-disclosure on some level, communication and personal growth remain static.

You may already know that animals reveal dominance and submission. For instance, Jane Goodall's study of chimps in East Africa demonstrates various modes of dominance and submission. Studies of birds, such as chickens, show that a "pecking order" of dominance and submission is established in a coop, where the birds literally peck one another to establish a hierarchy. After the order is established, the pecking becomes symbolic, where one bird acts as if it is going to peck, while the other bird bows in submission. Likewise, dogs lie on their backs and expose their throats to display symbolic submission.

Humans also display modes of dominance and submission in their interpersonal communication. How do you feel, for instance, when talking with a close personal friend? More than likely, the dominance-submission variable is not operating. How would you feel visiting a foreign ambassador in his or her office? Perhaps you would feel a bit more submissive. The same feeling is generally true in various relationships, such as employer-employee, officer-enlisted person, nurse-patient, parent-child, and teacher-student.

In the case of intercultural communication, dominance and submission may be inculcated by group expectations, minority status, or racial differences. For instance, for many years it was widely believed that men were inherently better than women in industrial work. From at least World War II on, however, it was discovered that women could rivet, paint, weld, and operate lathes as well as men. Once this particular cultural barrier was bridged,

Submission and Dominance Relationships

Many of our interpersonal-intercultural experiences lead us to speak and listen based on roles we expect rather than personal relationships.

women flocked to the job marketplace and now hold responsible positions in many job areas once believed to be capably held only by men. The resultant communication on the job in these cases is hopefully less culturally dominant and submissive.

Dominance and submission stem from other causes related to culture. For instance, certain submissive-dominant behavior can be explained by roles and status.

Roles. Roles are behaviors performed because of attitudes or expectations of position. A person may communicate and behave in a certain way because his or her role demands such behavior. A law enforcement officer who seems hard and unbending in his or her work role may be highly sympathetic and jovial with family or friends. The clerk at a local department store who communicates cheerfully, demonstrating all measure of judiciousness and consideration for the potential customer, may be cruel and inconsiderate at home. Many of our interpersonal communication experiences may well be characterized by communication expected from the role rather than from the "real" person.

Status. Our perception of the status of another person also helps explain relationships of submission and dominance. As a person from another culture visiting a host culture, you may be perceived to have high status, which may lead to some ambiguous situations. For instance, a cultural rule in the Middle

East indicates that the higher-status person pays the check in a restaurant. At first, you may be confused, especially if the other person dramatically insists on paying. However, this insistence is a way of saving face when the higher-status person wins the battle of the check and pays—usually to the relief of the lower-status person, who insisted in the first place to maintain his or her pride (Yousef and Briggs 1975).

In Asian, African, and Middle Eastern cultures, age is an indicator of status. As chapter 3 indicated, many cultures revere their elderly, showing honor and respect in ways not practiced by many Americans. If you were working as a manager in an international situation, you probably would try to respect this norm on the job by paying special attention to senior employees and offering occasional benefits. On crucial personnel decisions, some cultural members could be offended if you passed over an older employee for a younger worker. At least by consulting senior members of a work force for their wisdom, many managers have forestalled serious intercultural problems.

Formality in Relationships

Another perception we hold in our interpersonal relationships centers around the degree of formality we feel appropriate for various relationships. With some people, little formality is necessary, while for other relationships, formality is expected. For instance, there is probably little formality between you and your roommate or between you and a good friend. Perhaps, however, your formality level increases with a professor or whenever you enter a situation where you cannot predict the degree of formality expected. Thus, many of our relationships can be characterized by their formality or informality, shaped somewhat by the interpersonal relationships involved and the situations in which we are interacting. For example, consider the formality in a graduation exercise compared with the informality of being with a group of fraternity members at a football game.

This concept of formality and informality also has intercultural importance. For instance, if the person with whom you are talking comes from a culture in which interpersonal relationships are highly structured, even hierarchical, and your views are that relationships should be equalitarian, then some difficulty in that relationship may arise. For example, you may approach a conversation informally, using first person pronouns, using the other person's first name, and so on. The other person, approaching the relationship formally, may refer to titles, make frequent references to one's position in life, and so on. Naturally, this conflict over appropriateness of formality can cause embarrassment and extreme discomfort.

To his discussion of formality in relationships, Sarbaugh (1979) added that, the more differences between two interacting parties—or heterogeneity, to use his term—the more difficult it is to predict the social roles and norms expected. This inability to sense what is expected creates a great deal of frustration. Thus, part of intercultural communication effectiveness involves some attempt to assess just what level of formality is expected. For instance, in the United States, if you are talking with a retired man or woman, what terms of address are appropriate? There are a number of retired people who prefer formal methods of address and others who prefer that you call them by their first name. Before embarking on one level of formality or another, try to determine what the other person prefers; often, that person's conversation reveals a preference. In the same way, many cultural norms dictate formality—so, listen for any cues that can help you set the tone appropriate for a conversation.

Interpersonal Attraction in Relationships

One other aspect of the interface of intercultural relationships is the process of interpersonal attraction. Researchers have confirmed that many people in the United States develop a positive attitude toward others in the sense that they like their presence, they respect their abilities, and they admire their looks and clothing. McCroskey and McCain (1974) described these elements as social, task, and physical factors of interpersonal attraction. We can extend these factors to indicate other possible characteristics that create interpersonal attraction from an intercultural standpoint.

Holmes (1974), for instance, argued that beauty is a matter of cultural norms, not merely individual tastes. In her study rating blacks, degree of interpersonal physical attractiveness was conditioned by standards of beauty based on features from several racial groups. Thus, the criteria for judging blacks stem from norms of beauty toward blacks. We can extend the principle, then, to indicate that interpersonal physical attraction is conditioned by cultural norms.

Furthermore, interpersonal-intercultural attraction is a function of common goals or even common frustrations; we are probably more likely to develop interpersonal attraction with another person sharing the same experiences. For example, the black phenomenon of perceiving one another as "brothers" and "sisters" testifies to the mutual bond and liking affected by a common set of experiences. The same principle seems likely for any number of group and cultural experiences—circumstances that people face together forge a bond of trust and make interpersonal attraction easier.

Interpersonal Work Relationships

Many of our perspectives on management and standard operating procedures cannot always be applied on the job in intercultural situations. Effective managers who work internationally often recognize the need to alter their organizational structure and their own personal management styles because of cultural needs in several of the following areas.

Speed and efficiency. Many cultural clocks seem slower than the North American orientation toward time. The job gets done in these cases, not because someone is insisting on speed and efficiency, but because workers respect others and try to build personal relationships. As Ruben (1977) emphasized, competence can be handled in such a way that people feel a part of the completed project and learn from the process. In many cultures, getting the job done has to be less important than involving everyone in the project, within limits, of course.

The cultural clock. Adapting to a culture's time orientation is one of the simplest, yet most helpful, changes we can make when living in a second culture. For example, one U.S. firm waited two years in Japan for an important decision. The American executives were surprised to learn that "time isn't money" in that country but that time is necessary for the indispensable "preliminary" of establishing relationships before negotiating.

Cultural rules of employment. Because of status and equality norms, some cultural rules toward employment are different than American rules. For example, in Iran, a worker who has become ill sends his brother in his place to work that day. In fact, loyalty is a very strong theme in many parts of Latin America and the Middle East, so much so that a worker who changes jobs too often is viewed as shiftless and disloyal. Ackermann (1976) told how a promotion of a manual laborer to foreman by a U.S. mining operation in the South Pacific led to his murder. In that culture, advancement above one's peers violates tribal rules of equality—and hence, the death.

Nonverbal communication. In parts of Africa, Latin America, North America, and the Middle East, an indication of "yes" can also mean "I hear you" but may not necessarily be an agreement. In Asia, pointing the soles of your feet or your toes is offensive, just as standing too close or too far can be offensive. In some cultures, a handshake implies welcome; in others, it implies distance.

Work and friendship. North Americans are accustomed to keeping work and leisure separate. They work eight hours and then go home to engage in social life. In many cultures, such as Japan, the Middle East, and Latin America, work, play, and friendship are blended within the total person. In these regions, a foreigner must be known for some time before a company will reveal itself and negotiate. On this point, Ackermann (1976) advised U.S. businesspeople to "ride out" with patience the times of establishing friendship and not be overly insistent.

Meaning of friendships. In a number of cultures, friendships are long term. The friendship opens commitments to hospitality, gift giving, and, in Latin America, godparenting. The North American concept of friendship is casual, with upward and social mobility overriding long friendships in favor of friendships that come and go. This difference makes the North American who is friendly vulnerable to being criticized as "hypocritical" because the person does not follow through with the friendship.

Role expectations of a manager. In some cultures, management is expected to assume responsibility for the total life of the employee, including sickness, personal problems, and children's welfare (Yousef and Briggs 1975).

Speaking in a straightforward manner. In your culture, you probably are expected to come to the point. What phrases like "get to the point" and "small talk before the main point" really indicate is that North Americans do not like wasting time, including in their conversational and speech patterns. However, in other cultures, such as Middle Eastern and Latin American cultures, people are considered rude if they come to the point too quickly, before ap-

An individual with ethnocentric attitudes makes the assumption that his or her cultural ways are best and right, even before careful evaluation and investigation of alternatives. Judgmental attitudes generally limit, rather than facilitate, intercultural communication. Ethnocentrism can be a factor in such diverse areas as social change programs or sex discrimination.

propriate timing and relationships are built. So, they talk around the point. If the intercultural manager speaks too straightforwardly too soon, some indigenous employees may think the manager abrupt and rude.

Need for Acceptance in Relationships

Nearly all of us have a need to be accepted by others. That need accounts for our often seeking cultural and group identities. Some people, however, need more acceptance than others and may, in fact, be "joiners." One study showed a correspondence between men who joined a fraternity and their simultaneous need for acceptance and their fear of rejection (Brady 1975). Sometimes, an individual may talk incessantly, making mutual conversation difficult. While this person seems boring, he or she may be expressing a deeper need for acceptance. Likewise, the extremely quiet person may be expressing a need for acceptance and a fear of rejection by his or her silence. Because of their needs, such personalities are often motivated to maintain group loyalties (Hovland, Janis, and Kelley 1953). It is also likely that such individuals are susceptible to persuasion from others from whom they want to feel acceptance, while they may resist counternorm communication (contrary to their value system) from sources irrelevant to the need for acceptance or the fear of rejection (Abelson 1959).

Consequently, an overriding factor in certain interpersonal communication experiences stems from acceptance needs. For instance, one's use of threatening messages or sarcasm can have a negative effect on other people, especially people from a contrast culture not accustomed to such treatment.

Intercultural communication partially takes on its quality by each person's self-concept.

To establish and maintain rapport, one should use positive "bridge-building" communication. A sense of empathy can build rapport, respect, and mutual trust.

Have you ever noticed how some people seem able to stick with a point of discussion and solve problems while other people avoid working toward solutions? "Copers" are those individuals who generally work through problems or conflicts, while "avoiders" are those individuals who usually are either unable, or do not want, to seek solutions to issues. While everyone at times may choose to ignore problems and even flee various issues instead of maintaining an open line of communication, avoiders *consistently* avoid seeking solutions. Getting overwhelmingly angry, hiding behind a newspaper in the cafeteria, pretending not to see another, giving the "silent treatment," or acting pompously and dictatorially are manifestations of avoidance behavior. An avoider can experience more frustration during various stages of culture shock.

Coping Relationships

Of course, cultural behaviors can include avoiding or coping. The Japanese man who sits silently or quietly exits during a confrontation may be responding culturally, not personally avoiding. He may choose another time or place to resolve a question. The American who seems intent on pressing for a contract with a Kuwait businessman may not be personally coping but insisting on a cultural pattern of efficiency or time management.

Inevitably, even our best efforts at establishing and maintaining intercultural relationships are sometimes shattered by our discovery that others like what we dislike or dislike what we like. The resulting communication and attitudes have implications for many interpersonal and intercultural conflicts and methods of resolving them.

Balancing interpersonal conflicts. Fritz Heider, an early social psychologist who examined the problem of interpersonal conflict, observed how a given person perceives different objects of reality or topics under discussion and how he or she perceives another person (Heider 1958). In its extended form, this notion of balanced relationships suggests that, if you and another person like the same thing and like each other, a balanced relationship exists. However, the relationship is unbalanced when people who like each other do not like the same thing or when two people who like the same thing do not like each other. The first component in this description of interpersonal relationships is A's orientation toward a topic X, which includes A's attitude toward X (approach or avoidance) and various beliefs about X (cognitive attributes). The second component is A's orientation toward person B. A and B can have positive or negative attractions toward each other while holding favorable or unfavorable attitudes toward topic X. When there is an unbalanced state (A and B like each other, but A feels positively about topic X while B feels negatively about X), there is a tension to restore balance through communication.

Balance can be restored in several ways. For example, suppose a Mexican American named Roberto (A) and a black named Wes (B) like each other (they have been friends for two years and work as department heads in the same department store in San Antonio). Roberto likes a new accounting system recently installed (X), but Wes hates it and speaks negatively about the new system (X). In this obviously unbalanced situation (potentially producing some degree of conflict), several possibilities exist for change. To restore balance, (1) Roberto may convince Wes to change his attitude toward the new system (or Wes may convince Roberto); (2) Roberto may change his feelings about Wes or Wes about Roberto; (3) they may agree to tolerate the inconsistency and remain friends; or (4) each may work elsewhere.

These outcomes are augmented by some possible cultural differences. For example, both Roberto and Wes may unwittingly sift their perceptions of the other through some cultural stereotypes. Thus, Wes may think that Roberto is trying to win points with their store manager, also a Mexican American, and, for a moment, falls prey to the stereotype that Mexican Americans always stick together in groups. Roberto lets himself believe that Wes dislikes the system because Wes, according to Roberto's stereotype of other blacks, is not very innovative and prefers inefficiency to progress. Such misunderstandings occur frequently. By analyzing such topical likes or dislikes into their components, suggested by balance theorists, we can anticipate interpersonal outcomes.

What about when interpersonal conflict develops between person A and person B, rather than topical conflict? For instance, Larry was a flight instructor who personally disliked his student Abdul from Iraq who was living in the United States. Abdul assumed that he could bargain with Larry for free flight time and also waited to read the flight instruction manual until after several hours of Larry's personal instructions. Larry, however, had a set fee and expected Abdul to read the manual well in advance of any personal instruction. Thus, their topical disagreement was highlighted by Larry's personal dislike of Abdul, and, later, attempts to reconcile topical disagreements were thwarted by interpersonal conflict. Because Larry disliked Abdul, there was little motivation to work through their differences.

Because the relationships between person A, person B, and a topic are variable, balance theory provides one way of analyzing and predicting interpersonal outcomes. By examining the personal attitudes between two or more people and their respective attitudes toward salient topics, we can better understand why we are motivated to change or why we choose to ignore development of interpersonally oriented intercultural relationships.

Intrapersonal conflicts. Have you ever found yourself rationalizing your actions after you just bought something that you really could not afford? Or have you ever felt uncomfortable, worrying about a statement a highly respected person made to you, when that statement contradicted one of your beliefs? Or have you ever done something that violates your conscience or religious beliefs? The phenomenon of conflict after a decision or in the presence of information different from our beliefs is called cognitive dissonance. The theory of cognitive dissonance suggests that two cognitive elements (or beliefs), A and B, are *consonant* when no inconsistency exists between them but *dissonant* when inconsistency exists (Festinger 1957). For example, suppose a person violates a cultural or religious belief. The need to rationalize, following actions discrepant from one's belief, is a need for reducing internal pressures. The resulting intrapersonal conflict is cognitive dissonance. Or, suppose you bought a car for $8,000 and soon afterward learned that you could have bought the same car for only $7,000 from another dealer. Again, dissonance is aroused.

In the presence of dissonance, we tend to rationalize in several predictable directions:

1. Ignore the inconsistency. In some cases, people will not only ignore the situation (hoping it will go away perhaps) but flee any situation where conflict might arise, such as by getting up and leaving an intolerable conversation.

2. Discredit the source that brought inconsistency to our awareness. If someones's statement causes psychological discomfort, we may simply think "he doesn't know what he is talking about" and thus reduce that inconsistency.

3. Reduce the importance of the unchosen alternative. In the car example, we may become convinced that the dealer of the $7,000 car would not provide good service.

Table 11.1   Guidelines for Assessing Interpersonal Communication Skills

Do You Check Contextual Variables?

1. With whom are lines of communication (networks) open or closed in various groups?

2. Why are these networks open or closed? Are you "turned off" to someone's personality?

3. What is the frequency of communication among various group members? Do clique groups deny access to the group to others who could benefit from group participation?

4. Are hierarchical lines of communication within a formal group, such as an organization, open? How can those communication links be improved?

What Intercultural Relationships Are Operating in Any Given Interpersonal Contact?

1. Do you emphasize overlap of experience in communicating with others?

2. Do you emphasize areas that will build credibility?

3. Are you "open" in reception of information?

4. Is your verbal message consistent with your nonverbal message? Do your actions match your words?

5. Do you look for the "what" and the "why" of a message—what a person says and why that person is saying it?

6. Do you find yourself dominating most conversations? Do you only make statements or do you periodically ask questions in conversation?

7. Do threatening or nonstatus quo messages that affect you cause you to "screen out" such messages?

Are You Aware of the Listener as You Engage in Communication?

1. Do you consider the knowledge, education, and background of the listener and speak in terms the listener understands? Do you use jargon and slang?

2. Is it easy for others to tell you what is on their minds? Why?

3. Do you work considerately with others who fear rejection? Do you provide reassuring and positive feedback in your communication?

4. Do you "stay with" problems and work toward solutions or do you avoid working out problems?

5. Do you periodically compliment others? Do you separate an issue under consideration from the person?

4. Magnify the importance of the chosen alternative. Not only can we minimize the importance of one cognitive element, but we can magnify the importance of the other. For instance, we might assume that the $8,000 car has numerous advantages over the $7,000 car, such as a preferred color and other minor features.

5. Change attitude or behavior. In some cases, we change our inconsistent attitudes and behaviors toward consistency. If we say we love humankind,

but our actions indicate that we hate Frenchmen, then we could stop hating Frenchmen or quit believing we love humankind.

6. Seek reinforcing information. Find information supporting our choice.

The important point is that many interpersonal, as well as intrapersonal, frustrations can be explained through a rudimentary awareness of our need to rationalize intrapersonal conflict.

The problem of intrapersonal conflict is magnified greatly when the source of the conflict is cultural. Several aspects of culture shock stem from unfulfilled expectations and not knowing how to approach certain new situations. In the same way, when discrepancies between our cultural expectations and a host culture's expectations collide, the resulting frustration is likely to be internalized. Often, we then seek the reduction methods indicated. The person who eats pork against his or her conscience may actually change toward a more positive attitude toward pork. Or that person may feel that the immediate situation forced him or her into eating pork. Or that person may decide that he or she just doesn't want to think about it and may thus ignore the whole thing.

In the processing of intracultural conflict, we affect others around us. Our own patience and suspension of judgment may give others the freedom they need to adapt to the cultural or environmental causes of intracultural conflict.

The chapter thus far has focused on awareness of intrapersonal and interpersonal variables that affect communication outcomes. Let us now examine some ways of monitoring our interpersonal-intercultural skills. Perhaps some of the questions in table 11.1 will stimulate further thinking into ways of developing better interpersonal receptivity.

Assumptions of Intercultural Effectiveness

For some time now, specialists in intercultural problems have examined the role of effectiveness in intercultural encounters. Obviously, the more effective the intercultural communicator, the greater the advantages that accrue. Among the advantages are the abilities to form better interpersonal relationships, to develop broader economic bases for business, to create more-penetrating friendships, to stabilize ethnic identity, and generally to conclude intercultural tasks more efficiently. The social and economic rewards of intercultural relationships cannot be enjoyed without an understanding of some of the basic assumptions of intercultural effectiveness. We now discuss four of those assumptions.

Intercultural Effectiveness Is a Skill

Sometimes, the skill is cognitive, primarily through a better understanding of a condition or situation under consideration. Sometimes, the skill is behavioral, primarily involving a set of actions appropriate for varying conditions in intercultural communication. In any case, one of the assumptions in this text is that intercultural skills produce a condition of intercultural effectiveness. How that skill is applied and understanding the dimensions of what skills are necessary is, of course, the purpose of this chapter.

| Intercultural Effectiveness Is Desirable | Too many social and economic benefits are lost without adequate attention to the effectiveness and intercultural skills issues. Thibaut and Kelley's (1959) social exchange theory reminds us of the interest most people have in producing the maximum amount of "social reward." Such a statement is not meant to dismiss altruism, but personal motivation behind social relationships can often be attributed to saving face, social advantage, some degree of a self-esteem extension, and the like. |

| Intercultural Effectiveness Is Related to a Positive Communication Climate | Gudykunst (1977) identified positive communication climate as a factor in producing effective intercultural contact. Gudykunst, Wiseman, and Hammer (1977) argued for a third cultural perspective, rather than one's own cultural perspective, for producing maximum intercultural communication effectiveness. Furthermore, the cultural synergy notion advocated by Moran and Harris (1982) indicates that communication climate, or at least the creation of a non-threatening climate, opens a door for communication, better management, and productive relationships. In the discussion that follows, we will see how effective skills connect with conditions of ascendency, adequacy of communication systems, proper understanding, and tolerance. |

| Intercultural Effectiveness Variables Can Be Identified | One thrust of research in intercultural effectiveness involves exploring the cognitive variables related to adjustment (and hence to effectiveness) and to define ways to measure those variables. Once they are measured, then we have a predictive profile by which to evaluate a person's skills for intercultural tasks. When deficient, training is provided. In fact, the understanding of intercultural effectiveness deficiencies is the fundamental beginning point for intercultural training. The critical question in the process is the nature of the instruments that assess intercultural adaptability and its correlates. A related issue is the nature of the training program to correct the deficiencies and the delivery system by which to develop adequate intercultural skills. These topics have spawned the development of a growing number of consulting firms dedicated to the goal of assessing and treating problems in intercultural effectiveness. |

Cognitive Variables That Explain Intercultural Effectiveness

In addition to the basic assumptions of intercultural effectiveness just discussed, let us examine the cognitive variables that correlate with intercultural effectiveness. These variables represent the boundaries of this field of intercultural communication skills and its relationship to intercultural effectiveness.

A number of researchers have identified correlates of intercultural effectiveness. Some of these studies have focused on task effectiveness, while others have mainly noted intercultural adjustment and stress issues. Our purpose here is to survey the parameters of the variables in that research. For that reason, the predictor variables are presented here without necessarily referring to the full nature of the dependent variables, the sample used, the length of the study, or the rank order of the variables.

Without intercultural effectiveness skills, a person is likely to remain isolated interpersonally.

Ruben's (1977) reference to research in Canada and Kenya revealed a number of variables related to cross-cultural effectiveness. First on the list is that insistence on getting the job done can lead to ineffectiveness, at least for skills transfer and development. This role behavior is likely to become even more dysfunctional in cultures where occupational roles and expectations are at odds with cultural norms. A person who works for an organization that exhibits an intensive communication style is likely to experience failure within a culture that appreciates a more leisurely pace of work and task behavior. So, developing a cultural fit between one's interpersonal style, one's corporate culture, and the culture in which one is working is important.

Insistence on Task Behavior

Self-oriented behavior also was researched and discussed by Ruben (1977). He referred to his study with Kealey, in which they discussed how self-centered roles became highly dysfunctional. For instance, they noted that calling attention to oneself, bragging, and showing disinterest in the ideas of the group usually spelled disaster for intercultural effectiveness. In Japan, even trying to make excuses for why something did not work out does not work as well as a simple apology. In general, extraordinary self-praise or self-blame usually do not work well in intercultural interaction.

Self-Oriented Behavior

Ethnocentrism	The deleterious effects of judgmental attitudes and a feeling of being superior to others from another cultural group are well documented. Ruben (1977) noted that judgmental attitudes erect barriers to effectiveness. In a series of investigations correlating a scale to measure ethnocentrism (developed by Hood 1982) with culture stress, Dodd (1985) found a significant correlation, indicating that highly ethnocentric individuals are less likely to adjust well during a transitional experience. Gudykunst and Kim (1984) explained that prejudice and ethnocentrism lead to less effectiveness in intercultural encounters. Furthermore, Tucker and Baier (1985) reported that the ability not to criticize or put down foreigners was significantly linked with intercultural adjustment.
Tolerance for Ambiguity	The ability to react to new but ambiguous situations with little difficulty is a significant skill in intercultural effectiveness (Ruben 1977; Tucker and Baier 1985; Gudykunst and Kim 1984; *Overseas Diplomacy* 1973; Grove and Torbiorn 1985). In other words, if you can handle situations you do not immediately understand, then you probably have a high tolerance for ambiguity. Intercultural communication by nature poses ambiguities; other people, institutions, organizations, and even your attitude toward yourself just do not seem to make any sense. General confusion and disorientation may result just from being in another culture. Fluidity and flexibility are really important for building relationships in intercultural climates.
Empathy	A number of researchers report that the ability to put ourselves in the shoes of others is an important relationship skill. That same ability also links with intercultural effectiveness. To understand things from another's point of view is critical in a number of circumstances, including communicating innovative ideas (Rogers 1983) and performing up to our potential in intercultural communication (*Overseas Diplomacy* 1973).
Openness	Observers like DeVito (1986) have noted how openness and flexibility in personal communication style are important for maximum interpersonal relationships to develop and to be maintained. Dogmatism has been significantly correlated with lack of adjustment by linking measures of flexibility with intercultural adjustment and performance (Tucker and Baier 1985). While it is good to share how we feel about things, we become obnoxious when we communicate in a way that beats people over the head or that leaves no room for disagreement or further dialogue, especially when someone else has a differing opinion.
Cognitive Complexity	Cognitive complexity refers to the ability of a person to perceive a wide variety of things about another person and to make finer interpersonal discriminations than cognitively simple individuals. Using a sample of Americans working in five countries of South America, Norton (1984) found that cognitively complex individuals scored significantly lower on measures of culture stress than

cognitively simple individuals. Gudykunst and Kim (1984) later made the observation that category width, another way to describe cognitive complexity, makes for greater effectiveness. In general, cognitively complex individuals make better and more accurate judgments in developing impressions about others. They also can see situations in their larger contexts and come up with more differentiated descriptions—they just see more possibilities about people and situations.

Research also shows that our ability to feel comfortable interpersonally is significantly correlated with maximum intercultural adjustment (Norton and Dodd 1984). Other research indicates that interpersonal trust, interpersonal interest, interpersonal harmony (Tucker and Baier 1985), and interaction (*Overseas Diplomacy* 1973) are correlated with effectiveness. Thus, if you do not feel comfortable with your interpersonal relationships in your home culture, you probably will not feel any more comfortable in a host culture different from your own.

Interpersonal Comfort

The amount of immediate and personal control we sense about our communication environment has been significantly correlated with intercultural effectiveness. Tucker and Baier (1985) found a significant correlation between personal control and intercultural adjustment and performance. Other research also has highlighted significant correlations between personal world view, a kind of fatalism tendency, and cultural adjustment (Dodd 1985). These findings suggest that how you view your ability to take charge of your communication climate has a significant impact on adaptation in a new culture and your ultimate success in being interpersonally effective. The implication of taking control is not that you develop a domineering attitude but that you remain confident even when it seems things are not going too well.

A Sense of Personal Control

Innovativeness refers to our ability to try new things, to engage in some social risk taking, particularly where new information and developing social relationships are concerned. Evidence suggests that our ability to try new things is linked with intercultural effectiveness (*Overseas Diplomacy* 1973). Being a risk-taker does not mean advocating social deviancy or taboo-breaking behavior. On the contrary, innovativeness means the ability to make significant strides in developing and accepting new ideas within a context of social acceptance. A willingness to experiment with new approaches and especially a willingness to learn are highly linked with intercultural communication success. And, too, there is value in trying some new things a step at a time, a suggestion that allows you and those around you to absorb the change that may occur.

Innovativeness

Clearly, our self-esteem predicts intercultural effectiveness. A negative self-esteem can shake the foundations of our personal outlook (Bennett 1977), thus inhibiting effectiveness. Also, self-confidence and initiative directly correlate

Self-Esteem

with personal adjustment and performance (Tucker and Baier 1985; *Overseas Diplomacy* 1973).

All of us have self-doubts once in a while, and even those occasional negatives can chip away at intercultural effectiveness. As Shakespeare said, "Our doubts are traitors and cause us to lose the good we oft might win by fearing to attempt." Fear can freeze our emotions and our spirits. At the root of some fear is low self-esteem. Beyond those momentary losses of confidence, however, most of us can really perform beyond our expectations.

One of the needs discovered in intercultural counseling is that some individuals need genuine, self-confidence-building programs before they go overseas. That need is also present for an entire family going together to an intercultural assignment.

Communication Apprehension

Recent studies have revealed that our personal anxiety about communication in groups, interpersonally, and publicly significantly impacts upon intercultural adjustment and intercultural effectiveness. Research shows that the higher the communication apprehension, the lower the intercultural effectiveness (Dodd 1985). As expected, effectiveness is inhibited by lack of communication confidence (McCroskey 1982).

Other Variables

A number of other variables correlate with intercultural effectiveness, including interpersonal communication and friendships, acculturation motivation, age, occupation, organizational memberships, language competency (Kim 1977), showing respect for others, interactive skills (Ruben 1977), positive motivations, positive expectations, trust in people, patience, sense of humor, attitude toward drinking/drugs, family communication (Tucker and Baier 1985), degree of similarity/difference with host culture, host culture familiarity, and degree of rigidity of host culture (Gudykunst and Kim 1984). Hammer, Gudykunst, and Wiseman (1978) found three factors explaining communication effectiveness: (1) ability to deal with psychological stress, (2) ability to communicate effectively, and (3) ability to establish meaningful interpersonal relationships. Researchers and trainers also emphasize the advantages of intercultural training (Grove and Torbiorn 1985).

The purpose here is not to be exhaustive of all the variables that contribute to an understanding of intercultural effectiveness, but to provide a background by which to better perceive and evaluate the question of skills. Effectiveness is assumed to be an integral part of the skills development process, and thus by understanding intercultural effectiveness, we have a clearer knowledge of skills needed in various settings. Table 11.2 summarizes the various predictors of intercultural communication effectiveness.

A Model for Intercultural Skills

In one way, applying the various predictors of intercultural communication effectiveness discussed in the previous section to our personal repertoire of abilities is the clearest approach to developing effectiveness. Obviously, however, a number of climate and situational factors also need to be considered.

Table 11.2   Predictors of Intercultural Communication Effectiveness

Effectiveness	Ineffectiveness
High people, less task emphasis	High task, less people emphasis
Few self-statements	Many self-statements
Low ethnocentrism	High ethnocentrism
High tolerance for ambiguity	Low tolerance for ambiguity
High empathy	Low empathy
High openness, low dogmatism	Low openness, high dogmatism
Cognitive complexity	Cognitive simplicity
Comfort with interpersonal relations	Discomfort with interpersonal relations
High personal control, low fatalism	Low personal control, high fatalism
High innovativeness	Low innovativeness
High self-esteem	Low self-esteem
Low communication apprehension	High communication apprehension

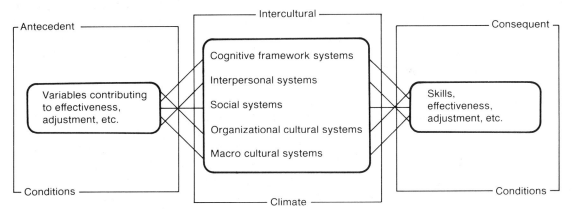

Figure 11.1
A model for intercultural skills.

The model presented in figure 11.1 is another way to look at the research into intercultural communication skills. As we can see, the model explores the interaction among antecedent, process, and consequent conditions. In other words, beyond merely exploring variables that predict intercultural effectiveness, we need to examine the intercultural climates that intervene and affect the ultimate effectiveness outcomes. Those climates include intrapersonal and cognitive frameworks, interpersonal systems, social systems, corporate cultures, and macrocultures that affect our perceptions, values, and social skills relating to effectiveness.

In the long run, intercultural communication skills are not "push-button" substitutes for understanding. Communication strategies are never mechanistic, artificial ways around loving, warm, personal involvement with people and the hard work required to make relationships work. There is more than a "pen pal" mentality at stake. The utilization of a skill orientation can make an intercultural relationship smoother, though not necessarily at first easier. In that way, intercultural skills are really the application of an eclectic awareness of factors contributing to effectiveness and a personal motivation to make these work in our relationships.

Developing Skills in Building Intercultural Relationships

How can you perform better in intercultural contexts? Perhaps the strategies that follow will add more skills to your understanding of the principles already introduced in this chapter.

1. *Work to emphasize areas of similarity with others.* To the extent you can underscore commonality, generally the better the interpersonal relationship.

2. *Try to accept differing opinions.* In this way, you can remain open and receptive. Dogmatism has a way of blocking intercultural communication.

3. *Make your verbal messages consistent with your nonverbal messages.* Listen to yourself and try to see yourself talk. Discrepancies between the verbal and nonverbal send a mixed message that in the long run discredits you.

4. *Avoid dominating conversations.* Listen to how much time you spend communicating while in a group. You may be dominating others in the group, and it may not be long before they find you a bore. Listening to others, inviting their explanations, and showing genuine interest are communication suggestions.

5. *Avoid being submissive in conversations.* Although domination can prove to be harmful, if you are overly submissive, people may decide that you have nothing to contribute, a condition that leads to intercultural relationship demise.

6. *Be an affirmer.* You do not have to be a backslapper or act obsequiously to be confirming in your communication behavior. Your intercultural counterparts will appreciate your attempts at being understanding rather than critical.

7. *Practice communication clarity and conflict resolution.* Consider these brief examples as potential beginning points for better intercultural effectiveness:

Condition	Sample response
Need for clarity	"Did I understand you correctly, Hassan, when you said _____ ?"
	"Let me be sure I have this down; I understand you to say _____ ."
Certainty that message was understood by other	"Would you mind going over that in your own words and let's see if we're thinking the same thing."
Conflict	"Thu, I wouldn't upset you for the world. Could you tell me more of what you see?" (As Thu speaks, listen carefully and be

willing to respond positively toward the person, despite any disagreement over the issue.)

"I think I see what you mean. Let's see if we can work this out. Perhaps there's another viewpoint we haven't considered."

This chapter highlights the settings of interpersonal communication, particularly focusing on the influence of intervening or mediating elements, including homophily, credibility, self-disclosure, submission and dominance, formality, interpersonal attraction, work relationships, need for acceptance, and ability to cope. The chapter also reports on balance theories applied to intracultural-intercultural communication and personality variables. Finally, the chapter focuses on assumptions and variables related to the intercultural effectiveness process.

This Chapter in Perspective

1. Observe children at play. List mediating variables that you observe in their communication and give examples. Are racial differences noticed by children? If not, why not? Report these findings to your class and exchange observations with other class members. How do children reflect and pre-shadow adult intercultural communication?

2. Do a field study in which you observe dyads, or pairs, of people. Keep records. Compare nonverbal communication between friends with nonverbal communication between strangers.

3. Read a news magazine account of an intercultural contact. After reading the story, list at least five ways in which most people display poor interpersonal-intercultural communication.

Exercises

Abelson, Herbert I. *Persuasion.* New York: Springer, 1959.

Ackermann, Jean Marie, "Skill Training for Foreign Assignment: The Reluctant U.S. Case." In *Intercultural Communication: A Reader,* 2d ed., edited by Larry A. Samovar and Richard E. Porter. Belmont, Calif.: Wadsworth, 1976.

Bennett, Janet. "Transition Shock: Putting Culture Shock into Perspective." *International and Intercultural Communication Annual* 4 (1977): 45–52.

Berlo, David K., James B. Lemert, and Robert J. Mertz. "Dimensions for Evaluating the Acceptability of Message Sources." *Public Opinion Quarterly* 33 (1969): 560–76.

Berscheid, Ellen, and Elaine Walster. *Interpersonal Attraction.* Reading, Mass.: Addison-Wesley, 1969.

Resources

Brady, Robert M. "Predictive Correlates of Adoption Behavior in a Social Context: A Multiple Discriminant Analysis." Unpublished Master's thesis, Western Kentucky University, 1975.

Brooks, William D., and Philip Emmert. *Interpersonal Communication*. Dubuque, Iowa: Wm. C. Brown Company Publishers, 1976.

Burke, Jerry. "The Effects of Ethnocentrism upon Intercultural Communication." *International and Intercultural Communication Annual* 3 (1976): 20–34.

DeVito, Joseph. *The Interpersonal Communication Book*. 4th ed. New York: Harper and Row, 1986.

Dodd, Carley H. "A Profile of Variables Correlated with Culture Shock and Personal World View." Unpublished research, Abilene Christian University, Abilene, Texas, 1985.

Festinger, Leon. *A Theory of Cognitive Dissonance*. Evanston, Ill.: Row, Peterson, 1957.

Goetziner, C., and M. Valentine. "Problems in Executive Interpersonal Communication." *Personnel Administration* 27 (1964): 24–29.

Grove, Cornelius L., and Ingemar Torbiorn. "A New Conceptualization of Intercultural Adjustment and the Goals of Training." *International Journal of Intercultural Relations* 9 (1985): 205–33.

Gudykunst, William B. "Intercultural Contact and Attitude Change: A Review of Literature and Suggestions for Future Research." *International and Intercultural Communication Annual* 4 (1977): 1–16.

Gudykunst, William B., and Young Y. Kim. *Communicating with Strangers: An Approach to Intercultural Communication*. New York: Random House, 1984.

Gudykunst, William B., Richard I. Wiseman, and Mitch R. Hammer. "Determinants of a Sojourner's Attitudinal Satisfaction." In *Communication Yearbook* 1, edited by Brent Ruben. New Brunswick, N.J.: Transaction, 1977.

Hall, E. T. *The Silent Language*. New York: Anchor, 1973.

Hammer, Mitch R., William B. Gudykunst, and Richard L Wiseman. "Dimensions of Intercultural Effectiveness." *International Journal of Intercultural Relations* 2 (1978): 382–93.

Heider, Fritz. *The Psychology of Interpersonal Relations*. New York: Wiley, 1958.

Holmes, Barbara. "Racial Ethnocentrism and the Judgment of Beauty: A Restudy." Paper presented to Speech Communication Association, Chicago, December 27–31, 1974.

Hood, Kregg. "Correlation of Ethnocentrism and World View." Unpublished manuscript, Abilene Christian University, Abilene, Texas, 1982.

Hovland, Carl I., Irving L. Janis, and Harold H. Kelley, *Communication and Persuasion*. New Haven: Yale University Press, 1953.

Jourard, Sidney. *The Transparent Self*. Princeton, N.J.: Van Nostrand Reinhold, 1964.

Kim, Young Yun. "Toward an Interactive Theory of Communication—Acculturation." *Communication Yearbook* 3 (1979): 436–53.

Korman, A. I. "A Cause of Communications Failure." *Personnel Administration* 23 (1960): 17–21.

McCroskey, James C. "Oral Communication Apprehension: A Reconceptualization." Paper presented to the Speech Communication Association, Louisville, Ky., November, 1982.

McCroskey, James C., Virginia P. Richmond, and John A. Daly. "The Development of a Measure of Perceived Homophily in Interpersonal Communication." *Human Communication Research* 1 (1975): 323–32.

McCroskey, James C., and Lawrence R. Wheeless. *Introduction to Human Communication.* Boston: Allyn and Bacon, 1976.

Moran, Robert, and Philip Harris. *Managing Cultural Synergy.* Houston: Gulf, 1982.

Newcomb, Theodore, "An Approach to the Study of Communicative Acts." *Psychological Review* 66 (1960): 393–404.

Newmark, Eileen, and Molefi Asante. "Perceptions of Self and Others: An Approach to Intercultural Communication." *International and Intercultural Communication Annual* 2 (1975): 54–62.

Norton, M. Laurie. "The Effects of Communication Effectiveness and Cognitive Complexity on Culture Shock." Master's thesis, Abilene Christian University, Abilene, Texas, 1984.

Norton, M. Laurie, and Carley H. Dodd. "The Relationship of Self-Report Communication Effectiveness to Culture Shock." Paper presented to the Speech Communication Association, Chicago, November 5, 1984.

Overseas Diplomacy. U.S. Navy, Bureau of Navy Personnel, 1973.

Rogers, Everett M. *Diffusion of Innovations.* 3d ed. New York: Free Press, 1983.

Rogers, Everett M., with Lynne Svenning. *Modernization among Peasants: The Impact of Communication.* New York: Holt, Rinehart and Winston, 1969.

Rokeach, Milton. *The Open and Closed Mind.* New York: Basic Books, 1960.

Rosegrant, Teresa J., and James C. McCroskey. "The Effects of Race and Sex on Proxemic Behavior in an Interview Setting." *Southern Speech Communication Journal* 40 (1975): 408–20.

Ruben, Brent. "Human Communication and Cross-Cultural Effectiveness." *International and Intercultural Communication Annual* 4 (1977): 95–105.

Ruhly, Sharon. *Orientations to Intercultural Communication.* Palo Alto, Calif.: SRA, 1976.

Samovar, Larry, Richard Porter, and Nemi Jain. *Understanding Intercultural Communication.* Belmont, Calif.: Wadsworth, 1981.

Sarbaugh, Larry. *Intercultural Communication.* Rochelle Park, N.J.: Hayden, 1979.

Scheidel, Thomas. *Speech Communication and Human Interaction.* Glenview, Ill.: Scott, Foresman, 1972.

Shaw, Marvin E. *Group Dynamics.* 2d ed. New York: McGraw-Hill, 1976.

Thibaut, J. W., and H. H. Kelley. *The Social Psychology of Groups.* New York: Wiley, 1959.

Tucker, Michael F., and Vicki E. Baier. "Research Background for the Overseas Assignment Inventory." Paper presented to the SIETAR International Conference, San Antonio, Texas, May 15, 1985.

Tuppen, Christopher J. S. "Dimensions of Communicator Credibility: An Oblique Solution." *Speech Monographs* 41 (1974): 253–60.

Wheeless, Lawrence R., and Janis Grotz. "Self-Disclosure and Trust: Conceptualization, Measurement, and Inter-relationships." Paper presented to the International Communication Association Convention, Chicago, April, 1975.

Yousef, Fathi, and Nancy Briggs. "The Multinational Business Organization: A Schema for the Training of Overseas Personnel in Communication." *International and Intercultural Communication Annual* 2 (1975): 74–85.

Intercultural Communication and Communicator Similarity

Objectives

After completing this chapter, you should be able to:

1. Determine the effects of homophily on intercultural contact.

2. Delineate basic dimensions of homophily.

3. Give examples of how homophily aids and / or mitigates information flow.

4. Utilize a measure of interpersonal homophily.

Many of our interpersonal relationships begin and end because we discover similarities that draw us toward another person or because we find differences that repel us. Human beings tend to categorize others as "one of us" or as something "less." This propensity greatly affects our intercultural relationships, for we hang mental labels on others of "similar" or "different" and often act in a manner consistent with our evaluation. This chapter examines our intercultural perceptions of similarity and difference and the effects of those feelings on information sharing.

Imagine for a moment an ambassador from Saudi Arabia talking with an ambassador from Sweden, or a British agricultural extension representative attempting to persuade a Boran herdsman from Kenya, or a middle-class white selling furniture to urban blacks, or a white school teacher persuading a Mexican-American community to adopt youth recreation programs. The common element in these examples is their simultaneous interpersonal and intercultural relationship. Yet, each of these situations involves very different people, and the differences between the people are important. Again, many intercultural communication relationships begin and end with images of similarity or difference between two parties.

As chapter 1 indicated, a fundamental focus of communication is the creation of commonality—approximating unity of ideas. However, perceived differences can, from the outset, obviate any hope of clarity and instead foster mutual suspicion, distrust, and ambivalence. Furthermore, in intercultural communication, individual differences, however they are perceived, are magnified by the addition of cultural differences. This perception of differences is a basis for a primary assumption about intercultural communication: the need to recognize differences and bridge them through communication. The term used to refer to those perceived differences is *heterophily*. The degree of similarity in interpersonal perception is called *homophily*. Homophily and heterophily are important for one reason: They form the perceptual relationship basis for information sharing. The tendency to communicate with those similar to us is called the *homophily principle*.

Dimensions of Homophily

Like credibility, homophily can be broken down into its component parts. The five dimensions of homophily are: (1) appearance homophily, (2) background homophily, (3) attitude homophily, (4) value homophily, and (5) personality homophily (McCroskey, Richmond, and Daly 1975).

Appearance Homophily

The research investigating the kinds of factors that people use to evaluate similarity or difference reveals that physical appearance is one of the first ways we judge other people. In general, persons who have similar physical characteristics judge one another as similar, and thus homophilous. This feeling applies not only to generalized appearance, but includes looks, size, and even clothing. The problem of cultural stereotyping, as we discussed in chapter 3, is partly related to appearance homophily. For instance, a North American student and an Iranian student see the other approaching in the hallway. Based

According to the homophily principle, we tend to interact with other individuals similar in social characteristics.

solely on appearance, they probably come to the mutual, though silent, conclusion that "this person is different from me." In turn, that heterophily perception may precipitate little more than a greeting—or possibly feelings of hostility on the part of one or both. Many people close their thinking at the point of appearance only, without reference to significant other indications of homophily or heterophily.

We also judge others on our perceptions of age, education, residence, and other demographic features, ratings of similarity that we call background homophily. For instance, McCroskey, Richmond, and Daly (1975) found that perception of social class, economic situation, and social status highly influenced most of their respondents' judgments toward others. In their study of Colombian villages, Rogers with Svenning (1969) reported that perceived differences in social status between farmers and their "hacienda" owners created a situation in which information passed among individuals within a social class. In other words, homophily was so predominant that information did not "spill over" to outside groups marked by their background homophily.

Background Homophily

Attitude homophily includes commonality of personal attitudes and opinions. Actually, people who share similar attitudes seem to maintain friendships and join together in other ways. Furthermore, perceived attitude homophily in person B, for example, not only reinforces person A's attitude, but also creates a positive relationship between these two people.

Attitude Homophily

Another element of homophily is a perception of similarity in morality, sexual norms, ways of treating people, and other general values (McCroskey, Richmond, and Daly 1975). Value homophily, sometimes referred to as morality homophily, requires an assessment of long-enduring judgments of good and

Value Homophily

bad conceptions. As an illustration, consider cultural values in Sweden's antispanking law. On May 21, 1979, newspapers reported passage of Sweden's new law prohibiting parents from spanking their children. The reasons advanced for this law included norms of antiviolence; supporters argued that spanking would lead to child beating and abuse. Various subcultural groups in Sweden, particularly some religious minorities, have argued against the law, claiming that it strips parents of their natural rights to correct their children by what they consider tried and proven methods. At its root, this clash focuses upon values of protection from all physical punishment, on the one hand, and values of physical punishment as a means to a "greater end" of child rearing, on the other hand.

Personality Homophily

In addition to these other dimensions of homophily, people also perceive similarity or dissimilarity of personality. For one thing, research studies indicate that we attribute greater feelings of friendship and attraction to people we perceive as similar to us (Byrne 1961). Also, friends are more similar in personality than nonfriends (Berscheid and Walster 1969). Furthermore, there is a tendency to project onto our friends the very characteristics we lack. So, we usually conceive of the ideal person in North American culture as a psychologically strong, self-sufficient person who is able to give emotional gratification. Curiously, then, there is a kind of personality projection in which we attribute personality characteristics we lack upon our friends (Beier, Rossi, and Garfield 1961). Furthermore, these projected characteristics are often characteristics of a culturally ideal person. For example, males typically attribute more masculine interests to their friends than to themselves, but not to nonfriends. If we expand this principle, then it appears that each of us conceives of culturally ideal persons, and we project on our friends these ideal personality characteristics that we secretly would prefer in ourselves. For example, if a person is introverted and perceives a culturally ideal person to be extroverted, then he or she will typically project extroversion qualities on a friend. It seems, then, that friendship develops not only because of personality homophily but also because within that homophilous bond is a phenomenon of attributing to friends positive, ideal cultural characteristics that we ourselves lack.

Homophily and Interpersonal Attraction

The principles we have discussed up to now suggest that we perceive others as similar or different—that is, we categorize according to these terms. But what causes us to like those individuals with whom we feel some sense of similarity? To answer, we turn to a brief discussion of interpersonal attraction, a concept related to homophily. Interpersonal attraction refers to the degree of interpersonal liking and a desire to maintain a relationship with the other person.

Physical Attraction

Research studies confirm our intuitions that interpersonal attraction is related in part to physical attractiveness (McCroskey and McCain 1974). However,

this effect is short-lived and not isolated from task and social attraction. Initially, physical attraction is the most typical reason for communication encounters. Without some degree of attraction, little chance exists for interpersonal affinity (McCroskey and Wheeless 1976). However, as two people know one another over a period of time, the other dimensions of attraction become more important.

Values in the United States seem to indicate an intense interest in appearances, despite the age-old warning that "beauty is only skin deep." North Americans seem to enjoy a fascination with beauty and good looks. By comparison, other cultures emphasize psychological dimensions of attraction, such as wisdom (ancient Hebrew culture), slyness (Iranian culture), and courage (Indian subculture). Also, one's idea of beauty is relative to a culture's norms of physical attractiveness. Oily skin, short hair, a pin through the nose, or slimness may be preferred, depending on one's outlook—and culture.

Task attraction is the degree to which we perceive the competence of another person, with whom we find it easy to work and with whom we would like to continue a job of some sort (McCroskey and Wheeless 1976). This attraction factor explains why we like people who can perform jobs especially well. The North American cultural ideal is often the person who excels in the execution of his or her skills. For example, in the United States, one of our mirrors of popular culture is the cinema. So, consider for a moment the movie *Airport*

Our circle of friendships is highly conditioned by homophilous individuals, usually interpersonally attracted by task and social skills.

Task Attraction

(or its sequels), in which the airport manager makes the right decision at the right time, risks his reputation and life for the sake of the passengers, but averts an imminent airplane crash. The audience is left not only with the thrill of high drama but with an admiration for his "skill" in performing the job. Admiration for task ability is evident in a number of cultures, though such competence takes many forms, depending upon cultural expectations. Among some black males in the United States, the ability to join in rhyming games, especially to joke insultingly with others, is a sign of linguistic competence and cultural attraction.

Social Attraction

In addition to physical and task attraction, we develop affinity toward others by assessing the degree to which we would enjoy spending time with them. Of course, we may enjoy a person socially yet decry the idea of working at a job with that person. In the same way, we may be physically attracted to a person's dress and looks but not wish to interact in either a task or social environment.

The homophily principle implies that, when two people perceive similarities, they tend to communicate more frequently and more effectively. Its relation to attraction and affinity stems from an extension of the principle. Simply put, the more we perceive ourselves as similar to another person, the more we like that person. And reciprocally, attraction can produce homophily. Homophily and attraction both are related to positive, rewarding communication (Byrne and Griffitt 1966) and to social and physical proximity (Rogers and Shoemaker 1971).

The Homophily Principle and Intercultural Communication

Obviously, we obtain a lot of information from interpersonal sources, many times from daily relationships—friends, family, and peers. And these relationships may alter our knowledge, motivation, and behavior more than we realize.

Homophily and Information Sharing: The Friendship Connection

Up to this point, the chapter has described the dimensions of homophily and interpersonal attraction. The consequence of homophily is best described in the homophily principle, which is to say that we share information with similar persons. Under this condition of perceived homophily, communication is generally more effective than heterophilous communication. Or to put it another way:

> When the source(s) and receiver(s) share common meanings, attitudes and beliefs, and a mutual code, communication between them is likely to be more effective. Most individuals enjoy the comfort of interacting with those who are similar in social status, education, beliefs, etc. Interaction with those quite different involves more effort to make communication effective. Heterophilic interaction is likely to cause message distortion, delayed transmission, restriction of communication channels, and may cause cognitive dissonance, as the receiver is exposed to messages that may be inconsistent with his existing beliefs and attitudes, an uncomfortable psychological state. (Rogers and Bhowmik 1971, 527)

A number of examples reflect the homophily principle: political voting choices are usually discussed among people of similar age and education; farmers talk with other farmers perceived to have attitude and value homophily; Chicago inner-city dwellers communicate with other inner-city dwellers of similar social status, age, marital status, and family size about family planning; Indian villagers interact mostly with other villagers of similar caste, education, and farm size about social questions.

Total homophily would be impossible, for then no one would be able to share anything with another person that the other person did not already know. Thus, opinion leaders are usually slightly higher in certain social characteristics than those they influence. Figure 12.1 illustrates the homophily principle, showing that those who seek information are within a range of similarity. This figure also points out how homophily and opinion leadership work jointly, since we typically do not seek advice from heterophilous people. In a study of Colombian villages, research findings clearly revealed that information sharing occurred within social strata and not across lines of social status, land ownership, and so on:

> For example, in the Colombian villages, there was the tendency for informal interaction to occur between farmers of generally similar social status. Seldom did a small farmer initiate a discussion about an innovation with a very large landowner (*hacendado*); perhaps the small farmer thought the *hacendado* would be an inappropriate role model for his adoption behavior, or maybe the *hacendado* was socially inaccessible to the small peasant. The lines of communication in a peasant village seem to flow horizontally within social classes, rather than vertically between those of different social classes. (Rogers with Svenning 1969, 235)

The homophily principle is further illustrated by a study in Ghana (Dodd 1973), in which respondents were asked their sociometric choices for opinion leadership. African villagers in that study preferred opinion leaders who were homophilous in terms of their filial relationship, village residence, and religious membership. They preferred friends or relatives, someone in their home village, and someone of the same religious membership across widely variant topics.

Homophily and Persuasion

A logical extension of the homophily principle is to ask if individuals are persuaded because of homophily. The affirmative response to that question is underscored by a number of studies linking homophily to persuasion.

For instance, Berscheid (1966) found that communicators who were homophilous with their audience members in a laboratory setting responded by changing their attitudes toward a topic more often than under conditions of heterophily. In a curious way, this laboratory finding matches a number of classic field studies that examined the role of homophily in persuasive campaigns. For example, in a now classic study of 393 farm operators in Kentucky, Marsh and Coleman (1954) found that farmers who tended to adopt a large number of new farming practices had a high number of kinship relations (first

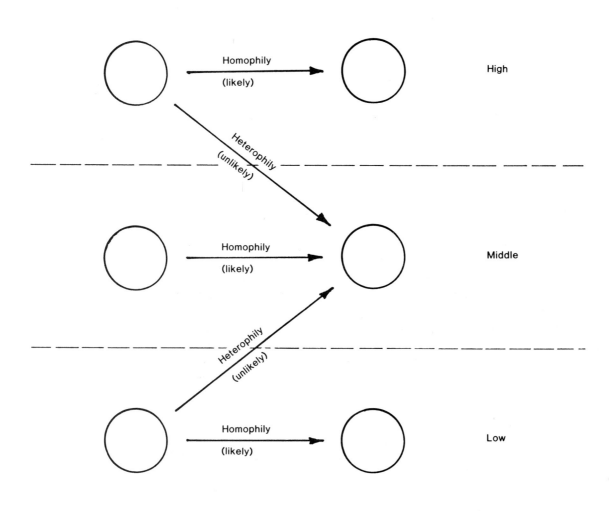

Figure 12.1
Homophily principle:
people communicate
and share
information with
individuals similar in
social
characteristics.

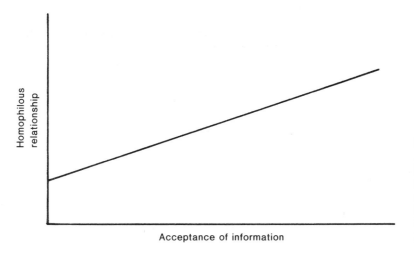

Figure 12.2
Acceptance of information increases corresponding to increases in homophilous relationships.

Acceptance of information

cousins or closer), close friendships, and work ties with other families and individuals who likewise had adopted a high percentage of new farming practices. This study supports a basic function of homophilous relationships, namely that homophily and adoption of ideas and products are correlated (illustrated in figure 12.2). As homophily increases, there is a corresponding increase in persuasion to buy new products and adopt new ideas, a phenomenon linked to these interpersonal ties.

Let us examine the relationship between homophily and persuasion from the standpoint of a medical subculture of physicians adopting a new drug. New drugs are usually introduced into the market through relevant medical journals and through sales personnel. The latter sources not only introduce the innovation but attempt to persuade their doctor-clients to adopt it by prescribing the drug for patients. In a well-known scientific research effort, Menzel and Katz (1955) followed the diffusion of a new drug in a New England community among 83 percent of the physicians practicing in the community. Not only did they discover the predominance of clique groups (figure 12.3), but also that clique group membership evolved as a result of homophily. Members of the three physician clique groups in this study were of similar age, ethnicity, religion, father's occupation, and speciality. Furthermore, adoption of the new drug followed lines of clique group membership, so that clique groups, marked by their homophily, tended to adopt around the same time.

The general homophily principle, however, differs depending on the social system. Traditional villages differ somewhat from modern villages in the kind of people with whom traditional villagers choose to interact. In other words, the type of community affects the homophily principle. Let us examine those differences by turning to some cases that have reported social system differences in communication situations where information has been passed interpersonally.

Homophily and Social Systems

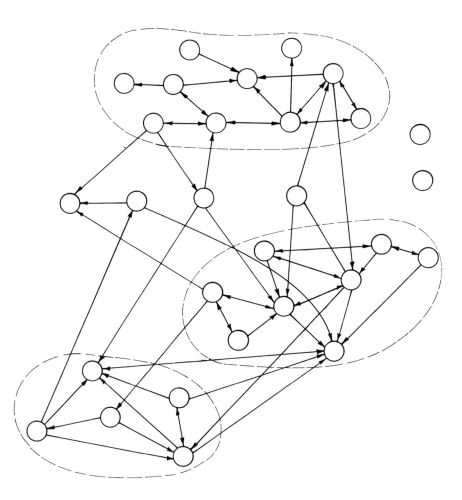

Figure 12.3
Illustration of new drug diffusion among New England physicians. The study showed who talked with whom on social occasions. Clique groups tended to adopt simultaneously.

In an extensive research project in two traditional and three modern Colombian villages, traditional villagers tended to interact homophilously. In other words, in the traditional villages, little information flowed downwardly, but rather, flowed horizontally; farmers considering agricultural innovations sought information from others with little more knowledge and competence than they themselves possessed. By contrast, modern villagers sought information from more competent individuals, who were also more innovative; this process necessarily led the modern villager farmers to interact with less homophilous individuals (Rogers with Svenning 1969).

Similar findings were reported in Bose's (1967) study of traditional Indian villages. He found a high degree of homophily on the basis of caste, education, and farm size in these traditional settings. However, in nearby Calcutta, income was the most important basis for predicting interaction and, thus, heterophily seemed to work in the large city.

In traditional towns and villages, information tends to flow horizontally and informally among people with homophilous social characteristics, illustrated by this Guatemalan village.

Optimal Heterophily

As we just discussed, the nature of a social system, traditional or modern, has an effect on how people seek information. Thus, in modern villages, people seek individuals who are technically more competent than they and who show some degree of increased innovativeness. However, this situation still occurs within a tolerable range of difference. People interact with others more *competent* than they on a task, but who are, nevertheless, homophilous in social characteristics.

The range of tolerable difference is called *optimal heterophily*. This concept clearly recognizes the simple fact mentioned earlier: If two people are perfectly homophilous, then one would know little more than the other about an innovation. So, if a person desires information about an innovation, he or she typically seeks someone else who is heterophilous in knowledge but homophilous enough in social characteristics to facilitate information sharing. For instance, suppose an Indian villager were deciding upon a new type of seed for seasonal planting on his farm. Depending upon motivation, the farmer would need information from someone more knowledgeable than he and yet someone with whom he could identify. A scientist would be too heterophilous; a close relative too homophilous. So, ideally, the farmer would discover someone with homophily in some characteristics but heterophily in knowledge. This situation calls for optimal heterophily.

This modification advocating moderate dissimilarity appears a necessary ingredient for message awareness, or as Rogers and Shoemaker (1971, 15) noted, "Ideally, they are homophilous on all other variables (education, social status, and the like) even though heterophilous regarding the innovation." Dodd (1973) found among respondents in Ghana that background heterophily clearly marked the message awareness stage of an innovation decision, but homophily characterized subjects' actual evaluation and ultimate adoption of an innovation. In other words, there can be a mix of homophilous and heterophilous

Table 12.1 Scale for Perceived Homophily

	Attitude Dimension	
Doesn't think like me:	1 2 3 4 5 6 7	:Thinks like me
*Behaves like me:	1 2 3 4 5 6 7	:Doesn't behave like me
*Similar to me:	1 2 3 4 5 6 7	:Different from me
Unlike me:	1 2 3 4 5 6 7	:Like me
	Background Dimension	
*From social class similar to mine:	1 2 3 4 5 6 7	From social class :different from mine
Economic situation different from mine:	1 2 3 4 5 6 7	Economic situation :like mine
*Status like mine:	1 2 3 4 5 6 7	:Status different from mine
Background different from mine:	1 2 3 4 5 6 7	Background similar :to mine
	Value Dimension	
Morals unlike mine:	1 2 3 4 5 6 7	:Morals like mine
Sexual attitudes unlike mine:	1 2 3 4 5 6 7	:Sexual attitudes like mine
*Shares my values:	1 2 3 4 5 6 7	:Doesn't share my values
*Treats people as I do:	1 2 3 4 5 6 7	:Doesn't treat people as I do
	Appearance Dimension	
*Looks similar to me:	1 2 3 4 5 6 7	:Looks different from me
Different size than I am:	1 2 3 4 5 6 7	:Same size I am
*Appearance like mine:	1 2 3 4 5 6 7	:Appearance unlike mine
Doesn't resemble me:	1 2 3 4 5 6 7	:Resembles me

Source: McCroskey, Richmond, and Daly 1975.
*Scale for these items should be scored in reverse direction, 7 to 1.

information sources. Which role is chosen depends on how much a person knows to begin with and how far along he or she is in a decision to act upon information (see Alpert and Anderson 1973).

Measuring Homophily

Two methods exist for measuring homophily. One is the method of mathematically developing adopter categories and then counting the number of times a homophilous pair occurs within the same adopter category.* For instance, Rogers with Svenning (1969) reported that 66 percent of the sociometric dyads were the same or close to the same adopter categories.

The second method for measuring homophily is the use of a scale, primarily focusing on interpersonal dimensions of a perceived homophily (McCroskey, Richmond, and Daly 1975). This scale, shown in table 12.1, has high reliability and validity and continues to be useful for perceived homophily. Its use has been demonstrated across samples of high school, college, and adult populations, though only in the United States.

*Adopter categories are derived by mathematically computing the mean and standard deviation for any sample of respondents based on their time of adoption. Each standard deviation away from the mean marks a new adopter category. Ho (1969) discussed this method of deriving a homophily score, as did Rogers with Svenning (1969), who used an averaging method. The method discussed in this chapter, which involves measuring interpersonal perceived homophily through interpersonal scales, is easier to calculate and provides about the same results.

Skills improvement for intercultural contexts can be heightened by an awareness of the homophily principle. The following list is a brief extension of the homophily principle into some practical areas:

1. *Deemphasize background in cases of wide economic disparity in background.* Too often, a person may unconsciously view wealth and power as a solution to many problems, rather than specializing in developing healthy intercultural relationships. It may be better to look to value and attitude relationships, where you can build friendships in the absence of appearance and background homophily.

2. *Seek a common ground.* If one person values material possessions, for example, a second person who finds these values extreme may feel little commonality. Build common ground by emphasizing areas of similarity.

3. *Tolerate differing values.* Inevitably, values between persons of different cultures clash. Despite these differences, you can build a "homophily" of respect and of tolerance for difference. Encourage communication about those differences and strive to build bridges of affection and empathy.

4. *Try to understand different views of knowledge.* Some people view knowledge as personal only, while only people perceive knowledge and attitudes as valid for everyone (Ruben 1977). Differences in knowledge and attitudes between two people should not be viewed as "I am right and you are wrong," but as differences to be shared. Rather than assume knowledge and attitude heterophily, suspend judgment and invite dialogue.

5. *Develop sensitivity to values.* By remaining alert to others' needs and values, you can turn heterophily into productive interaction. Heterophily gaps can serve to fill areas where you find yourself unknowledgeable, but you must initiate the discussion.

Developing Intercultural Communication Skills Concerning Homophily

---

The concept of homophily implies similarities in social characteristics. Heterophily implies differences, while optimal heterophily indicates a tolerable range of heterophily, where two people are socially homophilous but heterophilous on competence and information. Appearance homophily refers to similarity of dress, looks, and so on. Background homophily refers to similarity of residence, education, social status, race, and so on. Attitude homophily refers to perceived similarities on topics, while value homophily involves outlook and long-enduring judgments of good and bad. Personality homophily indicates similarity of behavioral predispositions.

This chapter also links interpersonal attraction factors (physical, task, and social attraction) with homophily, since homophily does not function in isolation. In addition, the chapter focuses on the influence of homophily in communication, such as in persuasion. Finally, the chapter reveals two methods

This Chapter in Perspective

of measuring homophily: counting the number of homophilous pairs within each adopter category and measuring interpersonal perceived homophily through interpersonal scales.

Exercises

1. Ask some of your friends to complete the interpersonal homophily scale in table 12.1 with regard to a person mutually known and somewhat respected. Now have them complete the same scale for someone in the news from a foreign country. What differences do you observe between the two?

2. Ask an international student to discuss with you the nature of interpersonal relationships in his or her country. In what ways does the homophily principle operate the same as in the United States? In what ways is it different?.

3. Observe interethnic, intercultural, and intracultural communication in a public place. Do you see some ways in which homophily operates in these situations? How? In what ways does heterophily operate? Why?

Resources

Alpert, M. I., and W. T. Anderson. "Optimal Heterophily and Communication Effectiveness." *Journal of Communication* 23 (1973): 328–43.

Beier, E. G., A. M. Rossi, and R. L. Garfield. "Similarity Plus Dissimilarity of Personality: Basis for Friendship?" *Psychological Reports* 8 (1961): 3–8.

Berscheid, Ellen. "Opinion Change and Communicator-Communicatee Similarity and Dissimilarity." *Journal of Personality and Social Psychology* 4 (1966): 670–80.

Berscheid, Ellen, and Elaine H. Walster. *Interpersonal Attraction.* Reading, Mass.: Addison-Wesley, 1969.

Bose, S. P. "Social Interaction in an Indian Village." *Sociologia Ruralis* 7 (1967): 156–75.

Byrne, D. "Interpersonal Attraction and Attitude Similarity." *Journal of Abnormal and Social Psychology* 62 (1961): 713–15.

Byrne, D. and J. Griffitt. "A Developmental Investigation of the Law of Attraction." *Journal of Personality and Social Psychology* 4 (1966): 699–703.

Dodd, Carley H. "Homophily and Heterophily in Diffusion of Innovations: A Cross-Cultural Analysis in an African Setting." Paper presented at the Speech Communication Association Convention, New York, November 10, 1973.

Ho, Yung Chang. "Homophily in Interaction Patterns in the Diffusion of Innovations in Colombian Villages." Unpublished Master's thesis, Michigan State University, 1969.

McCroskey, James C., and Thomas McCain. "The Measurement of Interpersonal Attraction." *Speech Monographs* 41 (1974): 261–66.

McCroskey, James C., Virginia P. Richmond, and John A. Daly. "The Development of a Measure of Perceived Homophily in Interpersonal Communication." *Human Communication Research* 1 (1975): 323–32.

McCroskey, James C., and Lawrence Wheeless. *Introduction to Human Communication.* Boston: Allyn and Bacon, 1976.

Marsh, C. Paul, and A. Lee Coleman. "Farmers' Practice-Adoption Rates in Relation to Adoption Rates of Leaders." *Rural Sociology* 19 (1954): 180–81.

Menzel, Herbert, and Elihu Katz. "Social Relations and Innovation in the Medical Profession: The Epidemiology of a New Drug." *Public Opinion Quarterly* 19 (1955): 337–52.

Rogers, Everett M., and D. K. Bhowmik. "Homophily-Heterophily: Relational Concepts for Communication Research." *Public Opinion Quarterly* 34 (1971): 523–37.

Rogers, Everett M., and F. Floyd Shoemaker. *Communication of Innovations: A Cross-Cultural Approach.* New York: Free Press, 1971.

Rogers, Everett M., with Lynne Svenning. *Modernization among Peasants: The Impact of Communication.* New York: Holt, Rinehart and Winston, 1969.

Ruben, Brent. "Human Communication and Cross-Cultural Effectiveness." *International and Intercultural Communication Annual* 4 (1977): 95–105.

Intercultural Communication and Communicator Credibility

Objectives

After completing this chapter, you should be able to:

1. Identify key elements of intercultural credibility across cultural circumstances.

2. Apply credibility factors to specific leaders in various cultures to understand their success or demise.

3. Apply credibility factors to create credible images in intercultural interactions.

4. Identify specific characteristics of charisma and charisma's application to intercultural communication demands.

Intercultural relationships involve interpersonal roles that are part of the communication climate in which we interact. The perceived credibility of another person in a relationship constitutes a specific kind of role: the communicator role of information giving and credibility.

A few years ago, Helen Sohns, a German nurse, worked among the Mataco Indians at the northernmost part of Argentina's border and described her attempts to introduce better birth delivery techniques. At first, the Indian women eyed her suspiciously, but, gradually, after a series of special lessons for birth attendants, her credibility as a trusted source increased. She particularly credited the following message, presented during her lessons, for some of her increased credibility:

> When you make bread, you need flour; when your husband makes a chair, he needs wood (most men here are carpenters). In the same way, a woman in whose body a baby is growing needs enough food to form the baby's body. If she does not have enough food, the baby will be weak, and her own body will suffer and get weak. Have you noticed how the women's teeth go bad after having a baby? That is because the baby takes what it needs to form its bones, and the mother's body suffers. Now, your custom is that a woman who is expecting a baby must eat very little during the last three months so that the baby will be small. It is true that we do not want an enormously big baby that will cause difficulty in delivery, but we do want a strong baby. There are some foods that make a person fat, such as bread, noodles, sugar, semolina, rice, etc. It is right that an expectant mother should not eat too much of these. But there are other foods which give a lot of strength and do not make a person fat, such as meat, fish, eggs, milk, fruit, and vegetables. A pregnant woman should eat plenty of these, so that the baby will be strong without being fat. (Sohns 1975, 314)

As a result of several efforts similar to this presentation, Sohns reported a greater sense of trust from the birth attendants in this traditional setting and found them calling upon her much more frequently and readily. What happened as a result of this speech that produced that heightened trust in this highly personal, intercultural communication situation? The villagers perceived trust, expertness, and a certain oneness with this nurse, or, as she went on to state, "They do not regard me as a rival now, but as a colleague."

This case is not isolated but has been repeated thousands of times around the world wherever people are speaking or listening, across time or topic. The interface between sources and receivers dramatically raises the question of why we believe someone—there is clearly a dynamic perception on the part of listeners that causes them to turn to another person in belief or disbelief, in trust or mistrust, in praise or blame. What are those qualities perceived between people? Can we infer elements applicable for raising credibility interculturally? Credibility in intercultural communication alters our relationships and impacts upon the information-giving and receiving roles of people. The exact nature of communicator credibility is the focus of this chapter.

Dimensions of Communicator Credibility

Communicator credibility refers to the degree of believability of a speaker. Going beyond mere believability, however, communicator credibility encompasses a number of factors, including authority, trust, co-orientation, charisma, and dynamism. These five categories have been derived from a number of research studies investigating the underlying dimensions of communicator credibility. For instance, early research identified expertness and trustworthiness as two major elements of communicator credibility (Hovland, Janis, and Kelley 1953). Later studies extended those earlier findings to include character (McCroskey 1966), dynamism (Berlo, Lemert, and Mertz 1966), and objectivity (Applbaum and Anatol 1972). Tuppen (1974) identified not only trustworthiness, expertness, and dynamism but added that the communicator who creates the impression that he or she stands for similar interests as the receiver—a factor called co-orientation—and the communicator who is thought of as overwhelmingly convincing also have communicator credibility.

Authority

Perceived authoritativeness does not indicate that the speaker is authoritarian, for that notion implies an element of dominance, perhaps even obstinacy. Rather, we refer here to one who holds specialized knowledge and insight. Research identifying elements of authoritativeness has referred to such adjectives as "reliable," "informed," "qualified," "intelligent," "valuable," and "expert." From an intercultural perspective, these items extend to encompass two basic features: expertness and eliteness.

Authority by expertness. Many cultures value training in speciality areas, so that, when particularly distinctive work needs to be accomplished, one typically calls in a "consultant" or some other expert. From a broader point of view, our values lead us to think of specialization as an ideal, a goal. The folklore phrase, "Jack of all trades and master of none," describes a person who is unskilled or unspecialized and may be a phrase of derogation. Specialities in North American culture typically hinge upon technology and productivity.

The notion of "expert authority" is universal. Cultural members seek advice from experts, but often the experts are skilled in a number of areas, particularly in working with people. Villagers, tribesmen, and others serve unique roles as experts in marriage, farming, religion, food, and building. In other words, these individuals possess characteristics of "polymorphic leadership," which means that they may be experts in several areas, not just one. In any case, the need for information competence leads us into role relationships where that need can be satisfied.

Authority by power eliteness. Unlike North American culture, where many people perceive themselves as relatively equal to each other, a number of cultures hold the view that credibility stems from special gifts—charms, mana, money, education, and so on. The few with power to rule are called elites. By eliteness, we mean those individuals who are set apart, not only because of their perceived authority by a group of individuals, but because they are generally accepted by a culture to be authoritative and because they hold special prestige in the culture for their authority. For instance, a village shaman is typically believed to hold certain powers and, consequently, authority. But this authority may be described as "elitist," since few people in the culture hold such power, authority, and thus, such prestige. This power base may at first seem unusual, but it is an important variable for vicarious strength, attraction, and information.

In a now classic study examining communication among immigrants in Israel following their independence, Eisenstadt (1966) reported upon the role of elites as influentials. He interviewed immigrants streaming into Israel from numerous parts of the world. He found that, upon their arrival, the immigrants sought information on basic survival aspects of living in the new culture. Eisenstadt examined the role of various sources of communication in this acculturation process. As the following percentages reveal, most of the immigrants found the most effective communication to come from authoritative sources, whom Eisenstadt classified as elites:

Formal, impersonal	10 percent
Personal appeal from official to immigrant	25 percent
Through leaders (elites)	65 percent

The 65 percent who found the elites' communication to be most effective stressed the perceived authority and yet personableness of the elites. The following statements highlight the role of elite communication in this situation:

"We do not want only to hear orders from far away people, even if they are very wise and know everything. Our rabbis know that the best way is to gather all of us in the synagogue and to tell us about it and to explain it to us. Otherwise, we do not listen. . . ."

"In our place, they (old leaders) were really very important and honored as they knew everything about our tradition, how to arrange things, the right ways to behave. But here it changes, it is otherwise. . . . They do not always understand this, and they cannot help us in getting our way here. That is why I became interested in the new (political) organizations and frequent these meetings. The organizers are here really important people and know how to advise you, and so some of us are going there." (Eisenstadt 1966, 581, 584)

These statements underscore the social tendency to seek authoritative information. Under conditions of ambiguity, people seek the information-giving roles that elites provide.

Trust Trustworthiness is another dimension of communicator credibility and relates to such features as honesty, unselfishness, virtuousness, and character. In other words, to the extent that we perceive a speaker to be trustworthy, we tend to attribute high credibility to that speaker. Trust has also been linked with interpersonal communication—we typically reveal highly personal information only to those we explicitly trust (Tubbs and Baird 1976). In the same way, a receiver typically attributes higher credibility to those whom the receiver feels are people of character and trustworthiness.

Trust and co-orientation are important factors in intercultural communicator credibility.

During the cold war years of the 1950s, for example, the credibility gap between the United States and Russia was a trust gap. Neither side could be certain that the other would not trigger a nuclear war. The tensions became so great that steps were taken to ease the tension that threatened a world holocaust. According to Windt (1973), for the Russians to be successful in gaining their concessions, Khrushchev needed to alter Americans' perception of his being a "communist devil" to one of his being a trustworthy source. During his visit to the United States in September of 1959, Khrushchev in fact attempted to create credibility by creating a perception of trustworthiness. For instance, in the Camp David talks with President Eisenhower, he modified his position and thus gave Americans "one piece of evidence that Khrushchev was not as unreasonable as he had been portrayed," for he "contributed to a modification of our perceptions of him. He conveyed the shadow, if not the substance, of a reasonable politician, a man prepared to negotiate" (Windt 1973, 204). In contrast to a demagogue like Hitler, bent on world destruction,

> Khrushchev was entirely different. A preacher of peace and understanding, he looked more like a businessman than a politician. One reporter likened him to "any prosperous, hard-working, penny-pinching farmer who has reached the chairmanship of the local school board by sheer weight of his own toilsome success with the field." Furthermore, he had a sense of humor he displayed publicly and often turned on himself. His wife, Nina Petrovna, added to his image. No Mata Hari she, but rather a kind and gentle-looking matron who moved another American reporter to write: "There was the feeling that anyone who had the good sense to marry her, stay married to her, and bring her over here couldn't be all villian, no matter what he was doing during Stalin's regime." (Windt 1973, 208)

In this way, Khrushchev skillfully replaced the devil image with that of a trusted politician, or as Windt continued, "His agile and human responses to situations conveyed to the American people a leader who broke the mold of their stereotyped dictator" (p. 208).

The importance of trustworthiness is heightened by noting Khrushchev's actual effectiveness on the American people during the 1959 visit. A Gallup Poll revealed Khrushchev's success, for it showed that public opinion shifted from "antagonism" before the trip to "no opinion" after the trip. In effect, the strategy of inducing credibility perceptions by building images of reasonableness and trustworthiness contributed to modified perceptions of Khrushchev.

According to Tuppen (1974), another factor of communicator credibility is co-orientation, which means that people judge those with whom they communicate in terms of oneness with the speaker. In other words, people develop a communication role concerning their common goals, values, and group loyalties. The concept is similar to homophily, where two communicators perceive each other by their degree of similarity or dissimilarity. People judge other people by their value systems, group memberships, likeability, and personal goals and quickly form attitudes based solely on those characteristics. So, one of the goals in intercultural communication is to seek mutual perceptions of wanting the same things, or in other words, to establish co-orientation. The German nurse's communication, which opened this chapter, clearly sought to establish identification with the villagers, as if to say, "We truly want the same things—we have a common goal." **Co-orientation**

Establishing identification with a person or a group from another culture marks a significant step in effective intercultural communication. To the extent that we create a perception of co-orientation with our cultural neighbors, we have formed an intercultural bond bridging the gap of culture through our communication. Consider, for instance, Indonesian President Achmed Sukarno's speech to the United Nations in 1970, in which he clearly allied himself with a prevailing theme at that time of rule by the will of the people in the third world:

> Today, it is President Sukarno who addresses you. But more than that, though, it is a man. Sukarno, an Indonesian, a husband, a father, a member of the human family. I speak to you on behalf of my people, those ninety-two million people of a distant and wide archipelago, those ninety-two million who have lived a life of struggle and sacrifice, those ninety-two million people who have built a State upon the ruins of an empire. (Prosser 1973, 165)

One of the crucial mistakes of third world leaders of a decade or two ago may well have been their failure to establish a perceived similarity between themselves and their people. In not co-orienting themselves with their people, leaders of nations can suffer dire consequences, as Prosser (1973) wrote:

> Among the four charismatic leaders whom Lacouture treats, Bourguiba, Nasser, Nkrumah, and Sihanouk, all were masters of propaganda and public relations. Still only Bourguiba remained in power in mid-1972. Sihanouk's

"government by laughter" fell because he was so insensitive to his inability to communicate effectively with his followers that he, like Nkrumah, dared to leave his country, opening himself to a bloodless coup. (p. 166)

Doubtless, few of us are in a position to topple national governments because we do not communicate with co-orientation concerns, but these illustrations should heighten our awareness of the dire importance of commonality and empathy in our various intercultural relationships.

In a perceptive research article dealing with political communicator credibility, Winn (1978) called attention to a heretofore overlooked fact of political ethos that has applicability to intercultural credibility. Blending historical forces, Gallup Poll findings, and a factor analysis of the Carter-Ford presidential debates of 1976, Winn concluded that credibility depends upon rhythms of history. Apparently, for a given people, political communicator credibility depends upon cycles of history, which in turn dictates their demand for certain dimensions of political ethos. For instance, Winn's factor analysis revealed four major factors in the Carter-Ford debates: leadership, consubstantiality, trustworthiness, and dynamism. Ford scored higher on leadership, but Carter scored higher on the consubstantiality dimension, which was defined broadly but similarly to co-orientation. Winn anticipated the ultimate victory by Carter, since American history was ripe for a sense of plain folks commonality in a post-Watergate era. At another time in history, the co-orientation of Jimmy Carter may have yielded to a perception of authority and leadership of some other political candidate, which may explain the 1980 Reagan victory over Carter.

The point of Winn's study for our discussion is that history repeats norms significant to communicator credibility. During one period of a culture's history, co-orientation may indeed be the most important factor in establishing credibility, but another era may demand some other credibility factor, depending upon historical rhythms. This insight suggests that we sensitize ourselves to culturally preferred avenues of credibility. At least we can avoid using culturally unacceptable modes in speaking to others and thus potentially help ourselves to gain credibility. Also, the ways of establishing credibility in one culture may directly conflict with credibility gains in another culture. The juvenile who acts "anti-social" in dominant Anglo culture may be performing heroically in a gang subculture.

Charisma

Another element of intercultural communicator credibility is charisma. Charisma is defined as a type of leadership arising from a leader's claim to extraordinary power to remedy a distressful situation and a people's attribution of and acceptance of consequent authority. To put it another way, people believe that a charismatic person has special gifts, even supernatural powers, to lead them out of a crisis. For instance, many British citizens believed Winston Churchill to be extraordinarily talented and accepted his charismatic authority to lead England out of World War II. In another direction, Jim Jones led converts to accept his "messianic role" as cult leader and to believe that he was the only one able to deliver them from various world crises, including nuclear fallout and worldly concerns.

While an in-depth exploration of charismatic leadership is the subject of an extensive work by Max Weber and later writers interpreting Weber, we discuss here five characteristics of charisma and credibility. Since studies of charisma are so often reported in terms of leader and follower relationships, the points that follow discuss charisma similarly since the focus of this chapter is on relationships.

Charisma is perceptual on the part of followers. Each of the factors of credibility is perceptual in some ways, but charisma is especially dependent upon the followers' faith that the charismatic figure can lead them into a promising future. Dow (1973) convincingly underscored this point when he wrote of charismatic leaders:

> who reveal a transcendent mission or course of action which may be in itself appealing to the potential followers, but which is acted upon because the followers believe their leader is extraordinarily gifted. By accepting or believing in the leaders' extraordinary qualities, the followers legitimize his claim to their obedience. (p. 188)

Contrary to some public opinion in the United States, Castro actually enjoyed a charismatic leadership perception created by his followers during the early stages of the Cuban revolution. Fagen (1973) reported a survey by a Cuban research organization directed by Lloyd Free. In this survey of one thousand Cuban residents, conducted in April and May of 1960, Free classified 86 percent of his respondents as supporters of Castro's revolution. Of these 86 percent, about half were described as *fervent* supporters and reportedly made such statements about Castro as:

> "Fidel has the same ideas as Jesus Christ, our protector and guide."
> "I would kiss the beard of Fidel Castro."
> "My greatest fear is that some mean person might kill Fidel. If this happens, I think I would die."

The point of charismatic leadership depending upon a foundation of perceived power is particularly heightened by the bravery perceived in Fidel Castro, as Fagen (1973) continued:

> The theme of historical blessedness and protection received popular reinforcement from the circumstances surrounding Castro's return to Cuba from Mexico in 1956 with eighty-two men and the avowed purpose of overthrowing Batista. Only Castro and eleven others escaped to the Sierra Maestra, where they launched the guerrilla action which culminated in the downfall of Batista two years later. All the elements of high drama and miraculous escape were attached to the story of the guerrilla band during these two years. At one time, Castro was reported dead, and subsequently, a price of $100,000 was set on his head. (p. 223)

Charisma is contextual. Charismatic leaders arise during times of extraordinary stress. In this way, charisma is contextual, so that a charismatic leader in one situation may be ineffective in another, or as Fagen (1973) emphasized, "There are no universal charismatics" (p. 215). To extend the idea further, charisma's contextual nature implies that there is no "right time" for a charismatic leader to emerge; rather, such leaders arise not because of facilitating conditions but often because of adversity (Dow 1973). For example, a man like Churchill could inspire his listeners to visualize victory, despite Germany's devastating air strikes on England during World War II. Each crisis context seems to produce charismatic leaders who believe in their control over the destiny of a particular crisis, much like Hitler, Churchill, DeGaulle, and Roosevelt during an intense saga of world history.

Charisma is missionary. The charismatic leader is highly motivated toward a mission, which Max Weber described as "new, outside the realm of everyday routine, extraordinary and revolutionary." The leader believes in shaping the destiny and history of his or her people. There is a type of bond, an identification between leader and led, that makes the leader's appeal one of a "secular savior" (Dow 1973). Beyond mass perception, the charismatic leader's self-concept is one of master of history, transcending the moral order of things and inspiring the people to maintain their confidence in the leader. A good example of this principle again springs from the Cuban revolution under Fidel Castro. He viewed himself as one who was appointed and protected as part of a larger, blessed historical movment, or as Fagen (1973) wrote:

> First, Castro perceives the Revolution as part of a greater historical movement against tyranny and oppression. . . . Second, the Cuban leadership and Castro in particular are seen as blessed and protected by the larger historical movement of which the Revolution is a part. Castro's famous speech ending, "Condemn me, it doesn't matter. History will absolve me," is a classic, early articulation of this idea. Finally, because the leader is seen as acting in concert with larger historical forces not always visible to more ordinary men, he alone retains the right to determine the "correct" behavior in the service of the Revolution. (p. 219)

Under stressful conditions, such as poverty, war, and so on, it is not surprising that leaders like Hitler can convince nations of their mission. Charismatic leaders like Ghandi, Churchill, and Roosevelt believed in their task and perhaps viewed themselves as extraordinary people able to lead their nations from stress into victory.

Charisma is unstable over time. A key element in Max Weber's classic work on charisma is that charisma is effervescent—over time, the charismatic leader usually suffers demise. Fagen (1973) cited several reasons why charisma is short-lived. One reason is that the leader's image of infallibility is naturally tarnished because of inevitable failures, leading writers to note a "natural entropy of the hero's charisma" (p. 215). A second reason, according to Weber, is that the charismatic leader, over time, naturally must attend to

Dynamism is an important factor in intercultural credibility.

the affairs of state, a concern that causes the leader to be perceived as bureaucratic. This new image stands contradictory to the charismatic leader's earlier denunciation of the previous regime and thus produces a popularity loss. This circumstance, stemming from the need to attend to daily administration, is called the *routinization of charisma*. Turning to our extended example of Castro once again, some evidence reveals a shrinkage of Castro's followers and a shift away from Castro as the primary symbol of the Revolution toward a variety of other symbols and even organizational memberships. Evidence of this shift, illustrative of Castro's loss of popularity, comes from a comparison of the number of Castro's pictures that appeared in the monthly magazine of the National Institute of Agrarian Reform. Volume I (1960) of the magazine revealed an average of 8.4 pictures per month, compared with only 2.8 for volume II (1961) (Fagen 1973, 220–21).

Charisma is passed on by social ritual. Almost every culture has ways of passing on official charisma or charisma of the office. Power is passed on by ceremonies, charms, incantations, and the like. In the Serbian culture, for instance, the mother spits over the head of her baby in a religious initiation ceremony as a method of passing on blessings and a good spirit. Many cultures practice "laying on" hands as a way of passing on special powers. Coronations of kings and inauguration ceremonies of heads of states illustrate formalized ways that cultures imbue recipients with *impersonal charisma* (Dow 1973).

However, impersonal charisma should not be confused with charismatic emergence as discussed up to this point. But at some point in a culture's history, the now routinized, somewhat bureaucratic leader transfers some symbolic power of his or her charismatic leadership.

Dynamism

Another element in communicator credibility is dynamism, which refers to enthusiasm and personal involvement. Dynamism is often described in terms appraising a communicator's aggressiveness, emphatic nature, boldness, activity, and energy.

Dynamism certainly intersects with charisma, since a charismatic leader is often dynamic. The key ingredients for dynamism involve verbal and nonverbal elements. The inflammatory rhetoric of terrorism, for instance, is marked by dynamic qualities both in rhetoric and in terrorist action. Campus protests during the 1960s in the United States are most clearly remembered for their dynamic qualities. Also, black rhetoric, particularly preaching, is highly dynamic and stylized in its execution.

Research in communicator credibility across a variety of situations in North America, at least, reveals that the importance of dynamism depends upon specific situations. For instance, Applbaum and Anatol (1972) found that authority and trust considerably outranked the importance of dynamism in a classroom lecture or a speech to a social organization. However, when subjects in their experiment rated credibility for a sermon in a church, dynamism jumped from the least important factor to the second most important factor. Only trustworthiness was rated as more important than dynamism in the church context. These results suggest that context even now highly influences what individuals expect; dynamism is more important in some contexts than in others. It depends upon the cultural expectations of time, situation, and norms. Many intercultural situations demand a strong dynamic quality, for many cultures do not share European and North American emphases upon scientific proof and "logic." In fact, persuasion in parts of Africa and Latin America occurs in significant measure through emotional appeal and dynamic delivery, not enthymemes and cold logic.

Effects of Credibility on Culture

Certainly the five factors of communicator credibility just discussed are not without effects on individuals and on the entire culture. As figure 13.1 illustrates, intercultural communicator credibility factors relate to three effects of consequent credibility for communication.

Climate for Persuasion

The first effect of communicator credibility in the intercultural situation is its effect on persuasion. Three decades of research and writers as far back as Aristotle confirm that communicators perceived as highly credible are more persuasive than communicators with low credibility. Although the exact parameters of that persuasion process are constantly evolving, we are certain that credibility produces a climate for change. Individual and group belief systems originate from experiences and evidence. When a highly credible communicator provides a frame of evidence of a set of verbal and behavioral

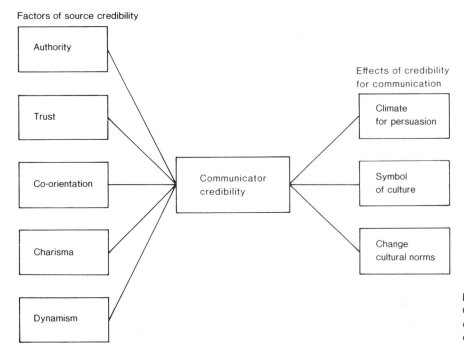

Factors of source credibility

Authority

Trust

Co-orientation

Charisma

Dynamism

Communicator
credibility

Effects of credibility
for communication

Climate
for persuasion

Symbol
of culture

Change
cultural norms

Figure 13.1
Communicator
credibility and its
effects.

experiences with which the listeners can identify, then individual and group belief systems are altered. Put another way, belief systems are protected by norms and other defenses, but a highly credible communicator opens a "crack in the door" through which further altering experiences can enter and change the belief system. In the earlier 1960s, for instance, many North Americans believed that the United States' actions were justified in the war in Vietnam, but after early repeated efforts by sources with low credibility and later, by more highly credible sources, the nation's mood and ultimately its war efforts were altered.

Communicator credibility also affects a culture in that the credible leader stands as a symbol of a culture. Among blacks in the United States, for instance, leaders like Malcolm X, Martin Luther King, and Jesse Jackson stand as symbols of black culture. Internationally, leaders like Ghandi of India, the Ayatollah Khomeini of Iran, Yassar Arafat, Nassar, Stalin, Sadat, and others are symbols of national direction, unity, and pride.

Symbol
of a Culture

A final effect of communicator credibility is that the credible communicator stimulates change in cultural norms. In a sense, communicators who are high in credibility and highly visible create an image that others emulate. This pattern of modeling or imitating is the foundation of learning theory and applies to the intercultural situation. For example, "heroes," politicians, entertainers, and other popular figures can shape not only public opinion but also norms and values.

Changing
Cultural Norms

Developing Skills in Understanding Communicator Credibility Relationships

Some of these principles of communicator credibility lead to applications to intercultural skills. The basic premise of this chapter is that intercultural contacts are influenced by a relationship between two people. Only in this case, we are emphasizing how we perceive a person's authority, trustworthiness, co-orientation, charisma, and dynamism and how these factors alter our intercultural communication. Some applications of these principles follow.

1. *Find cultural models.* Understanding culturally preferred models can help us grasp a role standard. For example, observing highly credible communicators within a culture can help us discover if the culture relies more on "emotion" or "logic," wisdom or science.

2. *Do not misuse authority.* Many visitors to a host country, for example, feel compelled to share knowledge. Unfortunately, some cultures take this behavior to mean that the visitor is acting without humility. In Japan, a U.S. naval officer stopped to assist a Japanese man whose motorcycle needed emergency repair. The officer acted judiciously, offering indirect advice, asking for permission to try an "experiment" on the motor. The reason for this indirect advice to the distressed motorcycle owner stemmed from the culture's value of not embarrassing a person by causing them to feel that they do not know how to do something. A quiet humility was appropriate—the cycle was repaired, and a friendship was established.

3. *Discover how to be trustworthy.* Studies among North Americans show that self-disclosure, friendship, and trust interact. The more trust we reveal, the more likely the chances of establishing and maintaining friendship, as long as we do not come across too strongly early in a friendship. Similarly, intercultural relationships rely on trust—and in some cases, the trust extends far beyond our own cultural expectations. For instance, trust in some cultures results from offering hospitality or showing wisdom and insight. Other cultures withhold trust unless there is some proof of loyalty, or in some cases, courage. Developing credibility in the context of intercultural relationships begins by probing ways to be trusted.

4. *Show personal concern for others.* Co-orientation is important and translates into a genuine concern for others. Build common ground interculturally; focus on similarities, not differences. Practice empathy.

5. *Be natural but flexible.* Sometimes, being "natural" can be offensive to other cultures. Then again, a person cannot be radically opposite his or her basic nature. So, be yourself, but talk and act as consistently as you can with the culture. Patience, humility, empathy, and willingness to try are characteristics that may help you maintain "naturalness" with yourself but flexibility in meeting people from other cultures. Couple with that a willingness to learn and a respect for others, and you will have overcome many beginning pitfalls.

This chapter indicates the nature of communicator credibility and its effects in intercultural situations. Authority, trust, co-orientation, charisma, and dynamism are foundational concepts. Their effects are found in their contribution to perceived communicator credibility, which in turn produces a climate for persuasion, a symbol of a culture, and an impetus for changing cultural norms.

Obviously, these factors and their effects do not work independently—they work in concert. However, any one factor may be dominant, depending upon cultural expectations and specific crises facing a culture or a nation at a point in time.

1. Ask your friends what they admire most about specific national leaders. Then ask them what they like least about the same national leaders. How does this list compare with the factors mentioned in this chapter?

2. Examine newspaper articles about various cultural leaders both in the United States and abroad. What features are emphasized in these articles? How do these emphases match the five credibility factors found in this chapter?

3. When a highly credible leader takes an unpopular stand on some major issue, list what people around you say about this leader. Does the leader's credibility seem to rise or lower? What kinds of messages produce the rising or lowering of credibility?

4. List examples of charismatic leaders whose routinization of administrative details leads to their unpopularity. What could such leaders do to retard this demise?

Exercises

Applbaum, Ronald, and Karl Anatol. "Factor Structure of Source Credibility as a Function of the Speaking Situation." *Speech Monographs* 39 (1972): 216–22.

Berlo, David, James B. Lemert, and Robert J. Mertz. "Dimensions for Evaluating the Acceptability of Message Sources." *Public Opinion Quarterly* 33 (1966): 563–76.

Dow, Thomas E. "The Theory of Charisma." In *Intercommunication among Nations and Peoples,* edited by Michael H. Prosser. New York: Harper and Row, 1973.

Eisenstadt, S. N. "Communication Processes among Immigrants in Israel." In *Communication and Culture,* edited by Alfred G. Smith. New York: Holt, Rinehart and Winston, 1966.

Fagen, Richard R. "Charismatic Authority and the Leadership of Fidel Castro." In *Intercommunication among Nations and Peoples,* edited by Michael H. Prosser. New York: Harper and Row, 1973.

Hovland, Carl, Irving Janis, and Harold Kelley. *Communication and Persuasion.* New Haven: Yale University Press, 1953.

Resources

McCroskey, James C. "Scales for the Measurement of Ethos." *Speech Monographs* 33 (1966): 65–72.

Prosser, Michael H., ed. *Intercommunication among Nations and Peoples.* New York: Harper and Row, 1973.

Sohns, Helen. "Training Mataco Indian Birth Attendants." *Missiology* 3 (1975): 307–16.

Tubbs, Stewart, and John W. Baird. *The Open Person.* Columbus, Ohio: Charles Merrill, 1976.

Tuppen, Christopher. "Dimensions of Communicator Credibility: An Oblique Solution." *Speech Monographs* 41 (1974): 253–66.

Windt, Theodore Otto. "The Rhetoric of Peaceful Coexistence: Khrushchev in America, 1959." In *Intercommunication among Nations and Peoples,* edited by Michael H. Prosser. New York: Harper and Row, 1973.

Winn, Larry James. "Jimmy Carter and the American Political Image." Paper presented at the Southern Speech Communication Association, Atlanta, Georgia, April 8, 1978.

Chapter 14

Intercultural Communication and Opinion Leadership

Objectives

After completing this chapter, you should be able to:

1. Understand intercultural communication patterns between opinion leaders and those they influence.

2. Identify opinion leaders in a culture.

3. Assess the effect of opinion leadership on intercultural relationships.

4. Identify the overlap between friendship and opinion leadership.

5. Discuss opinion leadership roles as part of an intercultural communication network.

Several years ago, while conducting fieldwork in Africa, I learned an important lesson about opinion leadership. One purpose of this trip was to speak with large numbers of villagers and to collect data for a research project. Upon entering a village where few foreign outsiders had traversed for a while, I went directly to the chief's hut—though not without the fanfare of a couple of dozen children and about a half a dozen dogs. Although the chief was meeting with the other elders of that village, my arrival seemed no bother, and they welcomed me to visit with them. After a visit of some forty-five minutes, in which I explained the purpose of my visit and engaged in conversation of several current topics, the chief suddenly asked me, to my surprise, if I wanted them to ring the "gong gong." Being too embarrassed to question what the "gong gong" was, I simply said yes. With such affirmation, the chief and other leaders went to the front of the chief's hut and rang a large bell, after which all the village family heads gathered within a matter of minutes. Unfortunately, I was speechless by the process, so that the few words I spoke were probably not worth the trouble it had taken the villagers to gather. However, the remainder of my stay in that village was filled with warm reception from many households.

This incident solidifies a number of elements of a larger concern—and a principle of intercultural communication often discussed in the literature as opinion leadership. My going to the chief and village leaders tapped an interpersonal network that legitimized my work in that village. The larger principle is that, within almost any cultural system, there are individuals to whom others go for information and advice. In a small village, these opinion leaders may indeed be village elders, or they may be less formal leaders who are nevertheless influential. Understanding the dynamics of opinion leadership in intercultural communication is the goal of this chapter. Opinion leadership is a significant communication role relationship between people. It is a role filled with interpersonal empathy, warmth, and intimacy.

Opinion Leadership as an Information-Seeking Role

Even in the most individualistic and technological societies, people are linked to other people in a chain of interpersonal networks. One cannot escape interpersonal communication input from peers, work associates, kin, and others. In one sense, every person we meet has some influence on our decisions, but all people do not exert equal amounts of influence. Those individuals, however, who have a greater influence on the opinions of others are called *opinion leaders*. Lazarsfeld, Berelson, and Gaudet (1968) found as early as 1940 that ". . . in every area and for every public issue there are certain people who are most concerned about the issue as well as most articulate about it" (pp. 49–50). An opinion leader influences others in a social community but is similar in social characteristics with those whom he or she influences.

By definition, opinion leadership is not to be confused, necessarily, with community leadership. Classic research (Lazarsfeld, Berelson, and Gaudet 1968) emphasized that "the opinion leaders are not identical with the socially prominent people in the community or the richest people or the civic leaders.

They are found in all occupational groups" (p. 50). The Berelson, Lazarsfeld, and McPhee (1954) survey of voters and their opinion formulation in the 1948 presidential election revealed similar ideas about leadership:

> The banker and mayor and union officer may be "opinion leaders" in a distant sense, but ordinary voters listen to nearby influences. For this reason, one might properly speak less of leaders than of a complex web of opinion-leading relationships. It is true that one can single out those individuals who are more likely than others to be at the center of several such relationships and call them "opinion leaders," as we do in this analysis. (p. 109)

These studies highlighted the principal assumption of opinion leadership: People influence people where there exists a dynamic of respect and communication. Sherif and Sherif (1967) indicated that interpersonal communication influences individuals as much or more than the mass media. They further identified several terms for these influencing agents, calling them opinion leaders, gatekeepers, influentials, initiators, and tastemakers. Again, opinion leaders are not necessarily community leaders or elites but are more likely to be family, friends, coworkers, and other informed associates. For example, according to Erbe (1962), the family is essential in the dissemination of information to the mass of the community. Community workers, Peace Corps volunteers, and other intercultural information sources have found such a mesh of interpersonal networks to function in settings ranging from villages to modern cities.

For almost the first half of this century, laypeople and researchers assumed that the mass media were all-powerful, able to sway passive audiences, shaping them into malleable culture moved by the whims of those who controlled the mass media. World War II propaganda in Nazi Germany, Orson Welles's "War of the Worlds" broadcast in 1938, and the influence of Madison Avenue advertising in radio and on television created a perception of mass media power. This theory of mass media was called the *hypodermic needle theory*, conveying the image of a message being injected into the minds of passive audience members.

However, researchers using this model overlooked the important information roles where people sought advice. When Lazarsfeld, Berelson, and Gaudet (1968) investigated the influence of communication on voters' choices during the 1940 presidential election, they were convinced that they would show that the mass media had caused the voters to pull the lever for one candidate or another. To their surprise, they discovered that fewer voter choices were influenced directly by the media than by interpersonal sources. When these interpersonal sources appeared to influence three or more people, they were called opinion leaders. This cultural pattern continues almost universally today.

There is even an interpersonal network spin-off following media news. For instance, Steinfatt, Gantz, Seibold, and Miller (1973) highlighted the importance of interpersonal sources of communication in serious news events, such

Opinion leadership lends interpersonal influence in a context of information seeking.

as assassinations. They compared several cities for news sources and reported the predominance of interpersonal communication sources for the following events:

Event	Percent Hearing from Interpersonal Sources
1. John F. Kennedy assassination	
a. San Jose, California, sample	50 percent
b. Iowa City, Iowa, sample	55 percent
c. Dallas, Texas, sample	57 percent
2. George Wallace assassination attempt	70 percent

Not only do these figures accentuate the importance of interpersonal communication sources in news events, but they illustrate the prominent role of interpersonal communication networks.

Starosta (1974) underscored the highly interpersonal nature of information sources within Ceylon:

These disquieting conclusions are replicated in my own field study of three villages in central Ceylon, where many villagers relied almost exclusively on the words of neighbors, shopkeepers, and "others in the market" for their information. . . . The radio set or the newspaper is always to some degree an intruder. The villager who would have a prescribed ritualistic response for his dealings with the village headman might be overwhelmed by the tremendous volume of ideas that would flow from the media to the degree where he would set up defenses against the influx of impersonal and alien stimuli. (pp. 307–308)

The interpersonal nature of influence has been documented in similar ways in hundreds of studies in cultures around the world.

Not all interpersonal communication is with opinion leaders, but all relationships with opinion leaders are interpersonal. Because this bond is unique, subtle, and influential, it represents a significant intercultural communication role relationship.

We now examine personality and demographic features that distinguish opinion leaders. Can we delineate a profile of opinion leadership? The answer, according to past research, is yes.

Characteristics of Opinion Leaders

Interest and Media Exposure

One characteristic of opinion leaders is their high interest in the issue and in pertinent mass media. For instance, early studies reported that opinion leaders, compared with followers, were more interested in elections, more exposed to the mass media, and talked more about issues. Sherif and Sherif (1967) concurred that "the opinion leader is typically more exposed to appropriate mass communications than are his followers" (p. 305). Other research emphasized that opinion leaders for cosmopolitan issues, rather than local issues, were likely to read national news magazines; by contrast, opinion leaders for local issues typically did not attend to national news magazines (Katz 1963). Opinion leaders' keen interest in issues stems, to some extent, from their high exposure to the mass media. That is, the mass media contribute to an opinion leader's knowledge (Rogers 1983).

As noted earlier, information does not "leap" from source to receiver in one giant step but in several steps. Decisions concerning grazing domains among herdsmen in Kenya, for instance, are made through respected leaders who pass on advice, decisions, and information through dialogue. Among U.S. voters, research indicates that opinion leaders pass information and advice from various media and personal sources to those whom they influence and to still other opinion leaders through a complex chain of opinion leaders. This passing of information through interpersonal sources on a "grass roots" level is called the *multi-step flow*. This phenomenon emphasizes interrelationships that are important conduits for effective social communication transmission. As figure 14.1 illustrates, this process allows opinion leaders to pass on interpretations as well as information. While the media supply opinion leaders with information, the interest and knowledge of opinion leaders make them perhaps more knowledgeably competent than those they influence—one reason for a role relationship to develop for information seeking. Opinion leaders are information rich.

Accessibility

Opinion leaders tend to be interpersonally accessible in two ways. They are accessible geographically by their residence near major pathways, and they are accessible psychologically, often demonstrating gregariousness. Rogers (1983) observed that opinion leaders live in strategic locations and demon-

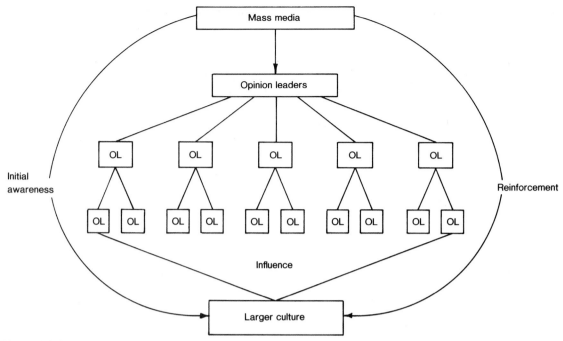

Figure 14.1
Multi-step flow of
information.

strate more interactions than other people. Since the opinion leadership relationship is ongoing, then certainly accessibility contributes to that relationship
and to the social participation qualities of opinion leaders.

Socioeconomic
Levels

Opinion leaders typically emerge from the upper levels of each occupational
division. Educationally, within each socioeconomic status level, opinion leaders
tend to come from the more educated members of the group. They also tend
to be slightly higher in income than those they influence.

Other
Characteristics of
Opinion Leaders

Observers of intercultural relations and of the spread of ideas within a social
system note several additional generalizations about opinion leaders as a source
of personal influence: (1) personal contact is more frequent and more effective
than mass media influence; (2) opinion leaders associate with and share the
same characteristics as those they influence; and (3) close associates hold
common opinions and are reluctant to deviate from group consensus (Katz
1963). The Lazarsfeld and Menzel (1963) summary also described opinion
leadership in terms of dyadic similarity:

> As informal leaders, they were asked to name persons they knew and associated
> with, and to whom they would go with questions about the election. Ninety-two
> percent of the replies referred to family members, friends, neighbors, and co-
> workers, who tended to be male, slightly older, slightly better educated, and
> slightly higher placed occupationally than the persons who named them, and to
> belong to markedly more organizations. (p. 110)

The psychological and physical similarities continue to be operative in these information relationships (Richmond 1980).

In some cultures, opinion leadership is usually *monomorphic,* meaning that a person is an opinion leader in a specialized topic. Monomorphic opinion leaders are influential in a limited field, while *polymorphic* leaders exert influence in a variety of sometimes unrelated spheres.

In one early study, monomorphic leadership was tested in four topic areas: political opinions, purchase of household groceries, fashions, and motion picture preferences. The results showed little overlap of leadership; a leader in one field wasn't likely to be influential in another unrelated field (Lazarsfeld and Menzel 1963).

In contrast to the prevalence of monomorphic leadership in the United States are intercultural instances of polymorphic opinion leadership. For instance, Dodd (1973) reported that 76 percent of his African sample preferred the same person for advice/information on such divergent topics as farming, disputes, and religious questions.

Whether a culture has a monomorphic or polymorphic style mostly depends on its specialized information needs. In general, the monomorphic style is found in technical information cultures, while the polymorphic style is found in less technically information-oriented cultures (Ho 1969; Korzenny and Farace 1977).

Richmond (1980) noted some specific attributes of polymorphic opinion leaders, compared with their monomorphic counterparts, at least on a relatively "closed" university campus in the United States. She reported that the polymorphic opinion leaders in this system revealed a likelihood to try more new things (innovativeness) and showed less apprehension in their communication.

Task information. Overall, opinion leaders function as channels, advisors, and sources of information within a context of cultural relationships. These leaders emerge in small groups because their talents are especially needed at that time. Consequently, the same person is unlikely to become a leader in a different group setting, unless the conditions are similar (Barnlund 1962). In other words, group leadership depends on the group task and the constituency of group membership. Similarly, opinion leadership depends upon task relevency. Interpersonal roles of opinion leaders include being channels of interpretive information and sources of social pressure and social support.

Group network reinforcement. Opinion leaders also function to reinforce group norms and to keep group members from deviation. Opinion leaders' personal influence stands as an intervening variable between a message and the kind of response the individual makes (DeFleur and Ball-Rokeach 1976). Figure 14.2 illustrates the structural communication channels between opinion leaders and those they influence. The diagram points out that opinion leaders have a "built-in" network of interpersonal links. Even persuasive efforts are

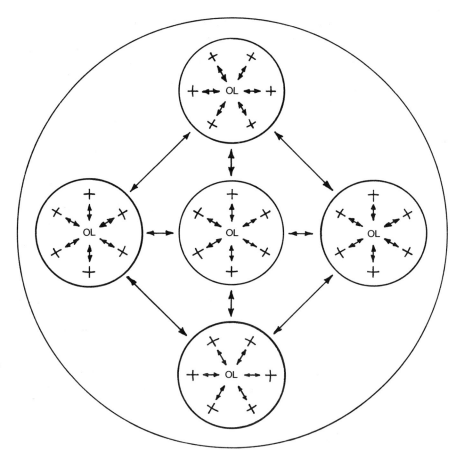

Figure 14.2
Opinion leadership communication as part of a social network. Opinion leaders pass information on to those they influence, and opinion leaders influence one another within a cultural communication network.

likely to be more effective when the message is focused toward opinion leaders, who in turn influence, or at least pass on information, among those homogeneous groupings of people with whom they typically interact.

Optimum communication role conditions. Opinion leaders pass information and influence people within a context of low-key, informal relationships. However, this network of information is affected by several conditions (Korzenny and Farace 1977):

1. *When informal opinion leaders also serve formal roles, influence is multiplied.* If an opinion leader also works as a manager or supervisor on a job, then the two roles merge, resulting in a "double" opinion leader link. The boss is also an opinion leader. So, when appointing managerial positions, and when a concern for interpersonal relations is important, appointing the informal opinion leaders to important positions in a formal structure may be a significant step.

Table 14.1 Comparison of Opinion Leadership Assessment Techniques

Technique	Concept	Example
1. Sociometric choice	Ask respondents to whom they go for information and advice about a particular topic.	A respondent says: "I go to person A for information about a new type of seed."
2. Self-report	Ask respondent if anyone has sought his or her advice over a certain period of time.	Person A responds: "Yes, three people have asked me about this new type of seed."
3 Key informant report	Ask a person of the culture in question to tell you who is influential on specific questions.	The informant indicates: "Well, most people would probably go to Person A, since he really understands new things about farming."

2. *Opinion leadership is concentrated in traditional social systems.* As we have already indicated, traditional information systems utilize polymorphic opinion leaders. However, this monopoly of information can also be a monopoly of power, unless the opinion leaders are innovating or unless information is regularly and widely dispersed.

3. *Opinion leadership reflects the cultural norms.* Opinion leaders do not usually overstep cultural norms, but they generally reflect those norms while bringing about social change. In some ways, they are very similar in social characteristics to those they influence, except on knowledge and competence, where they are often quite ahead.

Measuring Opinion Leadership

The next question, beyond understanding characteristics of opinion leaders and their interpersonal dynamics, involves how to identify opinion leaders. Over a period of years, three techniques have emerged: the sociometric choice technique, the self-report technique, and the key informant report. From all indications, these three techniques basically correlate, which is another way of saying that they produce similar results. Table 14.1 summarizes these three methods, which are outlined in more detail in the paragraphs that follow.

Sociometric Choice Technique

With the sociometric choice technique, the researcher asks the respondent to whom that person would go for information and/or advice about a particular topic. The exact nature of the specific questions depends upon the culture, the topic under consideration, and so on. Typically, however, the sociometric choice technique asks respondents for their choice of a person in specific categories, some of which are noted in the following:

1. *Value relationship:* Asking the respondents which people they value for the way they do their work. *Example:* "Which two farmers do you consider good farmers?"

Opinion leaders are respected partly for their competence and their knowledge.

2. *Communication-task relationship:* Asking the respondents to whom they would most likely go for advice regarding a decision. *Example:* "To whom would you likely go for advice on adopting a new farm program?"

3. *Communication-social relationship:* Asking the respondents with which people they like to socialize. *Example:* "With which two farmers do you most frequently visit?"

4. *Liking relationship:* Asking the respondents which people they like the most. *Example:* "Which farmers do you like the most?" (Van den Ban 1973).

The chief advantage of the sociometric choice technique is that it immediately taps interpersonal networks, providing the researcher with a complete profile of who respects whom. Generally, if the same person is mentioned as a so-ciometric choice by five or more people, then that person is probably an opinion leader. The disadvantage of this technique is its cost and time, since usually a large sample is needed to discover these relationships.

Self-Report Technique

The self-report technique is largely a matter of asking respondents if anyone has come to them over a certain period of time. For instance, a typical question might ask if anyone has specifically asked for your advice on certain topics within the last six months. If a respondent reports that he or she has had as many as three or more requests for information, then there is a likelihood that the respondent is an opinion leader. An immediate problem with this method, however, is that many advice sessions are couched in normal, everyday conversations in which information is shared and objections are answered. Often, opinion leaders may not remember the specific content of these conversations and thus may not report them as direct advice sessions. In other words, opinion leadership is far more subtle than many people, especially the opinion leaders themselves, imagine. A second problem is that self-report data frequently lack quality because of memory loss over time; respondents cannot always accurately remember details over a period of months. One way to combat this problem in self-reporting of data is to use a number of questions to stimulate recall, at the same time taking care not to lead the respondent. Still a better way is to conduct a study in which issues and answers are able to be recalled.

A third method of locating opinion leaders is to ask a key informant of the culture in question for that person's analysis of people to whom others go for information and advice concerning topics under consideration. This method extends anthropological field methodology by working closely with informants who typify the culture in question. These informants are more than "guides," for they should be able to discuss a number of factors about the culture, serve as translators (when necessary), and serve as a case study of a person typical of the culture. The problem in using this method involves a need to ensure representativeness. Therefore, the researcher may use several key informants as the opportunity arises. One advantage of this technique is its low cost and time efficiency. The disadvantage is one of accuracy because of limited input.

Key Informant Report

It is possible to influence a culture by "targeting" opinion leaders. We have seen that there is a pattern of information systems that link people in social networks, and in those networks, people seek information from opinion leaders. To share information with opinion leaders is to heighten the possibility of that information being passed along to the other cultural members with whom the opinion leader has some relationship. One extension of the principle is to market ideas and products through these information webs.

Dangers of Using Opinion Leaders as Information Facilitators

However, two dangers arise from utilizing opinion leaders as information facilitators. One danger is that labelling an opinion leader can destroy his or her credibility. For instance, a seed company once identified an opinion leader in a farming community and put a sign in his lane by the main road, inviting all farmers to come by and talk with this particular man, who they explicitly labelled as a leader. After that, fewer and fewer people came by to visit, although the visits were plentiful before the sign was erected. Appointing an opinion leader to a formal position can be helpful, but it may be best not to call attention to the formal relationship.

A second danger arises in inviting an opinion leader from one community to communicate with another community. Since opinion leadership is usually localized, removing an effective informal leader from the immediate environment and placing this person in a "strange" culture helps neither the person nor prospective receivers of information. In West Africa, for example, a particular change program typically recruited intelligent young men with high credibility in their home villages, trained them in a nearby city, and sent them to advance a change program in other villages. In addition to the culture shock experienced by the young trainees, the program met with limited success because of the differences in background and respect across villages. Sometimes, a man from one clan would enter a village composed of individuals predominantly from another clan. These heterophilous differences were large enough to severely diminish otherwise productive work. An opinion leader cannot always transfer the characteristic to other situations.

Developing Intercultural Skills Concerning Opinion Leadership

Two skills in particular are highlighted here. The following simple but effective suggestions can increase effective strategic understanding of opinion leadership:

1. *Facilitate a heightened sense of respect for yourself and foster interpersonal relationships by personally adopting some opinion leader qualities, such as gregariousness, amiability, and empathy, as well as knowledge about the topic of concern.* When you interact with other people, for instance, if you "cut them off" or in some way show disrespect, it is unlikely that such people will continue a long-enduring friendship with you. So, look for rapport-building efforts that often begin with a keen interest and a lot of listening.

2. *Know when and how to involve opinion leaders in message facilitation.* Opinion leaders can add credibility to a message in a way that often reduces the "emotional blinders" and suspicions that sometimes prevent adequate attention to a topic of potential interest. When someone you respect asks you to listen to something, you are more likely to do so than if an impersonal source invites your attention.

This Chapter in Perspective

Opinion leaders are information-rich people in role relationships with others similar to them in a communication network. They have high interest and competence in the subject, accessibility, access to relevant information, and are similar to the people they influence. An opinion leader in one particular group probably will not be an opinion leader in another group, unless the needs and conditions of the groups are similar. Functionally, opinion leaders open channels of information. They also reinforce group norms and individual opinions and provide a source of social support.

Some opinion leaders serve a communication information role for only one topic area (monomorphic opinion leadership). Other opinion leaders function as information sources across a variety of topics and are called polymorphic leaders.

1. Ask people in your class to whom they go for information concerning some topic of significance. Who are the opinion leaders? What characteristics do they seem to have? Do they offer opinion leadership on a number of topics? Why or why not?

2. Spend some time in an organization, asking who talks with whom about various topics. Why do patterns of informal communication emerge? What are the interpersonal networks and relationships in the organization? In what ways is a "closed" organization like a culture? In what ways is it different from a culture?

3. To discover the role of the mass media in shaping our opinions, ask five of your friends to describe in some detail how they think a medium, such as television, affects their thinking about world events. Then ask about ways that their interpersonal relationships affirm, deny, or in any other way alter mass media messages. On political or social issues, for instance, is it common for interpersonal relationships to interact with the mass media messages?

Barnlund, Dean C. "A Consistency of Emergent Leadership in Groups with Changing Tasks and Members." *Speech Monographs* 29 (1962): 45–52.

Berelson, Bernard R., Paul F. Lazarsfeld, and William N. McPhee. *Voting.* Chicago: University of Chicago Press, 1954.

DeFleur, Melvin L., and Sandra Ball-Rokeach. *Theories of Mass Communication.* 3d ed. New York: David McKay, 1976.

Dodd, Carley H. "Homophily and Heterophily in Diffusion of Innovations: A Cross-cultural Analysis in an African Setting." Paper presented at the Speech Communication Association Convention, New York, November 10, 1973.

Erbe, William. "Gregariousness, Group Membership, and the Flow of Information." *American Journal of Sociology* 67 (1962): 502–16.

Ho, Yung Chang. "Homophily in Interaction Patterns in the Diffusion of Innovations in Colombian Villages." Unpublished master's thesis, Michigan State University, 1969.

Katz, Elihu. "The Diffusion of New Ideas and Practices." In *The Science of Human Communication,* edited by Wilbur Schramm. New York: Basic Books, 1963.

Klapper, Joseph T. *The Effects of Mass Communication.* New York: Free Press, 1960.

Korzenny, Felipe, and Richard Farace. "Communication Networks and Social Change in Developing Countries." *International and Intercultural Communication Annual* 4 (1977): 69–94.

Lazarsfeld, Paul F., Bernard Berelson, and Hazel Gaudet. *The People's Choice.* 3d ed. New York: Columbia University Press, 1968.

Lazarsfeld, Paul F., and Herbert Menzel. "Mass Media and Personal Influence." In *The Science of Human Communication,* edited by Wilbur Schramm. New York: Basic Books, 1963.

Menzel, Herbert, and Elihu Katz. "Social Relations and Innovation in the Medical Profession: The Epidemiology of a New Drug." *Public Opinion Quarterly* 19 (1955): 337–52.

Merton, Robert. "Patterns of Influence." In *Communications Research,* edited by Paul F. Lazarsfeld and Frank N. Stanton. New York: Harper and Brothers, 1949.

Richmond, Virginia. "Monomorphic and Polymorphic Opinion Leadership within a Relatively Closed Communication System." *Human Communication Research* 6 (1980): 111–16.

Rogers, Everett M. *Diffusion of Innovations.* 3d ed. New York: Free Press, 1983.

Rogers, Everett M., and F. Floyd Shoemaker. *Communication of Innovations: A Cross-Cultural Approach.* New York: Free Press, 1971.

Sherif, Carolyn W., and Muzafer Sherif, eds. *Attitude, Ego-Involvement, and Change.* New York: John Wiley and Sons, 1967.

Starosta, William J. "Toward the Use of Traditional Entertainment Forms to Stimulate Social Change." *Quarterly Journal of Speech* 60 (1974): 306–12.

Steinfatt, Thomas M., Walter Gantz, David R. Siebold, and Larry Miller. "News Diffusion of the George Wallace Shooting: The Apparent Lack of Interpersonal Communication as an Artifact of Delayed Measurement." *Speech Monographs* 59 (1973): 401–12.

Van den Ban, A. W. "Interpersonal Communication and the Diffusion of Innovations." In *Intercommunication among Nations and Peoples,* edited by Michael H. Prosser. New York: Harper & Row, 1973.

Chapter 15

Intercultural Communication, Innovation, and Change

After completing this chapter, you should be able to:

1. Identify variables that influence the rapid spread of information among cultural members.

2. Describe the decision-making process of individuals when confronted with information needs.

3. Categorize early and late adopters of innovations by their personality characteristics.

4. Develop strategies for effective intercultural efforts at social change and development.

5. Summarize the factors that predispose a person or culture toward innovativeness.

6. Understand factors related to group and organizational innovativeness.

What would you do if you were asked to introduce a YMCA program in a predominantly Hispanic community? How would you involve elderly people in a community nutrition program? Working with a medical team as a communication specialist, how could you invite highland Indians in Ecuador to engage in different eating habits to correct a culturewide nutritional deficiency? Suppose you were interested in a summer field trip to Guatemala to help in a reforestation project where woodland mountainsides have been stripped for firewood. What process of communication would initiate and sustain a reforestation effort among villagers? If you were working at a summer camp, how would you involve surrounding communities in a program of volunteerism to help you with large projects at the camp?

A partial answer to these questions is contained in earlier sections of this book, where you read about the nature of culture and about relationships needed for effective intercultural communication. The rest of the answer comes from an understanding of information diffusion and of the management process to implement innovations.

One area of communication research deals with how innovations—that is, new ideas—spread within and between cultures. This research is called *diffusion of innovations*. Actually, diffusion research answers one of the most basic questions in communication: "Who talks with whom?" But, diffusion is a process of interpersonal communication applied with the goal of persuasion, social change, or community development. Diffusion research examines not only a number of communication, social, and demographic variables in the *process* of diffusion, but explores the consequences of message awareness—adoption or rejection of an innovation. Meanwhile, the entire process occurs over a period of time, since people hear messages and respond to them at different times. Thus, diffusion is the "grass roots" spread of new information usually aimed at social change.

For example, a few years ago, the Kenyan government offered herdsmen new land with low-interest loans, near a new beef-producing location. The spread of this information, the decisions that were made, and the consequences that ensued are typical categories that social change researchers would investigate. Of course, the emphasis throughout this discussion of diffusion and social change is communication—in its many forms—and the behavioral results of these persuasive communication attempts from one culture to another. This chapter also explores descriptions of and strategies for the ways in which information impacts on cultural groups and how the information flow can be managed. The innovation and change process within organizational cultures receives special emphasis.

The study of diffusion began in the nineteenth century among anthropologists.* In the early days of anthropology, debates raged over the importance of invention, compared with diffusion. However, as this area of anthropology developed, its focus sharpened on a general concern about the exchange of ideas and technologies among societies. The classic case of the steel axe introduction among the Yir Yoront in Australia (Sharp 1952) underscored a definitive anthropological concern about the relationship of culture and social change. The stone axes were symbols for masculinity and authority. Their replacement, Sharp argued, led to the demise of that culture. Since values were undermined, prostitution, drunkenness, and other social breakdowns became rampant, and the culture lost its traditional structure. Later, applied anthropology based its concern on social consequences of an innovation by analyzing cultural values of a society and the "cultural fit" of an innovation in that society (Firth 1958; Arensberg and Niehoff 1964).

The largest and most enduring tradition of diffusion research originated in rural sociology. As early as 1925, researchers examined the relationship of adopted innovations to their cost of diffusion. In the early 1940s, the classic study of diffusion and adoption of hybrid seed corn in Iowa (Ryan and Gross 1943) influenced subsequent research. This investigation examined roles of communication in persuading farmers to use this improved strain of corn seed. The discoveries from that research effort made a lasting impact on the direction of social research, including intercultural communication.

From that historical point, investigators pursued what could be called communication-related aspects of the social change process. Communication researchers studied the diffusion of news events via interpersonal and mass media channels. For instance, the Dallas assassination study (Greenberg 1964) and other news event diffusion studies (Deutschmann and Danielson 1960) stemmed from a communication perspective. More recently, diffusion research has focused interculturally.† Trends aim toward a theory of communication and social change in organizational innovation and management, as well as in the traditional concerns over community development. Oddly enough, however, it was not until the mid-1950s that other scholars became aware that fields other than their respective disciplines were also conducting diffusion research and had been doing so for over a decade.

*In an anthropological sense, "diffusion" is the view that explains change in a society as resulting from the introduction of innovations from another society. Kroeber (1937) noted that early diffusionists contributed primarily to calling the importance of diffusion to the attention of social scientists.

†The topics of social change communication efforts are varied, ranging from agricultural practices to family planning. Scholars continue to try to explain the social change process, including the nature of the innovation (Rogers 1973), the nature of the interpersonal relationships involved (Korzenny and Farace 1977), the nature of intercultural contact and attitude change (Gudykunst 1977), and other variables (Rogers and Shoemaker 1971; Rogers 1983). For the rhetorical nature of social change, see Starosta (1974, 1975, 1976).

A number of social change efforts are aimed at the adoption of health innovations. By analyzing the communication-diffusion process, field workers facilitate their work.

Cultures do not remain static but change both in technology and in ideology over time. Whether it be improved farm implements, new weed sprays, color television, computers, laser beams, or ideology, we can trace the movement of information within a social system over a period of time. Some innovations alter world events; some innovations have little impact. But common to almost any social change is communication.

Components of Diffusion

The basic components in the theory of diffusion and social change are: (1) the *innovation,* (2) which is communicated through certain *channels* (3) over *time* (4) among members of a *social system* (5) with certain *effects.* These categories stand as a type of model, highlighting major components. We would be remiss if we did not acknowledge the work of Everett Rogers and his various co-authors, since he has prolifically synthesized much of the diffusion research and theory. Close to three thousand diffusion studies have been conducted (Rogers 1973, 1983), with a number of aspects of diffusion applied to numerous communication variables.

The Innovation as a Cultural Message

An innovation is an idea or product perceived as new by an individual. Since perception is a subjective measure of the innovation that does not make it objectively new or acceptable, then we can think of an innovation as having two components: (1) an *idea* component and (2) an *object* component, which is the physical referent of the idea. All innovations contain the first component, but not all innovations have a physical referent. For instance, adoption of improved farming methods is easily observable. Other innovations, how-ever, such as political ideology, rumors, and news events, may not be as di-rectly observable. Like any other persuasive message, an intercultural innovation message contains inherently motivating features. Let us examine a few of these.

The following five characteristics of innovations can make innovation messages innately motivating:

1. *Relative advantage* is the degree to which the innovation appears better than its predecessor. For instance, a government development officer must show how a village water system has advantages over the old method of carrying water from the river.

2. *Compatibility* represents the degree to which the innovation is congruent with existing beliefs, attitudes, values, experiences, and needs of the re-ceiver. In intercultural efforts to persuade nationals to use a certain crop fertilizer, one obstacle sometimes facing change agents is cultural attitude and world view toward the earth. Among certain Central American In-dians, for instance, the adding of fertilizer is considered sacrilegious. Con-sequently, a successful field worker must outline persuasive messages that demonstrate the cultural compatibility of the innovation. One solution for Central American Indians has been to describe the fertilizer as "food" for the earth.

3. *Complexity* is the extent to which the innovation appears difficult to un-derstand and to use. As you might expect, simplicity is linked to adoption.

4. *Trialability* is the degree to which an innovation can be sampled or tried on a small-scale basis. For that reason, free samples constitute one reli-able strategy for marketing new products in the United States.

5. *Observability* is the degree to which an innovation can be viewed and scrutinized before actual adoption. For instance, if a target population can see a comparison of a fertilized crop and an unfertilized crop, chances for adopting fertilizers are heightened.

These five factors must be carefully considered in message development for planned social change (Rogers 1983).

Individual Choices about Innovations

The time it takes for a message to spread throughout a social system is an important and distinct consideration in the diffusion process. However, per-sonal choices depend not only upon available information but also upon the characteristics of the people making those choices.

When we face an especially important decision about a purchase, for ex-ample, or about engaging in some behavior, we almost always go through a period of awareness of the possibilities, talk with others if it is a major deci-sion, and then continue a mental debate until a decision is made. Intercultural communication concerning some innovation also causes people to engage in a

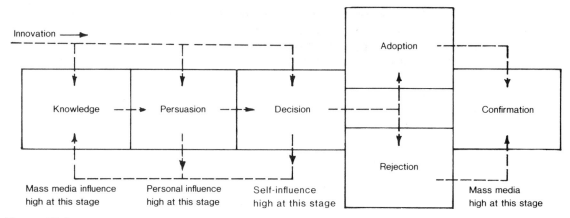

Figure 15.1
Innovation-decision process and channels of influence at various stages.

mental, decision-making process. Figure 15.1 presents a model to depict this process. In the knowledge stage, the individual becomes aware of the innovation and gains some understanding about it. The persuasion stage marks the person's evaluation of the innovation. During the decision stage, an individual may run a small-scale trial of the innovation, on a limited basis if possible. At any rate, a potential adopter must debate mentally, choosing to adopt or reject the innovation. In some cases, a small-scale trial may constitute an important part of the decision to adopt. Many times, marketing firms apply this principle as they distribute free samples of everything from soap in the mail to sandwiches at the grocery store. At the confirmation stage, the person seeks reinforcement for the innovation-decision that has been made. The alternatives, of course, are continuance or discontinuance of the decision. The dotted lines in the figure indicate that these stages may be short-circuited, compressed, and even reversed.

Research also shows that mass media impact during the decision-making process is especially high at the knowledge and confirmation stages. Our discussion in chapter 8 demonstrated how the mass media not only reinforce attitudes but serve to initiate awareness. The model in figure 15.1 again emphasizes that the mass media serve an awareness function as well as a reinforcement function. The model also shows that self-influence is greatest at the decision stage.

This relationship between stages of a person's decision and the channel of communication that that person uses during any one stage is well illustrated in an analysis of the swine flu inoculation program conducted by the U.S. Department of Health, Education, and Welfare during the summer and fall of 1976. Highlights of a report (Dodd 1979), derived from a survey of an elderly and of a college subculture, reveal general principles supported in several other diffusion research efforts. These data, along with the principles the data support, are presented here as a case sample to generate specific insight into the relationship of information sources to personal decision making:

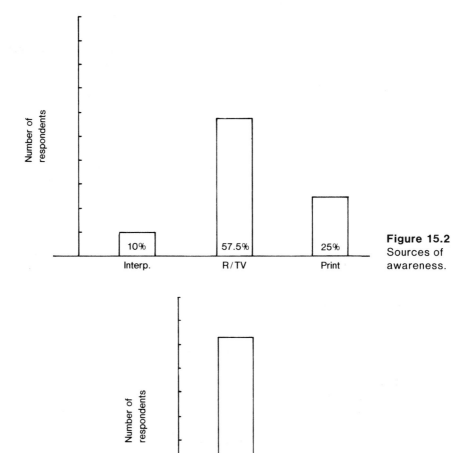

Figure 15.2
Sources of awareness.

Figure 15.3
Source of additional information.

1. *Communication sources differ at various decision-making stages.* As figure 15.2 shows, the respondents indicated that they *first heard* about swine flu vaccine from the electronic media (television news, 50 percent, and radio news, 7.5 percent), the print media (25 percent for newspapers and magazines combined), and interpersonal sources (10 percent). The remainder of the subjects were undecided or had no answer. Overall, 82.5 percent learned from a media source in gaining first awareness.

   After first becoming aware, 59 percent of the sample indicated that they *sought additional information* concerning the vaccine (see figure 15.3). Of that group, only 16.7 percent sought additional information from the media, with 83.3 percent seeking it from interpersonal sources. Of

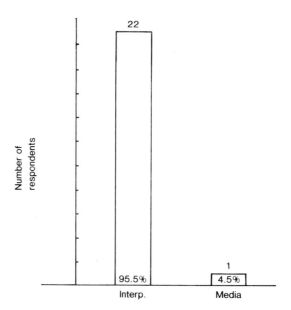

Figure 15.4
Source of advice.

those seeking interpersonal sources for additional information, 75 percent sought that information from a medical person, such as a doctor or nurse, with other minor percentages scattered among friends, relatives, and so on.

Furthermore, subjects were asked if anyone *advised them* concerning the swine flu inoculation—this question thereby extended the previous question. As figure 15.4 reveals, 95.5 percent of the respondents who received advice concerning the swine flu vaccine received that information from an interpersonal source, while only 4.5 percent received advice from mass media sources. Of those who received advice from interpersonal sources, 79.2 percent received that advice from a medical person, such as a doctor or a nurse. Thus, this finding parallels the previous item dealing with seeking additional information. Again, information sources serve different needs at various stages of decision making.

2. *Media sources predispose individuals to early awareness and adoption.* A number of investigations show that high media exposure relates to early adoption of innovations (Rogers 1983). In the swine flu inoculation study, adopters were significantly more inclined to seek additional information, after first becoming aware, than rejecters. As figure 15.5 reveals, vaccine adopters were more than four times as likely to seek additional information than rejecters (82.6 percent versus 17.4 percent). As we have already indicated, the bulk of the additional information came from interpersonal sources, particularly medical personnel.

Also, there is a clear positive correlation between newspaper readership and vaccine adoption. The greater the newspaper exposure, the greater the likelihood of adoption, so that vaccine adopters were four times

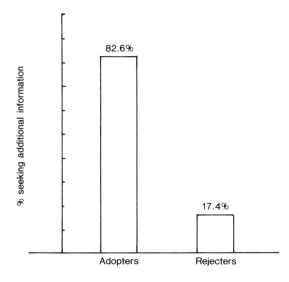

Figure 15.5
Relationships of seeking advice with vaccine adoption.

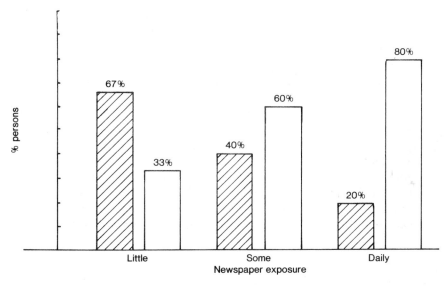

= adopt

= reject

Figure 15.6
Relationship of newspaper exposure with vaccine adoption.

more likely to be daily newspaper readers than rejecters (figure 15.6). These data reveal some form of predisposition toward adoption perhaps mediated by newspaper exposure. But whatever the effect of newspaper exposure in creating a climate for adoption, again, interpersonal sources were simultaneously enacted.

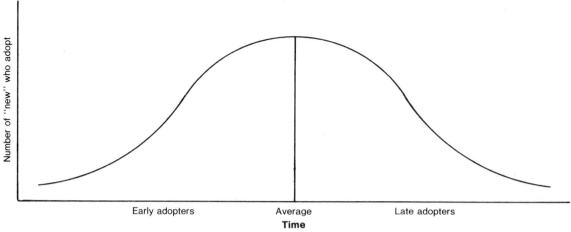

Early adopters   Average   Late adopters
Time

Figure 15.7
This bell-shaped curve shows the theoretical adoption of an innovation over time by the members of a social system. The curve develops when the number of new people adopting the innovation are plotted against time.

Characteristics of Individuals Choosing Innovations

Whenever individuals choose an innovation, some people adopt early, and some people adopt late or not at all. The measure of time of adoption, called innovativeness, can be plotted mathematically. An average plotting across a number of studies results in a bell-shaped curve, illustrated in figure 15.7. The curve's significance lies in dividing the curve into mathematical segments (called standard deviations) which, to make a long story short, allow us to *categorize* people across these consistent units. Immediately, we observe that an entire sample can be divided into those who are early and those who are late, simply by splitting the sample in half at the average time of adoption. The question, then, that remains is whether some kind of systematic difference lies between the early people and the late people. The answer, from previous research studies, is unequivocally "yes." In fact, investigations have taken the question a step further by analyzing not just the early and late adopters but also the percentages that fall under this bell-shaped curve within the early group and the late group. Furthermore, researchers have been able to detect personality differences among these categories. Among the early group, we can identify several categories: innovators (first 2.5 percent who adopt), early adopters (next 13.5 percent who adopt), and the early majority (the next 34 percent who adopt). These three groups constitute the first half of all adopters of an innovation. The late group of adopters fall into two categories: the late majority (the next 34 percent after the average) and the final adopters (the last 16 percent). An understanding of each of these categories, which we now examine in more detail, can help us to better analyze a potential group of adopters at various stages (Rogers 1983).

1. *Innovators* make up the first 2.5 percent of the population who adopt under the bell curve. Their most salient characteristic has been described as "venturesome." They are eager to try new ideas and usually can afford to take risks. For one thing, they are often "deviant" from their social system,

meaning that they do not necessarily follow the norms of the locale where they live. In fact, other more normative members of the social system may think them very unusual. In addition, innovators are open to irrational adoption and consequently are subject to making many mistakes. Perhaps their irrationality is one reason why the majority of their social system do not necessarily look upon them with favor. However, as Marsh and Coleman (1954) pointed out, residents may go to innovators for information *if* the social system is highly innovative. Generally, however, innovators are not opinion leaders of society.

2. *Early adopters* comprise the next 13.5 percent of the population who adopt an innovation. This group is best characterized by the word *respect*. As a whole, they are more innovative than the majority of the social system, but not so much as to be deviant. They are usually more local than innovators and adhere closely to community norms. In a sense, they are not too far ahead of other people in the culture, as the innovators are, but they are knowledgeable enough and respected enough to be a type of role model. The early adopter category is especially important in that it contains the highest number of opinion leaders.

3. The *early majority* are the 34 percent of the population who adopt an innovation just before the average person of the social system. Not many leaders stem from their ranks, but they serve as an important legitimizing link in the diffusion process. A key word for this category is *deliberate*.

4. The *late majority* are the 34 percent who adopt just after the average member of the social system. For the most part, adopters in this group are cautious, since they approach innovations with healthy skepticism. They may well see the value of an innovation but do not move to adopt it until public opinion favors the innovation or until peer group pressure is strong enough to motivate their adoption.

5. The *final adopters* are the final 16 percent of the population who are the last to adopt an innovation or who may never adopt at all. They are highly traditional, usually basing decisions on those of previous generations. Often quite suspicious of innovations, innovators, and change agents, this group is oriented toward local issues, and members of this group may function as negative opinion leaders.

One reason why people adopt an innovation stems from the personal characteristics we just discussed. We also need to examine, however, what social and communication factors mitigate the relatively early or late adoption of an innovation. In other words, why do some people adopt earlier than others in their social system? Why are some social systems resistant while others are open to change? These kinds of questions have led to research exploring the question of innovativeness.

Variables Leading to Early or Late Choices

Innovativeness refers to the degree to which a person is earlier than others in the social system in adopting an innovation.* Diffusion researchers usually investigate this facet of adoption behavior by testing variables that correlate with innovativeness. Correlation simply means that, as one variable goes up, another variable may go up or down. In other words, correlation measures the degree of relationship between two entities, or the amount of "linking" between two concepts. Diffusion research often utilizes a technique called multiple correlation in which a number of variables jointly correlate with a single variable under investigation. For example, if we found that the more that people read newspapers and magazines, the sooner their adoption time, then we would have a positive relationship between these two "predictor" variables and innovativeness. In fact, we can examine many variables that correlate with time of adoption, or innovativeness.**

The point is to discover what factors cause people to adopt early, late, or not at all, and this pursuit is called "predicting" innovativeness (or "explaining" innovativeness). The term *explained variance* is analogous to a percentage rating of how much joint explanation a set of predictor variables offers to account for adoption, with a maximum of 100 percent explained variance. In other words, the larger the percentage of explained variance, the stronger the relationship, or correlation, of a set of variables with innovativeness. Now, let us examine some reasons for innovativeness.

In their study of modern and traditional Colombian villages, Rogers with Svenning (1969) reported that the following five predictor variables explained 34.9 percent of the variance in agricultural innovativeness in modern villages: empathy, opinion leadership, farm size (labor units), farm size (land units), and schoolteacher contact. The two best predictor variables were empathy and opinion leadership. In traditional villages, they found that the following twelve predictor variables explained 66.4 percent of the variance in agricultural innovativeness: magazine exposure, home innovativeness, empathy, farm size (land units), farm size (labor units), opinion leadership, farm intensification scores, farm production, desire to increase farm size, self-perceived innovativeness, farmland cultivated, and reputation as a good farmer. Magazine exposure was the best single predictor in the traditional villages.

Rogers with Svenning (1969) also reported that the following seven variables accounted for 53 percent of the variance concerning home innovations in modern villages: cosmopolitanism (travel to large towns), political knowledgeability, lack of farm fragmentation, social status, self-perceived opinion

*Actually, little research has tested empirically the parameters of social system innovativeness (though, see Davis 1968 and Saxena 1968). For that reason, most of the discussion in this section focuses on individual innovativeness.

**The term *prediction* "refers to the fact that we are using information about one variable to obtain information about another" (Runyon and Haber 1971). The term does not necessarily imply "futurity." A strong correlation between X and Y, for instance, indicates that the presence of X "predicts" Y and the presence of Y "predicts" X.

leadership, functional literacy, and farm size. Concerning home innovativeness in traditional Colombian villages, predictor variables of present debt, cosmopolitanism, empathy, formal education, farm intensification scores, farm size, and contact with the federal agricultural bank explained 52.9 percent of the variance. In sum, these field studies underscored the importance not only of outside communication sources (magazines, nearby towns, and contact with lending sources), but also social and economic characteristics.

In another study of Colombian peasants, Paul Deutschmann and Orlando Fals-Borda (1962) found that mass media exposure, farm size, education, cosmopolitanism, awareness of innovations, use of written farm accounts, age, and level of living were variables that contributed up to 56.3 percent of the innovativeness variance. Whittenbarger and Maffei (1966) explained 44.4 percent of the variance in innovativeness with variables of information-seeking activity, knowledgeability, farm size, and attitude toward credit.

Among peasant farmers in India, Chattopadhyaya and Pareek (1967) used fatalism, authoritarianism, and liberalism to explain 59 percent of the variance in innovativeness. Also in India, Moulik, Hrabovsky, and Rao (1966) explained 81 percent of the innovativeness variance with the following variables: attitude toward an innovation, knowledge of the innovation, economic motivation, innovation proneness, and contact with extension agents. However, Junghare (1962), whose research was also conducted in India, explained only 23.8 percent of the variance in innovativeness with six variables: change agent contact, formal participation, socioeconomic status, education, economic status, and age.

In a study correlating social, communication, demographic, and cultural involvement variables with innovativeness, Dodd (1978) statistically classified correctly 72 percent of the respondents in his survey of West Africans.* The results clearly described early adopters of a religious innovation as relatively older persons who were either farmers or professionals, who had no church friends before conversion to the religious innovation, and who felt unfavorably toward others in their villages/towns. They read little, demonstrated little exposure to the cinema, tended not to belong to groups, but practiced giving advice in matters of settling disputes. They generally did not seek further information about the innovation beforehand but adopted quickly, although those few persons who did seek information generally discussed the matter with kin. In short, the people to adopt early were culturally uninvolved and could be described as lacking cultural interconnectedness.

In the same study, a late adopter profile revealed the late adopters as younger than early adopters, as either merchants or students who had friends who had previously adopted the innovation, and as people who felt favorably

---

*The term *correct classification* is a statistical term referring to the predictive power of a set of variables in classifying actual early and late adopters (see Multivariate Nominal Scale Analysis). Found in many advanced computer packages, the technique takes nominal level predictors (such as yes/no) and jointly correlates them with a single variable that also is nominal level.

Many people do not find social change beneficial, and thus they prefer ways of doing things that have remained intact for generations, such as this process of making fu-fu, a West African food.

toward others in their villages/towns. They read a lot, tended to be exposed to the cinema, belonged to educational and occupational groups, but did not practice giving advice on matters of settling disputes. They generally sought information from friends about the innovation before adopting. In short, late adopters seemed more culturally involved than the early adopters in this study.

These studies show that early and late adoption, or innovativeness, results from several elements. To the extent that each of these elements is correlated with innovativeness, we could anticipate a change in one or more of these elements to produce some corresponding change in innovativeness. Summarized from a number of studies, the elements that predispose a person—perhaps an entire culture—toward innovativeness are:

1. *Communication sources.* Orientation outside the social system, media exposure, and interpersonal communication contribute to innovativeness.

2. *Attitudes toward change.* Some individuals who are initially responsive to change in one set of innovations are often receptive to additional innovations.

3. *Leadership status.* A person who perceives herself or himself as an opinion leader typically adopts early.

4. *Social and demographic variables.* Education, literacy, and previous experience predispose individuals to early adoption.

5. *Personality characteristics.* Cosmopolitanism, venturesomeness, empathy, desire to achieve, and levels of aspiration also contribute to early adoption.

6. *Economic factors.* Size of organization, high income, and loan ability are some of the economic factors that can intensify innovativeness.

7. *World view.* A personal or cultural outlook toward fate, family, or spiritual fortunes can restrain innovativeness.

8. *Social system readiness.* Some cultures by nature embrace change; others reject change. Availability of funds or other support from government or private institutions also act as a catalyst for change.

9. *Cultural involvement.* Culturally interconnected and involved individuals typically display early adoption tendencies.

10. *Cultural cohesion.* Cultures, or especially subcultures, that are highly cohesive tend to adopt as a unit. Their adoption time is influenced by the previous nine factors just discussed.

Increasingly, development planners and social change experts consider all of these factors and the nature of the culture when they instigate planned change. The days of change programs without regard to personality, social, communication, and cultural factors are limited.* Instead, change efforts are relying upon a systems approach to form a holistic plan. Though we have presented social change variables as if they were dissected into many bits and pieces, these elements in actual practice can be coupled with cultural and rhetorical sensitivity to accomplish goals mutually beneficial to all people concerned.

Organizational Innovation and Change

The subject of innovation and change has been seriously investigated within organizations, as well as in the traditional areas of intercultural change, community development, and national development. The innovation and change process within organizational cultures is primarily a problem-solution orientation, by which managers and others attempt to assess organizational needs and then develop goals and plans to meet those needs, followed by strategies to reach the goals.

*Unfortunately, the mistakes of applying an authoritarian approach to management and social change continue. For instance, the ABC network program "Close-Up" (April 26, 1980) aired the social change dimensions of uranium mining in the United States. Almost without exception, inattention to the social change elements previously noted has caused tremendous difficulty in the mining regions and, according to the report, may lead to even more serious problems.

Discovering the Need for Change

We are assuming here that decision makers perceive the fundamental axiom for successful organizations: that change is inevitable. Without innovation and change, we become obsolete. Changes in world economies and national competition for goods and services call for clear directives to change or not exist, a point developed by Schmidt (1970, 1984). Besides those overriding concerns for change, however, are the following immediate conditions that signal a need for change:

1. *Change is needed when obsolescence is apparent.* When equipment failures are frequent and complaints are high about equipment, facilities, work conditions, and tools, then it may be time to investigate and assess those claims.

2. *Change is needed when productivity drops.* If task efficiency is low, innovation can stimulate growth. Changing systems, personnel, hardware, communication patterns, and so on can create a dramatic difference. The gap between actual performance and expected performance, or between actual procedures and expected procedures, can activate a manager to consider new alternatives (Schmidt 1984).

3. *Change is needed when there is a personnel shift.* When people leave or enter the organization, an opportune time exists to examine old procedures and goals and to build new ones with the different human resources available.

4. *Change is needed when morale and satisfaction are low.* When organizational satisfaction is consistently low, changes are needed. The obvious signs of dissatisfaction are tardiness, absenteeism, high employee turnover, and sabotage. The more subtle forms include higher than normal failure rates, emotional and psychological fatigue, lack of positive upward communication, a high number of rumors, frequent clique group interaction, and direct negative communication.

Factors Related to Organizational Innovativeness

Rogers (1983) collected a number of variables that correlate with organizational acceptance of new practices and procedures. Organizational innovativeness tends to occur when:

1. The leader has a positive attitude toward change.

2. Decentralization prevails. Innovativeness is blocked when power and control remain in the hands of a relative few. Decentralization of at least information sharing and some decision making can enhance overall organizational performance.

3. Organization members possess complexity—that is, a range and high level of knowledge and expertise.

4. The organization deemphasizes rules and procedures in members performing their roles. Extreme formalization kills innovativeness.

5. Organization members experience high social interconnectedness. Interconnectedness is the degree to which people have a number of social communication networks. New ideas can thus flow more rapidly, contributing to innovativeness.

Strategies for Innovation and Change

Many plans and methodologies have proven helpful in introducing change in organizations. The diffusion approach, discussed in the first part of this chapter, offers valuable insights to the problems of organizational change. The strategies listed here for consideration with planned, organizational change are especially heuristic for organizational innovativeness.*

The presence and communication of innovative information. When organizations consistently emphasize development and innovation, then members are obviously more inclined to accept change. Even if no norm for innovation is already established, decision makers can focus on and diffuse information about new processes. An up-to-date data base can stimulate the creativity of organization members. The key, though, is the communication and availability of new data.

Social network method. The social network methodology emphasizes the need to make contact with gatekeepers, opinion leaders, and liaisons in the informal communication networks that exist within the organization, as described in chapter 6. These are key people who are sufficiently influential in not only providing information to potential users, but in urging their acceptance of innovations.

Outside pressure. Obviously, organizations change in response to strikes, boycotts, demonstrations, pressure group demands, and legislation. Also, outside professional consultants can bring about change. The intervention strategy of consultancy can not only provide new data assessing needs for change, but the interventionist can often convince key leaders and top management of the structural, procedural, and economic methods that enhance performance.

Change in top leaders. Organizations change when the top management exercises personal and corporate change. During the economic recession of the 1980s, Lee Iacocca, president of Chrysler Corporation, accepted only a dollar a year for his otherwise $800,000-a-year job. He then asked the auto union working with Chrysler to make a wage concession, which they accepted. As a result, Chrysler went from virtual bankruptcy to become a highly competitive automobile manufacturer in just a few short years and even paid off its federal loan (which obtaining presented the federal government with an innovative change) early.

Job expectation technique. The job expectation technique (JET) is used to clarify job expectations among managers, peers, and subordinates. The method allows individuals to write their job descriptions. Relevant manage-

---

*The author is indebted to Schmidt's (1984) research, which guided the selection of these methodologies.

ment team members also contribute to the job description. By using this team-building approach, job perceptions are increased, role conflict and ambiguity are decreased, and quality-directed job effort results.

Management by objectives. Management by objectives (MBO) creates a system in which management and subordinates participate in setting goals for the subordinate. This method increases participatory style and communication and clarifies job expectations for a prescribed time period. The most common goals are set for six months or a year, after which evaluation is made and recommendations for the future are suggested.

Job enrichment. The job enrichment technique attempts to make the work itself more satisfying. The assumption here is that challenging and more satisfying jobs create more motivation. Job enrichment can include change of title, structure, implementation, responsibilities, and growth potential in a job category.

Team building. The team-building strategy involves providing team members with an opportunity to discuss possibilities for change. Because team members discuss their ideas for improvement and make implementation suggestions, they tend to work more cohesively. Also, the ideas are generally useful, although not every idea can be implemented. The Japanese model of "quality circles," a similar concept, has richly paid off for their corporate cultures and is being adopted by other nations.

Organizational development. Organizational development (OD) attempts to increase organizational effectiveness by connecting individual desires for growth with organizational goals. OD is not so much a technique in itself as it is a name for a total set of change strategies for the entire system over time. The heart of the planning really involves creating a support climate in which individuals can develop their methods for change (Schmidt 1970). By encouraging communication encounters among all levels of team management and employees, individual goals and organizational goals can be linked.

Developing Skills in Intercultural Communication, Innovation, and Change

This section lists some principles for a person seeking to engage in intercultural persuasion and social change. Though the list is not exhaustive, it does point to relevant considerations for the practitioner.

1. *Tailor a message to fit cultural values and past experiences.* As Rogers and Shoemaker (1971) recorded, a Peruvian village failed to adopt a badly needed innovation of boiling their drinking water because of their cultural value that only "sickly" people drank hot or warm things. Some years ago, a large drug-manufacturing firm in the United States developed a new headache pill to be taken without water. However, subsequent marketing revealed that the pill was unsuccessful. For a while, the manufacturers were baffled about the failure until finally they discovered that Americans simply had little faith in any headache medicine taken without water. The normal practice of taking water with pills pinpointed the failure. The

failure of a government attempt to install a water pump in a Zambian village is another example. The government reasoned that women could save time and improve efficiency by having water pumped from the river instead of walking the lengthy distance. The government project failed miserably, and the water pump fell into disuse for at least two reasons. One reason was that nobody had the mechanical skills necessary to keep the pump operational. A second and more important reason was that the trip to the river provided a means of conveying village "news." Women also exchanged views on children, crops, and household matters during these river visits. These examples illustrate why a study of cultural values and a perusal of past experiences is vital to an understanding of effective change.

2. *Consider need before an innovation's successful introduction.* After an unsuccessful introduction of irrigation among the Papago Indians, Dobyns (1951) concluded that introduction of change will be successful to the degree that those who are affected by the change are brought into its planning and execution and thus made to feel that the innovation is their own. Margaret Mead has stated, "Experience has taught us that change can best be introduced, not through centralized planning, but after a study of local needs" (Mead 1955, 258). Those local needs must involve indigenous planning.

3. *As a communication planner, concentrate on opinion leaders.* One failure in intercultural communication may well stem from a preoccupation with innovators in a culture rather than opinion leaders. Characteristics of opinion leaders have already been documented. The key method is to discover respected members of a social system and work with those members. Numerous intercultural failures occur from faulty planning and a disregard for cultural opinion leaders.

4. *Close the heterophily gap.* A "change agent" is a professional who works for adoption of an innovation within a social system. Usually, this person is heterophilous from most people with whom he or she is trying to bring about change. However, this person can close that heterophily gap by working with opinion leaders. Heterophily should be less of a barrier to opinion leaders than to their followers. In this way, information is introduced to the social system, and its dissemination is maximized.

5. *Anticipate and prevent undesirable social consequences of innovation adoption if possible.* The phenomenon of overadoption is not altogether uncommon. For example, after the introduction and diffusion of the weed-killer 2, 4-D, some farmers were so impressed with the results that they used it on their cornfields to excess and ultimate waste. Unsought overadoption occurred in the 1960s when some blacks pressed for activities not planned or sought by many black leaders (Fotheringham 1966, 211).

6. *Perform demographic analysis of the target culture.* Understanding significant demographic variables and their importance can enhance a change movement. For instance, dominant involvement with youth in a culture that advocates decision making among and respect for older cultural members can result in a youth movement with little future potential or leadership. Targeting the message toward specific demographic categories has several additional advantages:
   a. The message is more easily tailored to fit existing conditions of various age groups, professions and so on.
   b. The message has a chance of being spread by word of mouth among homogenous groups distinguished by their demography.
   c. The message can be aimed at "influentials" and informally respected persons in a village or other unit.

7. *Understand the use of the mass media.* Communication theory indicates that the mass media serve primarily to alert villagers to innovations, to reinforce villagers who already have adopted, and to develop a climate for change. Studies show, however, that the mass media do not influence adoption as directly as demographic, interpersonal, and cultural factors. Thus, the message must take on a "grass roots," interpersonal dimension. If the media are utilized, the communication planner must understand their strengths and limitations. For instance, a strategy utilizing a knowledge of demographic factors and interpersonal communication factors in conjunction with the mass media would be more effective than any one of these factors acting alone.

8. *Build bridges not walls.* The first people to adopt an innovation frequently are persons culturally disengaged from mainstream cultural life. Consequently, their rapid acceptance may produce a "credibility" gap for subsequent adopters who belong to the cultural mainstream. Therefore, work toward introducing the innovation to informal opinion leaders and to decision makers. Such a strategy need not ignore "innovators," but direct contact with opinion leaders does provide a legitimizing effect that lends credence to the message. Consequently, opinion leaders' influence, through their existing communication networks, accelerates message flow and impact.

9. *Don't seek the cultural recluse.* This suggestion is related to the previous point. More rapid growth and acceptance occurs among people who are culturally involved in terms of group membership, attention to the mass media, and favorable attitudes toward others in their villages. Therefore, try to choose adopter "prospects" carefully, avoiding the disgruntled, disengaged, and reclusive individual. The cultural recluse may temporarily swell the change agent's efforts but ultimately prevent long-range cultural penetration.

10. *Direct efforts toward members of existing homogenous units.* People organize themselves into units that approach similarity in viewpoint, lifestyle, and so on. While the most obvious units are the tribe, clan, and village, do not overlook nuclear and extended family units and friendship relations. Data reported earlier in this chapter revealed that the more accelerated adoption rate was accompanied by consultation with friends. Inviting sociological networks of "friendship units" or other salient units to hear jointly an innovation message is one useful strategy.

11. *Practice empathy.* Numerous studies show that empathy is highly linked with change agent success. Listen and show rather than "boss."

12. *Realize that some innovations may be harmful.* Though you may believe that some message or idea is necessary or important, not every culture agrees. If you are not wanted or are uninvited, then your effort may be futile. Cooperation is important. Remember that some innovations do not fit in a culture. Develop enough insight so that you do not give "steel axes" to a culture where such an innovation could bring harm.

This Chapter in Perspective

The theory of diffusion and social change provides insight into a "grass roots" movement of ideas from person to person within a culture. For instance, various characteristics describe early and late adopters of innovations. Understanding the decision-making process helps us to appreciate different sources of information at various stages of the decision process. This chapter also addresses the question of how individuals perceive innovations in terms of their relative advantage, compatibility, complexity, trialability, and observability. The variables that predispose a person or culture to innovativeness and social change are also examined. Finally, strategy considerations offer practical suggestions for intercultural communication efforts in persuasion.

Planners and communications development people need to weigh the ethics of social change in their deliberations and to consider genuine needs and a systems approach. Change planners must invite all the input possible in making policies and implementing them. Inviting cultural members to help in the formulation and planning stages can ensure highly ethical decisions and principles.

Organizational innovation and change is summarized here as a matter of several factors. The factors include systems elements, interpersonal variables, and personality areas. Noting the times where interpersonal change is possible is also a point discussed in this chapter.

Exercises

1. Make an appointment to visit some organization that works on community development and social change. It may be some social or governmental organization in your town or city. During the meeting, ask how

programs are developed, instituted, and communicated to the target populations. Find out what works well for this organization and what does not work well. How do their insights compare with the principles reported in this chapter? How could the principles in this chapter assist community agencies in communication?

2. Find current magazine and/or newspaper articles and interviews dealing with some new idea or new technology. Gather as much factual reporting as you can from these sources and then compare what various people are saying about the innovation. Do people who seem more interested in the innovation do or say anything different from people who seem opposed to the innovation? Why or why not? Try to sketch a profile, from reading these interviews and articles, that characterizes early and late adopters of this innovation.

3. Choose some new idea or technology, perhaps the same one you chose for exercise 2. Interview five people and ask each one to define what they like the best and the least about the innovation. Ask them also what characteristics could be presented about the innovation that would motivate people toward persuasion. Do these characteristics add to the list of innovation characteristics given earlier in this chapter? What is it about persuasive messages that makes them compelling?

Resources

Arensberg, Conrad M., and Arthur H. Niehoff. *Introducing Social Change.* Chicago: Aldine, 1964.

Broom, Wendell. "Sponsorship: Propaganda or Good News." Monograph of the Missions Center, Abilene Christian University, Abilene, Texas, 1964.

Chattopadhyaya, S. N., and Udai Pareek. "Prediction of Multiple Practice Adoption Behavior from Some Psychological Variables." *Rural Sociology* 32 (1967): 324–33.

Davis, B. E. "System Variables and Agricultural Innovativeness in Eastern Nigeria." Unpublished doctoral dissertation, Michigan State University, 1968.

Deutschmann, Paul J., and Wayne A. Danielson. "Diffusion of Knowledge of the Major News Story." *Journalism Quarterly* 37 (1960): 345–55.

Deutschmann, Paul J., and Orlando Fals-Borda. "La Communication de las Ideas entre Los Campesinos Columbianos." *Monografias Sociologicas* 14 (1962). Cited in *Communication of Innovations,* by Everett M. Rogers and F. Floyd Shoemaker. New York: Free Press, 1971.

Dobyns, Henry F. "Blunders with Bolsas: A Case Study of Diffusion of Closed-Basin Agriculture." *Human Organization* 10 (1951): 25–32.

Dodd, Carley H. "Predicting Innovativeness in the Adoption of a Nontechnological Innovation in Africa." *International and Intercultural Communication Annual* 3 (1976): 100–110.

Dodd, Carley H. "Insights into Church Growth in Ghana." *Strategy* 5 (1978): 2–5.

Dodd, Carley H. "Sources of Communication in the Adoption and Rejection of Swine Flu Inoculation among the Elderly." Paper presented to Southern Speech Communication Association, Biloxi, Mississippi, April 14, 1979.

Firth, Raymond. *Human Types*. New York: Mentor, 1958.

Fotheringham, Wallace. *Perspectives on Persuasion*. Boston: Allyn and Bacon, 1966.

Greenberg, Bradley S. "Diffusion of News in the Kennedy Assassination." *Public Opinion Quarterly* 28 (1964): 225–32.

Gudykunst, William B. "Intercultural Contact and Attitude Change: A Review of Literature and Suggestions for Future Research." *International and Intercultural Communication Annual* 4 (1977): 1–16.

Havelock, Ronald. *Planning for Innovation*. Ann Arbor, Mich.: Institute for Social Research, University of Michigan, 1973.

Junghare, Y. N. "Factors Influencing the Adoption of Farm Practices." *Indian Journal of Social Work* 23 (1962): 291–96.

Korzenny, Felipe, and Richard Farace. "Communication Networks and Social Change in Developing Countries." *International and Intercultural Communication Annual* 4 (1977): 69–94.

Kroeber, A. L. "Diffusion." In *The Encyclopedia of the Social Sciences*, II, edited by Edwin Seligan and Alvin Johnson. New York: Macmillan, 1937.

Lin, Nan. *The Study of Human Communication*. New York: Bobbs-Merrill, 1973.

Marsh, C. Paul, and A. Lee Coleman. "Farmer's Practice-Adoption Rates in Relation to Adoption Rates of Leaders." *Rural Sociology* 19 (1954): 180–81.

Mead, Margaret. *Cultural Patterns and Technical Change*. New York: New American Library, 1955.

Moulik, T. K., J. P. Hrabovsky, and C. S. Rao. "Predictive Values of Some Factors of Adoption of Nitrogenous Fertilizers by North Indian Farmers." *Rural Sociology* 31 (1966): 467–77.

Rogers, Everett M. *Communication Strategies for Family Strategies*. New York: Free Press, 1973.

Rogers, Everett M. *Diffusion of Innovations*. New York: Free Press, 1983.

Rogers, Everett M., and Nemi C. Jain. "Needed Research on Diffusion within Educational Organizations." Paper presented at the National Conference on the Diffusion of Educational Ideas, East Lansing, Michigan, March 26–28, 1968.

Rogers, Everett M., and F. Floyd Shoemaker. *Communication of Innovations: A Cross-Cultural Approach*. New York: Free Press, 1971.

Rogers, Everett M., with Lynne Svenning. *Modernization among Peasants: The Impact of Communication*. New York: Holt, Rinehart and Winston, 1969.

Runyon, Richard P., and Audrey Haber. *Fundamentals of Behavioral Statistics*. Reading, Mass.: Addison-Wesley, 1971.

Ryan, Bryce, and Neal C. Gross. "The Diffusion of Hybrid Seed Corn in Two Iowa Communities." *Rural Sociology* 8 (1943): 15–24.

Saxena, Anant P. "System Effects on Innovativeness among Indian Farmers." Unpublished doctoral dissertation, Michigan State University, 1968.

Schmidt, W. H. *Organizational Frontiers and Human Values.* Belmont, Calif.: Wadsworth, 1970.

Schmidt, W. H. "Communication, Change, and Innovation: A Selective View of Current Theory and Research." Paper presented at the American Business Communication Association International Conference, 1984.

Sharp, Lauriston. "Steel Axes for Stone Age Australians." In *Human Problems in Technological Change,* edited by Edward H. Spicer. New York: Russell Sage Foundation, 1952.

Starosta, William J. "Toward the Use of Traditional Entertainment Forms to Stimulate Social Change." *Quarterly Journal of Speech* 60 (1974): 306–12.

Starosta, William J. "Critical Review of Recent Literature." *International and Intercultural Communication Annual* 2 (1975): 108–15.

Starosta, William J. "The Village Worker as Rhetorician: An Adaption of Diffusion Theory." *Central States Speech Journal* 27 (1976): 144–50.

Whittenbarger, Robert, and Eugenio Maffei. "Innovativeness and Related Factors in a Rural Colombian Community." Paper presented at the Rural Sociological Society, Miami Beach, 1966. Cited in *Modernization among Peasants: The Impact of Communication,* by Everett M. Rogers with Lynne Svenning. New York: Holt, Rinehart and Winston, 1969.

AAt-2326